PERSONALITY
DEVELOPMENT

PERSONALITY DEVELOPMENT

C.L. KUNDU

Vice-Chancellor
Sanskriti University
&
Former Vice-Chancellor
Himachal Pradesh University

STERLING

STERLING PUBLISHERS (P) LTD.
Regd. Office: A1/256 Safdarjung Enclave,
New Delhi-110029. Cin: U22110DL1964PTC211907
Tel: 26387070, 26386209; Fax: 91-11-26383788
E-mail: mail@sterlingpublishers.com
www.sterlingpublishers.com

Personality Development
© 2017, C.L. Kundu
ISBN 978 93 86245 09 0

PRINTED IN INDIA

Printed and Published by Sterling Publishers Pvt. Ltd.,
Plot No. 13, Ecotech-III, Greater Noida - 201306, Uttar Pradesh, India

To
My Wife, Usha

To
My Children
Sanjay and Neenu

To
My Grandchildren
Bharat, Chaitanya and Rahul
Enakshi and Nitika

Preface

Studies in personality development undoubtedly constitute one of the central problems of present day Psychology and Education. A considerable amount of research done in the recent past in this field has greatly enriched our knowledge in regard to the theoretical aspect of personality and in regard to the techniques of assessment and its development. This field of study has assumed particular importance in the present context of industrial and technological advances taking place in our country. Time is not very far when services of psychologists will be required to a far greater extent than at present for providing expert guidance and help in the different fields of work such as vocational guidance and selection, child guidance clinics, education and industry, mental hospitals and jails, etc. In all these, *Personality Development* will unquestionably occupy an important place.

Roback in his book on History of American Psychology writes that the output of psychological books and articles in America exceeds the total output in all other countries combined, about eighty per cent of the world's research in personality area comes from American psychological laboratories. The popularity of the subject has reached such a stage that a few American psychologists have expressed jocularly that if psychology continues to grow as it has been, there will shortly be more psychologists than people in the United States. The Indian picture in the psychological research, particularly in the area of personality, is not very encouraging. Students in Indian Universities are forced to read books published in Western countries, containing Western researches and techniques. Though a few psychologists think that there is nothing like ' Western' or 'Indian' approach to personality and that psychology is one, there is widespread ignorance of the uniqueness of the subject when it is developed in tune with the cultural conditions of the respective countries. It is time that books on psychology and education; containing Indian researches and techniques were written. The present book is an attempt in that direction.

The aim of this book is to make available to the students and to the general reader, Indian investigations which are representative of the modern experimental treatment of important topics concerning personality. The title 'Personality Development': reflects contemporary trends in Psychology Education and Sociology with special reference to the area of personality development. The investigations reviewed have been selected on the basis of their importance to the area of personality and of their nature and interest to the student. In general, each chapter includes an introductory section designed to orient the reader to the topic under consideration, a review' of Indian studies pertinent to the problem, and a concluding discussion in which the experimental results are interpreted from the viewpoint of personality development and of their application to problems of everyday interest. All the researches in this book are presented in a manner designed to make their aims, methods, results and interpretations as clear as possible to the student who is not technically prepared to read the unpublished thesis in its original form. For this reason it became necessary to make some changes in the terminology employed by the original researchers and to present the results in a somewhat simplified form and to amplify the descriptions of the methods used in the various researches. Hence, no chapter in this book is in any sense a verbatim reproduction of articles or these on which it is based. However, the author has been careful to present with accuracy the factual material of every study. For permission to use the studies reviewed by the author, henceforth wishes to express his indebtedness to the researchers on whose unpublished works the author has drawn upon the preparation of the present book.

1.5.2017

C.L. Kundu

Contents

1

Personality: Indian Approaches

Cross-Cultural Research

Cross-cultural studies have revealed that every culture has a typical characteristic and distinctive concept of personality. Culture directs and gratifies individual needs very differently in different societies. This is due to the fact that every culture emphasises its particular values and thereby not only affects the emotions, perceptions, feelings and thoughts of the individual, but also characterises a different way of life. In this sense, the concept of personality differs from culture to culture; the characteristics of personality emerging out of a culture may differ in degree but not in kind. Cultural pressures are among the dominant factors that influence the basic personality pattern feelings towards parents, the siblings, the peer groups and the other socio-economic and political groups, feelings and attitudes towards the same and the opposite sex and the sense of guilt, emotions and hostility connected therewith, etc. Each culture has its own values and approved way of living that affect the thoughts, the feelings, the emotions, the actions and endeavours of its people These fundamental values of a culture, to which a child belongs, lend a pattern to his basic personality, a pattern that gets injected in the individual-self in interaction with the primary and secondary groups of that culture. These pressures, directly or indirectly, lead the child to adopt the socially approved way of life in his particular culture. In every society there are ways of cataloguing experience that the child must learn if he is to become an acceptable and socialised member of the group. This learning is a part of him and a vital force in shaping his personality. Culture is powerful and pervasive, changing the character of our biological drives, affecting our thinking, our emotions and our perceptions. There are distinct patterns of aggression, sibling rivalry, privacy, jealousy, love, frustration, play and participation in different cultures.

For instance, the Western culture emphasises egocentric and more realistic tendencies, whereas the Indian culture emphasises values such as a sympathetic attitude, self-sacrifice, cooperation, self-discipline and self-ideals. Sex and interest differences in Indian and American cultures bring about some differences in the choice of particular ways of life. While Indians, on the whole, prefer ways that stress self-control and social restraint and dislike the ways of sensuous enjoyment, the Americans prefer ways of enjoyment and progress in action and dislike receptivity, inner life and meditation. The outlook of Indians is oriented towards inner life, development of the self and preservation of traditions, while that of the Americans is oriented towards nature, society and a rich life. Perhaps, it is due to this factor that the Western and the Indian theorists and psychologists have defined personality in different terms.

Western psychological literature is gorged with various definitions of personality, but the one most commonly accepted by psychologists is the definition rendered by G.W. Allport. 'Personality is the dynamic organization within the individual of those psychological systems that determine his unique adjustment to his environment.' This definition emphasises

(a) that personality is constantly evolving and changing as a motivational and self-regulating aspect; (b) that it is neither inclusively mental nor exclusively neural: it operates from both body and mind; (c) that psycho-physical systems have motivational force for the full range of social and environmental aspects; (d) that the way in which the individual learns to adjust is unique; and (e) that the individual behaviour includes a great amount of spontaneous creative behaviour towards environment, involving mastery as well as passive adaptation.

While Allport emphasises the importance of psycho-physical system in components of the personality, Shaffer lays emphasis on the observable behaviour and remarks that: 'Personality consists of observable behaviour, and it is also individual and intrinsic. It is defined as an individual's typical or consistent adjustment to his environment.' According to the psycho-analytic theory propounded by Sigmund Freud, personality is made up of three major systems, 'Id',- 'ego' and 'super-ego' and the human behaviour is the product of interaction among these systems. But for Adler, personality is a unique configuration of self entity, motives, traits, interests and values that is expressed itself in a 'style of life'. Cattell made an attempt at factor analytic studies of personality and emphasises that personality is concerned with 'all behaviour of the person, overt or covert, under variety of environmental situations, and thus personality is that which permits a prediction of what a person will do in a given situation. Thus like Allport, Cattell views personality as a complex and differentiated structure of the dynamic traits. On the other hand, there are social psychologists who emphasize the role of a particular society in shaping the particular behaviour to the extent it fulfils the needs of individual, its excessive domination producing 'basic anxiety' causing conflicts and adjustment problems in the individual. For Sullivan, the individual cannot exist apart from his reactions to others. Throughout his life he remains a member of the social field. Personality, thus, is the relatively enduring pattern of recurrent interpersonal situations which characterise a human life.

There is one characteristic feature in all the above definitions and theories of personality: that personality is the individual's unique pattern of traits — the pattern that distinguishes him as an individual and accounts for his unique and relatively consistent ways of interacting with his environment.

This concept of personality has been questioned in India since the ancient vedic period. Indian philosophical-psychologists perceive some life force over and above these traits that enables the individual to think, to feel, to will and to act This 'life force' is a constant factor which persists amidst biological, psychological and environmental changes. Indian philosophers have named it as 'self consciousness' or 'self-illuminacy'. Even some western psychologists, operating on the factorial analysis of the personality, refer to some unknown 'X' factor operating over and above the various traits. They have called if self, 'self-concept' or 'self-perception'. But the Western concept of 'self refers only to ME' reaction of an individual as a mental process, while the Indian concept of 'self-consciousness' refers to something deep, inherent, intuitive, the transcendental self in the individual as a part of the universal self.

Indian School of Thought

The Indian schools of thought have treated men as 'a person' with variations in their ontological premises. For instance, Advaita reaches the startling conclusion that finitude has no reality in an ultimate reference and personality could be ascribed to a being in which all finite personalities merged without retaining a vestige of their distinctive experience. Sharma in his excellent treatise on Nature and Development of Human Personality in Ancient Indian Thought concludes that *Nyaya-Vaisesika* and *Purva Mimamsa* postulate plurality of soul, whereas *Samkhya* reduces all ontological principles to two only. But still they are entrenched in the common soil of Idealism of the *Astika-Parampara* (theistic tradition, owing allegiance to the Vedas). Apart from it, their emphasis upon the role of the individual in the attainment of spiritual advancement is unmistakable. There is certitude in the bold assertion that "the technique of expanding the self and increasing the dimension of personality received an elaborate treatment in the Indian system not to be found in other countries." The *Nyaya-Vaisesika*: offers a close peep into the nature of human personality and the way that leads to its full development. *The Nyaya-Vaisesika* reduces the entire universe, of which an individual human being is a part, into six (even seven) categories *(padarthas)* and classifies all existents under them. These categories are 'substance' *(dravya)*, 'attribute' *(guna)*, 'activity' *(karma)*, 'generality' *(samanya)*, 'individuality' *(visesa)* and 'inherence' *(samavaya)*. Non-existence *(abhava)* was added to this list by the later followers. The substances are enumerated as nine in number. Out of the nine substances, which serve as substrata of all, the first seven (earth, water, fire, air, ether, time and space) serve as the material cause of Nature without and the last two, soul *(Atman)* and mind *(Manas)*, provide a peep into human existence and personality. Further, analysis of these two substances yields what could be termed as the parameters of human personality.

According to *Nyaya-Vaisesika* there are three primary factors of human personality viz., Soul *(Atman)*, Mind *(Manas)* and Body *(Sarira)* along with the five senses of knowledge *(jnanendriyas)* and the five senses of action *(karmendriyas)*. The conceptualisation of human personality by *Nayaya-Vaisesika* requires further elaboration of its constituents so as to characterise its true nature. Its realistic ontology encompasses adequate details of psychodynamics apprising one of the determinants of human personality and their functioning.

The Self *(Atman)*

According to *Nyaya-Vaisesika*, the Self constitutes the pivot in the functioning of the human personality. This statement is well corroborated by the import of the sutras. *Nyaya* holds *Atman* as a unique ubiquitous substance to which all cognitions, feelings and conations belong. That the soul exits is indicated beyond doubt by desire *(iccha)*, aversion *(dvesa)*, *effort (prayana)*, pleasure *(sukha)* pain *(duhkha)* and cognition. "The nature of these attributes is psychic which means their mainstay *(asraya)* has to be other than the body.

Nyaya proves the existence of soul through inference whereat a *Vaisesika*, the existence of soul is proved through direct perception The 'I' intuited, gives us sufficient proof of existence of the soul. Other proofs such as the authority of the Vedas or inference of existence are the additional ones, A Yogi is capable of having direct perception of the 'I'-ness or the soul. Even perceptual cognition of the *self* results from a particular conjunction of the *Self* and the mind.

That there is plurality of soul is well substantiated by the argument that each individual's experiences are different from others and that each individual feels his ego. The activity and inactivity which are observed in one's own soul are indicators of the existence of other souls. The status at birth and the individual differences in men serve as further proofs of the existence of the self.

The Self is eternal *(nitya)* and indestructible *(anasvara)*. For Gautama saying that 'soul exists' is the same as asserting that soul is eternal. For Kanada also even though not an object of perception yet it is a substance that is eternal. It is all-pervading *(vibhu)*, Besides, the Self is not intelligence itself, but owns intelligence as its quality. It is the seat of *Ahamkara* (ego-sense). It is the knower, the subject and not mere knowledge the object.

Atman is neither the body nor mind or senses, but what controls them and synthesises their operations. It acts as a unifying factor of all types of cognition and action. Regarding the phenomenon of plurality of souls, there seems to be divergence of opinion. While some think there is only one *Atman*, variously differentiated on the phenomenal plane, others maintain pluralism which is explained in terms of soul's connection with mind and body.

An interesting feature of the newborn soul is that what determines the particular kind of body in which the soul is born is its past *Karma*, operating through *Adrista*, the invisible force generated by the karmic residium. Thus the possession of a particular body lends particularity and peculiarity to each human personality with which it stands identified. However, the assumption of *Adrista* as the force behind all human action leads to 'Hobson's choice' vis-a-vis human will. The conception of *Adrista* is supposed to take up the 'agency' from the Self, which is a continuum. But Adrista itself is supposed to be a link in the chain of causation and therefore, cannot be the sole determining factor.

Gopinath Kaviraj comments, that 'the ascription of causality (of action) to human will is out of question' for the simple reason that human will (*manusiya prayatna*) is occasional and determined by *Adrista* itself. This leaves a void to be filled in by postulation of the divine will (*Isvariya Prayatna*).

Nyaya Bhasya states that the Self (Atman) is described as one "who sees all, enjoys all, knows all and experiences all". Self, according to Nyaya is the mainstay of all human endeavours based on thought and experience. It is the repository of all mental propensities, instincts, desires and dispositions (the *samskaras*) of the past life. Hence it governs and regulates mind and the senses which serve as media for the soul to perceive and experience. This connection of self with the senses and mind for appropriating external and internal perceptions respectively is what results in the creation of consciousness.

Mind *(Manas)*

The other important factor of human personality visualised by *Nyaya- Vaisesika* is *Manas* (mind). Manas here refers to the totality of inner organ (the *antahkarana* of Samkhya). It is held as the sixth sense, over and above the five senses. It is through the instrumentality of *Manas* that a person is able to receive thought—thoughts that eventually influence soul. The appearance and non-appearance of knowledge, on contact of the Self with the senses and the objects, are the mark of the existence of Mind. Knowledge appears only when Mind attends. Without Mind, the direct contact of the *Atman* with the senses would lead us to a strange situation of perceiving many things simultaneously. But in reality the perceptions occur in succession, a situation that presupposes the existence of an 'intermediate instrument', the Mind. Mind thus functions as a coordinator between the senses and the soul.

Mind in *Nyaya-Vaisesika* does not function as an independent perceiver; as the real percciver is the Soul. Nor could Soul function in place of Mind, as the production of cognition, pleasure, pain, desire, aversion, effort and impression is all associated with Mind, and cannot be attributed to Soul which is an eternal substance, whereas the products of Mind, the non-inherent cause, do not enjoy that eternality. *Atman* acts and reacts only through the intermediary, the mind.

Nyaya-Vaisesika presents a logical argument to prove the existence of Mind as separate in each Soul. The ideas, thoughts and feelings belong to the internal world and do not depend upon any of the five sense organs for their occurrence. For all volitional and internally perceived experiences there is a need to postulate an organ other than the five sense organs. The phenomenon of the recall of the past experiences and ideas and their sporadic loss necessitates the acceptances of Mind as an instrument of experience. The senses, in any case, are capable of registering only a 'particular' class of sensory experiences. The existence of a sense organ that could receive and cognise *all* sorts of experience seems to be a safe inference in this context. Mind is held as an eternal substance. But Mind is not all pervading because it does not have simultaneous perceptions. This very fact leads to the position that each body has its own Mind. It means that each individual has his own way of looking even at the same object.

The other notable characteristics of Mind are, that it is atomistic: it has no magnitude. ('In consequence of non-existence of universal expansion. Mind is atomic or infinitely small'.) It is indestructible aad eternal like an atom. Besides, body and other objects of perception constitute the objective world, whereas Mind defies perception and is the subjective side to the individual. As organ of perception, it helps the soul to perceive. 'Though not directly subject to volition it still is approachable by volition.

Mind according to Sharma is fickle and restless. This quality of Mind blunts the intuitive power of the Soul and weakens the hold of the latter on the former, i.e. the Mind. But empowered with volition. the Soul is able to retain its overall hold over Manas. This 'restraint of *the* internal organ' (*Cittan*) is what is called yoga.

To quote Sharma, what stands out in *Nyaya-Vaisesika* as the *Summum Bonum* is the realisation that release from the sufferings caused by empirical existence is possible. Using the words of Max Mueller, Sharma says: "the soul is different from the body and they think that, if this belief in the body as our own is once surrendered, our sufferings, which always reach us through the body, will cease by themselves." Valid knowledge of things (reality) leads to proper appreciation of what is good and bad, and therefore, affects the *karmic* residium in human life, which together with *adrista*, occasion life and birth. Acquisition of valid knowledge is an ideal one can ill-afford to ignore in life. The valid knowledge of these and the valid means of acquiring the understanding *(pramana* and *prameya)* should ultimately pave the way for *Nihsreyasa* the highest good. One could rationally conclude that this school of thought upholds the common sense goals of human existence which lead to the highest good and the arresting of all painful experience.

According to Safaya the essence of human personality is *Atman* which is of the nature of pure consciousness. To Sankara, *Atman* is consciousness itself. Ramanuja believes that consciousness is its attribute. *Nyaya-Vaisesika* believes that consciousness is an adventitious *(aupadhika)* quality of the soul. Samkhya calls it an essential attribute of *Purusa* which is reflected in *Mahat*. Buddha does not believe in the existence of permanent self, but a stream of consciousness. Jaina endorses Ramanuja's view.

Consciousness or the soul characterised by consciousness is the essence of the human personality. The soul possesses body and mind as its agents. The triune of soul, body and mind is accepted by all the schools (except by Buddha). A detailed description of the psychophysical system and the gross body is given by Samkhya. The thirteen elements of mind and five elements of body constitute the total body (physico-mental) of *Purusa*. Upanishads have explained the five sheaths and its details are given by Vedanta. Since Buddha does not believe in soul, his concept of personality is a Pudgala which is a congregation of five *Skandhas* namely the *Rupa, Vedna, Samjna, Sanskara* and *Vijnana*. These roughly correspond to the five Kosas of Vedanta — *Rupa* with *Annamaya, Vedana* with *Manomaya, Samjna* and *Sanskara* with *Vijnana-maya* and *Vijnana* with *Anandamaya*.

To sum up, the Self as the essence of personality and the substratum of all consciousness has been declared by all the schools of Indian Philosophy (except by Bauddha). The Upanishads present the fullest details about the self and its identity with Brahman. Samkhya calls it *Purusa*, and talks of plurality of *purusas*, with one genus (as a common factor). Nyaya makes a little departure from Upanishads and Samkhya by mentioning that Self is intelligent only in relation to body and that consciousness is its adventitious quality. Nyaya, however, affirms the etenality of the self. The souls are many and each soul acts through its agent *Buddhi.* Advaita calls it the witnessing Self (*Sakshi*), the immutable (*Kutastha*) and explains the relation between Self and Brahaman through two theories, viz., Abhasavada and Avacchedavada. The reflection of the Self in ego is called Cidabhasa. The relation of Kutastha with Cidabhasa is explained as that between original face and its reflection in a mirror The theory of *Maya* and *Avidya,* according to which the Self is enveloped by ignorance, identifying non-self with Self, has a great psychological significance. The relation between the individual and Self and the Cosmos, primarily postulated by Upanishads, has been explained in detail by Advaita.

The Upanishads mention the *Linga-sarira* or the *Sukshma Sarira* which includes the five vital airs, the *Manas,* the *Buddhi* and the *Aharnkara.* In sleep and death, the physical body remains detached with the Self, but the subtle body accompanies the Self. It transmigrates alongwith the soul at the time of death. It contains the seed of the *Karma.* The subtle body, according to Samkhya, is atomic in size, and it contains eighteen adjuncts. It stores Vasanas and Samskaras. It is undetermined. It is not dissolved till liberation.

The Upanishads declare the supremacy of *Buddhi* in the illustration where the soul is mentioned as charioteer, *Buddhi* the driver, *Manas* the reins, Senses the horses, and Body the Chariot. All the organs proceed to intellect, and all the experiences are accomplished by it. Advaita mentions the further characteristics of *Buddhi.* It reveals the objects in waking state and becomes both object and perception in the dream state. According to Advaita its characteristics are change (*parinarna*), activity (*cesta*), suppression (*nirodha*), ideation in action (*sakti*), life (*Jivana*) and characterisation (*dharma*). Again, the mind has six powers viz., (1) Power of cognition and perception through the senses (*Vedana-Sakti*), (2) power of judgement (*Manisa-Sakti*), (3) Volition (*Iccha-Sakti*), (4) imagination (*Bhavana*), (5) retention (*Dharana*), (6) Memory (*Smarana*). Judgement also is of two types—ascertainment (*Nirnaya*) and reasoning (*Tarka*). Reasoning is either in the form of inference (*Anumana*) or discussion (*Paramarsa*).

The 'I' notion reveals the existence of ego or *ahamkura* as an aspect of the Self. It is not exactly the Self, but a reflection of the Self. Samkhya calls it an evolute of cosmic intelligence 'Mahat' iccha an individualised consciousness through the interaction of (*Purusa* and *Pradhana*). But Advaita explains it differently. *Ahamkara* is a transformation of *Avidya,* whereby the Self erroneously calls itself the experiencer and the enjoyer. So *Ahamkara* is superimposed on Self. Between ego and soul, there is the veil of *Maya* or *Avidya.* Once the veil is lifted, *ahamkara* is dissolved and the true nature of the Self is revealed. *Ahamkara* of a child is faint, but it develops gradually by the accumulation of desires, fears, *vasanas.* etc. *Ahamkara* can be burnt by the fire of knowledge (says Advaita), by devotion and self-surrender (says Ramanuja) and by deep meditation (says Yoga). *Ahamkara* is the root of all *Vrittis.* Destroy it and all the mental modes of psychosis and obsessive compulsive neurosis will die automatically.

Citta, another important aspect of Mind, is that modification of *antahkarana* that remembers and stores past impressions, tendencies, hereditary traits and *Sanskaras.* It corresponds to the subconscious mind of the Western Psychology. Samkhya does not mention *citta,* but Advaita describes it in detail, and explains its importance as the storehouse of *vasanas* and *sanskaras* (of this life and past lives). *Citta* is dissolved at the rise of right knowledge and cessation of ignorance (*Avidya*). The Yogic method of meditation purifies the *Sanskaras* in it to the extent that the whole mind (called *Citta* in Yoga) becomes transparent and capable of reflecting divine consciousness.

The *Citta* is the storehouse of past *Karma* and the impressions gathered in the past lives. These determine the present ability, present aptitude and the present status of the person.

But it does not mean that man is a mere creature of the past. He can build new *Sanskaras* in his *Citta,* change the very fabric of the mental habits, exhaust the past Karmas, resolve the unpleasant impressions, revive the past pleasant *sanskaras,* develop the latent powers and make full cleansing of the *Citta.*

The Upanishads describe *Manas* as the coordinating organ that synthesises the functions of senses. It is material in character and derives its power from Self. The subtlest part of food is turned into the energy of *Manas.* Samkhya calls *Manas* as the fifth principle arising out of *Ahamkara* under the influence of *Sattva.* It works as the internal organ of perception to experience, pleasure, pain, etc. It controls the ten sense organs and works as the cognitive, affective and conative organ. Its function is to ponder *(samkalpa) and* to propose *(viklapa)* It discriminates between the specific and the non specific. It has the common properties of sensation, perception and motor abilities. It identifies itself with each of the senses. Nyaya justified the existence of *Manas* as a separate sense on the basis of non-appearance of simultaneous cognitions. According to Mimamsa, *Manas* is an instrument of direct cognition, capable of perceiving pleasure and pain, though while perceiving the external objects it needs the five sense organs. But Sankara goes a step further in proclaiming that *Manas* can perceive even without the sense organs. Even the blind has some visual perception. A snake has no ears, but can perceive sound. Some lower animals do not have all the senses, but the perception is not altogether absent in the case of the sense that is lacking. *Manas* is fickle, it wanders from object to object. It is very difficult to steady it. *Manas* is related to time and distance. Time and distance are but modes of the mind. Short time and distance sometimes appear to be very long.

The gross physical body is composed of five elements. Each of the elements contains in it the other four in small proportions. Samkhya mentions in detail the five *Tanmatras,* the element potentials, which are connected with the five elements on the one hand and the five respective senses on the other. Kanada explains in details the minute atoms, their conjunction and character, which constitute the gross physical body. References about five vital airs have been made in Upanishads and details worked out in Vedanta. These roughly correspond to the various systems responsible for the functioning of the body.

The Upanishads mention the five cognitive senses and their functions. The details about these have been explained in Samkhya, which have further been accepted by other systems. Bauddha explains the nature of the five senses, the five *golakas* (sense organs), their substratum, object and nature.

Although Bauddha, Jaina, Mimamsa, *Kyaya-Vaisesika* do not recognize the five motor organs as senses, their details have been given in the Upanishads, Samkhya, Yoga, Advaita and Visista-dvaita, and these have generally been included among the senses. Western materialists, denying the existence of soul, consider the human personality as an off-shoot of matter — an aggregate of atoms. Vitalists go a step further, and declare personality to be a living unity with the power of self-adoption, self-preservation and self-reproduction. Sensationalists call it a bundle of sense-impressions with a purpose and a will. Rationalists add a thinking principle to these sensations. According to them personality is the subject of experience.

According to the Upanishads, the essence of human personality is *Atman* which is the same as *Brahman. Atman,* in conjunction with gross and subtle bodies, becomes subject to experience of pleasure and pain. Its true nature becomes veiled, as it were. The nature of 'veiling' is differently explained by post-Upanishadic philosophers. It becomes engrossed in five types of 'sheaths' *(Kosa)* and the total personality is called *Jiva.*

The Five Sheaths of the Individual

The five sheaths of the soul have been described in Taittiriya Upanishad. The person consists of the essence of food. The gross physical body is the product of food. This is the first sheath. Different from and within it is the Self that consists of life *(Prana)*. The breath *(Prana)* is the life of all beings. Different from and within it is the Self consisting of mind. Different from and within it is the Self consisting of intellect (Vijnana) which direct all deeds. Different from and within that which consists of intellect is the Self consisting of bliss *(Ananda)*. The true Self is beyond the five sheaths *(Panchkosas)*: material, vital, mental, intellectual and spiritual. The same reference in a different context is given in Bhrgu Valli of the Taittiriya Upanishad.

The five principles that are identified with *Brahman* are matter *(anna)*, life *(prana)*, mind *(manas)*, intellect *(vijnana)* and bliss *(ananda)*. This is the hierarchy of the factors of individual personality.

Vedic psychological philosophy, as interpreted by Yatiswarananda, the famous disciple of Lord Rama Krishna, regards consciousness 'as the essence of personality' and the secret of strengthening of personality lies in its proper integration of One's body, mind, ego, and spirit in a harmonious, intelligent and spontaneous way. Here, 'integration' does not mean the fractional unity in the Western sense, but a complete unity, to form into a perfect whole. Every cell in our body is like a tiny solar system and an organisation by itself. All such units form a part of the greater unit which we call a body. To impart movement to the body, these units must coordinate with the general movement; when this is not the case, disharmony or illness is definitely a result. So the body must be nourished with pure food, fresh air and an exercise which brings energy, strength, health and cheerfulness. Similarly, our mind is a 'synthetic whole' consisting of the faculties of cognition, feeling and willing. These faculties of mind are often at war with one another and create terrible confusion within the individual. There are conflicts of duties, conflicts of moral standards, conflicts of spiritual ideals. The individual may become the whirlpool of emotions struggling together if there is no integration which stands of purity, strength and harmony.

Likewise, 'ego' with a characteristic of constantly changing its centre of gravity, if perversed, may make an individual egocentric, selfish and mean; a danger to himself, to his family and to the society. It is by integration of its internal components that an individual can save himself from maladjustment

Thus 'integration', has its physical aspects, its mental aspects and also its spiritual aspects. In a properly integrated personality the 'ego' or individual's consciousness is in tune with the universal consciousness which directs and guides the mind and the body in a harmonious, intelligent and spontaneous way. The individual feels harmonized and integrated when one is master of one's own mind and spontaneously follows the spiritual life without conflicts. The process of mental purification is called 'sublimation' in psychological terms. It is a process of giving a higher turn to the desires of primary instincts. Such a blessed personality sees the supreme spirit in himself and in all beings. His mind is not shaken by misery nor upset by happiness, he becomes free from attachment, fear and anger and thus he is one with the 'supreme consciousness'.

In the view of Gandhiji, personality is the total pattern of these components – the self, the mind and the body.' It is through intimate contact with the external, social and physical environment that a proper manifestation of personality is achieved. Here, the social environment includes contact with parents, relatives, friends and the community- physical environment comprises air. water, sunlight, nature, plants, etc. Manifestations of the personality are the outcome of the interaction between the spiritual, mental and physical dimensions of self and the external, social and physical environment. Tendencies that emerge from individual self are of two kinds:

i) *Higher Tendencies* : Characterised as positive and good. These are ideal qualities such as self-control, non-violence, selfless service, truthfulness, fearlessness, detachment and simplicity. These tendencies are prompted by pure, kind and loving thoughts and feelings of the higher or ideal self.

ii) *Lower Tendencies* : There are negative and evil tendencies prompted by the action-oriented lower passionate thoughts and feelings. These are hypocrisy, falsehood, cruelty, gloominess and pride. Abnormal qualities, such as, withdrawal from community life, brooding, sex obsession, delinquency and criminality' also arise from the lower negative tendencies.

The above discussion of the theories of personality—Western as well as Indian—lead us to infer that personality is made up of many components, some of which we can explicitly observe and measure, i.e. physical characteristics such as height, weight, physique mechanism and chemistry of the body influencing our movement, speed and power, intellectual capacities, aptitudes and talent trait behaviour patterns, habits and interests, etc. and others which we cannot easily observe and measure, such as feelings, ideas, attitudes, towards self, convictions, motives, aspirations, purposes, commitments, etc. We may categorise the former components as objective and the latter as subjective. Psychologists judge the personality of an individual through specific qualities of his behaviour organised and integrated into a whole. These specific qualities are called the traits. To the psychologist, the personality constitutes 'the self and the 'traits'. The central figure in the personality pattern, especially in the Indian sense, is the 'concept of self, 'self-consciousness' or 'self-awareness' or the 'impression' of the individual about himself, his capacities, his characteristics, his worth and his abilities in relation to the 'universal self'. Thus, the position of the 'self and the 'traits' in personality is somewhat the same as that of the 'sun' and the 'planets' in the solar system or the 'core' and the 'spokes of the wheel'. Traits held together are influenced by the 'self concept'. The 'concept of the self or 'self-consciousness' determines the form the various traits will take.

Self: The Life-force

Psychologists declare that a man's personality is a collection of capacities, habits and attitudes which distinguish him from other men. The question arises—who is that who thinks, feels and acts? What is the most important factor in man that motivates him to do so? These questions are beyond the realm of pure psychologists and can best be answered by the philosophical-psychologists who believe that there is something in the man called the 'self in the form of '1 am'. 'I think' '1 feel', I perceive' and I act' giving a life force to the individual. But, as we have referred to before, the nature of the self as held by the West is different from the nature of the self held by the Indians.

So far as the nature of the concept of self is concerned there is a widespread confusion among Western psychologists. The truth in that inference is evident from the following widely held definitions and theories of 'self.

William James, a philosopher as well as a psychologist defined 'self as 'all that one is tempted to call by the name of Me'. He describes two aspects of the self—the 'material Me', i.e the clothes and the other mateiral connected with the body and the social 'Me', i.e. the recognition one receives from others or what one thinks of others and feels about them. According to Thompson Gardener and Divesta, the self is 'all of the perceptions, meanings and attitudes that the pupil has about himself. Justin Pikanas conceives "self as I' in somewhat wider terms, including evaluation of self, and defines self, as 'that group of perceptions, evaluations and other possessions which refer to one's own sense of the personal identity. Although processes such as thinking, willing and feeling are important. The emphasis remains on the self as object and a person's perceptions, feelings, attitudes as they have reference to himself.

Coleman's view of 'self is perhaps the *most comprehensive of all* other definitions given by the western psychologist. For *him the self* has two facts: the self as object and *self as a process.* The *self as* object is the individual's self-image. 'This *image incorporates the* perception of what he is really like (self-identity), his *value as a person* (self-evaluation), and his aspirations for *growth and accomplishment* (self-ideal). From this point of view, we *can* regard *the self as the core* of the individual's frame of reference — his *assumptions concerning* facts, values, and possibilities whereas *'self as a process* is *the* knower, the striver and doer'.

As revealed from the above definitions, for the West, the 'self is not an innate identity because man is not born with the sense of self. It develops gradually in life time, when he recognizes his body parts name and feelings, i.e. the self structure which provides him a sense of self-identity. This takes him to the things outside of him and thus he recognizes those things in relation to his self. It is this self-identity that provides the individual a sense of adjustment and sets some goals in terms of the extent of his awareness. 'It is our awareness of the self that makes existence meaningful, providing continuity between past, present and future'. Lastly, it is after the development of the sense of self-identity that the man evaluates himself in positive or negative terms.

The fundamental difference between the concept of the self, as conceived by the West and in India, is that, whereas the West emphasises the 'self' as a mental process and refuses to recognise it as an innate identity, the Indian theories recognise the existence of self as quite apart from mental processes with a logic that consciousness can never be produced merely by the conditions of knowledge, such as sensations or ideas, which are only the conditions of the manifestations. It is deep, inherent, intuitive and transcendental aspirations for peace, joy, knowledge, beauty and love. It is a peculiar illumination of *Jnana* or awareness which reveals the subject, the object and itself in the act of knowledge. Sri Aurobindo described it a life-force of 'self-directive knowledge inherent in consciousness which enables it to guide its own force inevitably along the logical line of the original self-perception.'

Theories of Self

Saksena, surveying the literature on the psychological nature of the consciousness in Hindu philosophy has derived four possible theories of 'self-consciousness' (a) Self as a mental perception, (b) Self not by perception but by inference, (c) Self as a higher and super-normal perception, (d) Self as self-luminosity.

He has further categorised the first two theories as realistic and the last two theories as idealistic. While realists make the self as essentially unconscious and imposes upon the process of self-consciousness of status of an object and derive the self subsisting reality of consciousness, the idealists on the other hand insist upon its transcendental, unchanging and distinctionless nature. *Sankhya-Yoga,* the renowned book of Indian psychological philosophy, representing the realistic view, describes how the perception takes place. According to this theory, 'Buddhi' or intelligence goes out to the object through the channel of sense organs and assumes the form of the object, but it cannot yet manifest the object as it is unconscious.

It manifests the object to the self only when the reflection of the self is cast upon the unconscious 'Buddhi' modified in the form of an object. Thus, the self knows an external object; only through the mental modification it casts its reflection. Vijnana-bhiksu thinks that there is also a mutual reflection of the self on the 'Buddhi' and of the reflected 'Buddhi' on the self, and that it is through this double reflection that the self comes to know the external object.

Yoga thus holds that the self is always a knower, the witness, the spectator in every act of cognition. But Jayanta holds that the self cannot be established by perception, nor is it self-apprehended. It is established by inference, and the qualities of pleasure, pain, etc. are the marks of this inference. He declares that there is no other way of knowing the self than the knowledge of it as an object. Parthasarathi Misra holds that the self is both a subject and an object in two different senses. It is a subject as consciousness but object as a substance, i.e. the mental perceptions.

Western theories of self also revolve round the first two theories, i.e. self as mental perception and as an inference. Freud gave a three- part model of the mental self, i.e. 'Id', 'Ego' and 'Super-ego', in his theory of psychoanalysis. 'Id' represents the inner self of subjective experiences having no knowledge of objective reality whereas 'Ego' distinguishes between the things in mind and the things in the external self. Super-Ego represents the traditional ideals of the society as interpreted to the child by his parents, enforced by the system of rewards and punishment.

It persuades the 'ego' to substitute the moralist goals for realistic ones. Thus, in a narrow sense, it represents the 'ideal self. For Freud, self-concept (or Ego) arises from the interplay between the biological and instinctual urges of the 'Id' and modifying influences of the culture and parental strictures forming the Super-Ego. The role of Ego in the self-concept, although in different terms, has been emphasised by Ramanuja in Indian psychological philosophy. He held that consciousness or the self could never be without Ego. Knowledge does not appear to itself. Self is not mere knowledge but the subject of it and the general principle is that whatever appears to itself appear as an I. Hence, what constitutes the inward self is not pure consciousness but 'Id'.

Jung and Adler are a bit closer to Indian concept of self. For Jung 'self' is the centre of personality around which all the systems are constellated. It holds the systems together and provides the personality with unity, equilibrium and stability. Self is a life's goal, a goal that people strive after but rarely reach. Adler gave the theory of 'creative self'. In this theory, self is sovereign in the personality structure. It gives meaning to life. It creates the goal as well as means to the goal and is active principle of life. He termed it as 'lifestyle' a manner for coping with the life's problems. Angyal developed the concept of 'symbolic self representing the totality of self conceptions. He regards that 'the relative segregation of the "symbolic self' within the organism is perhaps the most vulnerable point of human personality organism', because symbolic self may alter the reality of the biosphere. So the totality of all components organised by its position in general pattern of the biosphere constitutes the structure of personality.

Snygg and Combs developed the theory of 'Phenomenal Self'. For them the basic human need is to preserve and exalt the phenomenal self. His 'phenomenal self' includes all those parts of the phenomenal field which the individual experiences as a part of characteristic of himself. Thus, for him the behaviour is subjective and is always reasonable and purposeful because what the individual thinks and feels determine what he will do: and the self is composed of perceptions concerning the individual, and organisation of the perception in turn has a vital and important effect upon the behaviour of the individual. Rogers, who was influenced by the theory of 'phenomenal self', believes that in addition to the self-structure there is an 'ideal self' which indicates what the person would like to be: for him the self or self concept denotes "the organised, consistent, conceptual gestalt composed of perceptions of the characteristic of I or 'me' and the perceptions of the relations of 'I' or 'me' to others and to various aspects of life together with the values attached to these perceptions". It is a gestalt which is available to awareness though not necessarily in awareness. It is a fluid and changing gestalt—a process, but at any given movement, it is a specific entity. The theory of 'conceptual gestalt' propounded by Rogers is perhaps the most important theory propounded in the West. It differs from the other western theories of 'self, i.e. of Freud and his dissenting associates emphasising the 'self as an 'I-me' reaction *of* mental processes and other theories of self referring to 'I-me' reactions of an individual because Rogers' concept of 'self' apart from individual's '1 me' relationship includes relationship with others 'I-me' also. But it does not represent the 'idealistic self' of Indian philosophy which is super-normal perception with a characteristic of self luminosity representing the last two Indian theories of 'self.

According to Vedantic philosophy, experience or fact does not represent the individual's impressions and ideas as distinguished from things and relations; it represents or rather is actual things and relations as 'cross-sectioned' by the individual, plus his impressions and ideas about them. The 'plus' represents an analytic operation made by the individual in his 'fact'. Since between my fact and the whole fact no disparity in essential nature exists, the same name, 'experience has been give to the 'whole' also. It has been called 'experience whole' the 'absolute whole' involving the 'partial wholes' of the individual centres. And because experience essentially is a system of things and relations and a consciousness revealing and reflecting or representing them, it is conscious whole. Semi-conscious, sub-conscious and unconscious are pragmatically useful and important distinctions, which exist for universe or the cross section; but they do not exist for the whole as such; so our consciousness is the cosmic consciousness, and thus universal self is the embodiment of pure consciousness. Maslow, on the basis of the study of the great personalities like Beethoven, Lincoln, Thoreau, Roosevelt, Einstein, etc. has drawn out a long list of the characteristics of the 'self but two of them, i.c., 'capacity to mystical and spiritual experiences' and to transcend environment rather than just coping with it, indicate that the self is not a mere mental perception but something deeper in the individual as a part of higher consciousness.

Development of Self

It is the sense of self awareness that distinguishes the man from other animals because of the latter's lack of self-awareness. The extent of psychological maturity depends upon the degree of self-awareness. The person is called to be psychologically mature to the extent that he knows himself and uses his concept of himself towards greater understanding.

Indian philosophy dictates that the greater the knowledge of oneself, the closer is the perfection. It is revealed in the Sanskrit dictum, 'Aham Brahma Asmi', i.c. I am Brahma, the life-force. It is through thoughts and feelings that the individual forms the concept of'who' and 'what he is*. Thus, the individual makes an image of the self, or picture of self in himself. This self-image has two aspects—physical and psychological. Physical self-image is the importance of his body and psychological self-image is the concept of certain qualities or traits such as honesty, dependence, self-control, non-violence, etc. in relation to his behaviour.

Body Schema and Self

Body schema is the diagram of the body built up in the brain by which coordinated, purposeful movements of the body are carried out affecting the individual's ability to orient himself in space. A small baby is unaware of the body organs as part of his person but as the child grows and gains a gradual recognition of it by hitting and hurting himself, he develops the awareness of his body. This awareness plays a very important part in the child's building up his concept of the boundaries of his body, its position in space. Studies by Gesell reveal that eye-hand coordination is very important in a child's early experience of the development of manipulative or other forms of behaviour. Spatial coordinations such as left-right, up-down, front-back, etc. are all judged by reference to the body position, especially in the early years of the child's life.

Self-Identity

It is after the recognition of the body awareness that the individual evolves his own estimation of himself, as beautiful, ugly, strong or puny.

According to John Nash, 'the child's concept of himself as a physical person is difficult to separate from the concept that he builds up of himself as a total person.'

There is a period in the development when the body becomes interesting and important to a person especially in the adolescence, when physical attributes or deficiencies, whether actual or imagined, have a considerable influence on the concept of self-image. The structure of self provides the individual with a sense of his own identity. Self-identity, according to Coleman, plays an important role for the adjustive behaviour. It is in terms of his awareness of himself as something unique that he sets goals, hopes, prays, fears and makes decisions. He exists as the centre of a changing world of experience, and most events in his world are perceived and dealt with in relation to the 'I' and 'Me'.

With the growth of the individual's experiences the contents of self-image also broaden and include certain things outside himself in which he feels his personal involvement. With the process the Ego- extension begins in the individual and the social self begins to emerge.The emergence of first social sense in the child is impulsive, spontaneous and uninhibited by reasons of moral standards. When the child gradually grows, he beings to receive the punishment or rewards by his parents or other persons around him, as a threat or protection to his self. He learns to restrain his impulses, he develops positive or negative attitudes—individual as well as social. During this process, 'as individual's experiences and perceptions become more complex and as he becomes more competent and effective, he normally finds himself less concerned with the basic needs and more concerned with the needs at higher levels, i.e. needs involving acceptance by others, creativity, self-expression. Thus, age level plays a vital role in the accuracy and development of self-conception; ability to form a self-concept increases with age, intelligence, education and socio-economic level. As the individual matures, he possesses more differentiations and realistic self-conception.

Role of Self in Personality Development

From the above discussion on the theories and development of self-concept or self-awareness, it is evident that the self is the fundamental characteristic of the human being. Self, when well-formulated, determines the personality structure of the individual. Whether the individual will be adjusted or maladjusted in his life, depends largely upon the extent of his development of the self.

An integrated self or a stable positive self developed through various stages of development leads to better adjustment than the unintegrated negative self. Integration of the self-concept requires a coordination between the individual self and the ideal self. Formation of integrated or unintegrated self-concept, with positive or negative tendencies, depends upon the type of treatment the child receives from others at home and outside the home. A stable positive self-concept develops self-confidence, fearlessness, love and sympathy for others, truthfulness, self-control, etc. Consequently, the child will make better social adjustment and will enjoy greater social acceptance. An unstable self-concept with negative tendencies inculcates feelings of uncertainty and inferiority and leads to self-indulgence and social withdrawal. So the child experiences greater emotional reactions and makes poor adjustment. Experimental studies confirm that subjects with stable self-concept are better adjusted than those with unstable self-concept.

A well formulated and realistic self-concept procures job efficiency while a powerful self-concept enables a person to cope efficiently with life, strengthening his ability to deal with problems.

***

2

Personality: Western Approaches

The term personality actually comes from the Latin word *persona* which means masks used by actors on the stage, but personality in the modern usage of the term means the real individual and not the disguised individual.

Personality covers the whole nature of an individual and is therefore difficult to define. Psychology does not regard personality as a passive entity but as that dynamic character of the individual which finds expression through his conduct and activities. It does not enquire into what personality is but into what it does. So considered, to put it in the words of Woodworth, personality means "the total quality of an individual's behaviour." Personality is not, however, a mere aggregate but is the unity or integration of manifold manifestations like pleasure, love, hate, activity, inactivity and hope–despair of an individual.

Various Definitions of Personality

Watson agrees with Woodworth in recognising the dynamic nature of personality. According to him personality consists of the organism's responses to stimuli in its adaptation with an environment through the medium of nervous system. Watson ignores mental unity and emphasises nervous pattern or organisation consisting of stimulus–response units. Other psychologists like McDougall, Morton Prince and Gordon W. Allport also agree with Woodworth in laying stress on the dynamic character of personality. McDougall regards personality as a number of instinctive activities. In his own words, personality is the balance or harmony of two contradictory impulses: (i) submission or self-abasement; and (ii) mastery or self-assertion. Thus their conflict gives rise to various disorders of personality. Morton Prince also regards personality as consisting of instinctive tendencies or impulses. Allport came to the conclusion that personality is the unity of those qualities of the individual which enable him to exert influence upon other individuals. Stout thinks that personality means the embodied mind. According to him the mind acts in various ways through bodily organism as its medium.

In conclusion, we may say that personality is not a mere entity nor is it a mere collection or aggregate of a number of activities or qualities, but the unity of them all. By personality is meant the individual's physical and mental pattern with the help of which he acts. Personality is the total quality of an individual due to bodily pattern, mental integration and chemistry of internal functions. It will be in the fitness of things to mention here that Allport identified 50 different meanings of the term. He points out that two opposing viewpoints emerge in the description of personality: (i) Mask approach; (ii) Substance approach. In the mask approach, authors have emphasised the superficial aspects of human behaviour and have thus laid emphasis on outward appearance. The other class, i.e., substance approach has provided definitions which centre around the underlying nature of the person and which emphasises the basic determinants of the behaviour pattern.

Various Approaches to Personality

Early Approach

Those of Freud's contemporaries, who left their imprint on the understanding of abnormal behaviour, were Janet, Morton Prince and Pavlov. Janet offered the explanation that there must exist a level of psychological tension for proper unification and integration of mental phenomenon. He believed that the reduction in the energy level weakens the capacity of the individual to synthesise and that, as a result, systems of ideas and feelings are dissociated from the total personality. Janet recognised two principal types of neurosis—psychasthenia and hysteria. Treatments, guided by the aforementioned tension level theory, consisted of helping the patient to re-integrate the dissociated elements. Prince was one of the first to recognise the importance of association and conditioning in the causation of psychoneurosis. He employed hypnosis and automatic writing as treatment methods. Pavlov evolved the concept of conditioning as a form of learning. His work served as a stimulus for the emergence of the behaviouristic school of psychological thought. The core of Pavlov's theory of personality foundation through conditioning lies in his attempt to explain sleep and hypnosis as being the result of the spread of inhibitory influences over the excitation and cerebral context. The conflict between the neural area of the inhibition was regarded by Pavlov as the precipitating factor in the development of neurosis.

Psychoanalytic Approach

Freud developed the psychoanalytical approach for the understanding of personality and its development. Early disciples of Freud soon developed divergent theories.

The basic ideas in Freud's concept of personality formation and structure grew directly out of his experience in the treatment of neurotic patients. He recognised that many of the attitudes and feelings expressed by his patients could not come from consciousness and, therefore, must reside in the levels below consciousness. For convenience of presentation, the Freudian approach to personality has been discussed in the following paragraphs.

Freud observed that the verbal production of many of his patients would come from the unconscious. He divided mental activity into three levels—conscious, pre-conscious and unconscious. The conscious includes the overt thinking. The pre-conscious memories can be recalled with some difficulty. The unconscious contains attitudes, feelings and ideas that are not subject to voluntary control. Motivation, Freud believed came from a general biological energy, and contained constructive and destructive urges. The motivation for man's activities is guided by two principles—the pleasure principle and the reality principle.

Personality, according to Freudian theory, is formed on the basis of conflict. Conflicts may be evoked between pleasure seeking and reality, love and hate, and passivity and activity. Growth towards maturity is dependent on the individual's success in resolving these conflicts.

Three principal stages are described by Freud in his theory of the psychosexual development of the individual. These stages are—the infantile stage which further includes the oral, the anal and the phallic; the latent stage; and the genital stage. Freud explained the personality structure in three components—the id, the ego and the super ego. The id is thought of as the main source of the biological energy that expresses itself in the life and death urges. The ego is the 'me' or 'self' in which the individual differentiates himself from his surroundings and through which the integrative core of the personality is formed. Super ego develops as the ego internalises social and cultural norms.

Adler, after departing from Freud, developed his school of individual psychology. His psychology emphasised the will to power, the inferiority complex and style of life. According to Adler, the main goals of personality are social adaptation and the attainment of power. Development of neurosis is due to fear of inferiority feelings.

Jungian school of Analytic Psychology mainly emphasised collective unconscious and archetypes. Jung has introduced the concept of introversion–extroversion in personality types. He has introduced the word association test to study the significant conflicts of an individual.

Other psychologists like Rank, Fromm, Horney, Sullivan, Reik and Alexander, and French have also advocated their own systems of psychology.

Cultural Approach: The cultural dimension of personality is an important aspect that needs consideration. Certain regularities of behaviour, which are characteristic of a certain cultural system are absorbed in the conduct of an individual. Those who share a common culture, display certain common modes of behaviour. This is often referred to as cultural character. However, it is essential to distinguish those regularities which may be ascribed to social inheritance as distinguished from those which may be referred to an individual's innate characteristics called temperament or constitution.

Some individuals consider personality culturally from another point of view. They do not ask for the regularities which characterise every person who shares the culture, but ask rather what provisions the culture makes for the development of maximisation or minimisation of differences. So culture does not merely provide for the uniformities in the behaviour of those who share a common culture but also for individual differences. The extent to which differences in life history experience become significant in the life of an individual has a cultural component.

Different methods have been developed for studying personality in culture. Three methods of interest are: (1) the life history approach; (2) the observational cross-section approach; and (3) the projective tests. Each method has given valuable information on the genesis of personality under different cultural setups.

Eclectic Theory of Personality Organisation

There are many eclectic theories of personality organisation. We have selected Murray's approach as representing one of the more comprehensive and influential of these theories. In his theory of personality description and prediction, Murray has drawn most heavily on psychoanalytic and Gestalt principles.

Murray has conceived personality as consisting of an integrate aggregate of needs and perceptual press (see Fig. 1). Needs are defined as what the subject requires to reduce striving behaviour. Murray's list of manifest and latent needs covers a host of social as well as personal need-situations. The frequency and the intensity of these various needs define a principle component of an individual's personality organisation. A press of an object of person is defined as what it can do to or for an individual personality, i.e., the power it has to affect the well-being of an individual. It may be noted that needs and press are functionally related, because environmental press are often interpreted by the individual on the basis of current needs.

In Murray's theory the behaviour resolution of a particular complex of need-press is called a thema. A thema is the dynamic structure of an event, i.e., the general nature of the environment and the individual's response. According to the theory, one can infer the general nature of an individual's needs and perceived press by analysing a large variety of his thematic tendencies. These thematic tendencies are most revealing when the individual feels no need to cover up his 'real' needs and perceptions.

In order to secure this less biased type of information, Murray developed the Thematic Apperception Test, a series of ambiguous pictures about people in various situations. According to the psychoanalytic dynamisms of identification and projection, the individual is assumed to identify with one of the characters in a picture, and then project his own needs and press perceptions into his description of the behaviour and feelings of the picture-character (Murray, See Fig. 1).

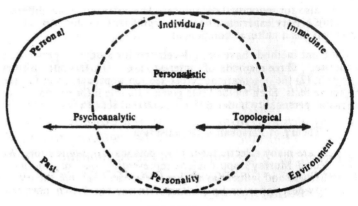

FIGURE 1

Protagonist Derivation	Murray Psychoanalytic	Allport–Personalistic	Lewin–Gestalt
Objectives	Reconstruction of past life experience to explain present organisation: thematic biography.	Present organisation of the individual personality as distinguished from other personalities: unique psychograph.	Establishment of general laws of organisation within the current behavioural "fied": B=P×R
Methods of Study	Free association and dream analysis: apperceptive tests of fantasy. The case history method.	Personality tests, judgments and ratings. Inter-correlations of expressive movements by statistical procedures.	Controlled environmental manipulation of experiment.
Leading Concepts	Need, press, thema; libido-theory; complex. Egodefence mechanisms and symptoms; the unconscious. Personal biography Gestalt.	Trait: Congruence and consistency. Functional autonomy. Uniqueness of the individual; individual personality structure as Gestalt.	Vector, valence, quasi-need; life space, boundary, barrier (topology). Contemporaneous motivation. Uniqueness of individual Gestalt.

FIGURE 2

Rosenzweig's (81) notion of a convergence of theoretical approaches to personality study among a limited number of investigators. " ... Allport emphasises the personality as it now appears within its own boundaries; Murray queries how it got that way from past experience; and Lewin studies its interaction with the present environment."

'We favour Murray's approach to personality theory because it borrows liberally from Freud's best thinking, and because it admits the possibility of more than one valid data-gathering procedure. Theoretically, such an approach might be able to synthesise the contributions of the available personality theories. It has already been responsible for the development of some of our more fruitful instruments for describing individual differences in personality organisation, e.g., the Thematic Apperception Test and the standardised stress situation. It shows promise of improving our predictions of individual behaviour sequences under known environmental conditions. Murray's theory supplies much of the operational precision that is so woefully lacking in Freud's formulations, yet it retains most of Freud's dynamic principles. In our opinion, it is a most promising approach to personality description and prediction.

TABLE 1

Aggregate of Needs*

1. *Positive Cathexis Supra:*
   a. Mother
   b. Female
   c. Father
   d. Male
   e. Brother
   f. Sister
   Infra:
   g. Brother
   h. Sister
   i. Contemporary
   j. Animal
   k. Possessions.
2. *n Affiliation*
   a. Friendliness
   b. n Sue: Dependence
   c. n Def: Respect
   d. n Nur: Kindness
3. *n Deference*
   a. n Blam: Compliance
   b. n Aff: Respect
   c. n Nur: Devotion
   d. Ego Ideal, Emulation
   e. Suggestibility

4. *n Nurturance*
   a. Sympathy and Aid
      Aggregate of Needs*
   b. n Aff: Kindness
   c. n Def: Devotion
5. *n Succorance*
   a. Crying
   b. n Aff: Dependence
   c. n Harm: Appealance
6. *n Harmavoidance*
   a. Timidity
   b. n Sue: Appealance
   c. n Nightmares
   d. Fears:
      i. Insup, Heights and Falling
      ii. Water
      iii. Darkness
      iv. Fire
      v. Isolation
      vi. Assault, Lightning
      vii. Assault, Animals
      viii. Assault, Human
         Hostility
         Father

Mother

Contemporaries

   ix. Illness and Death

   x. Miscellaneous

7. *n Infavoidance*
   a. Narcisensitivity
   b. Shyness of Competition
   c. Avoidance of Competition id, Inferiority Feelings
      i. General
      ii. Physical
      iii. Social
      iv. Intellectual

8. *n Blame avoidance and Superego*
   a. Sensitivity to Blame
   b. n Def: Compliance
   c. n Aba: Shame and Self-depreciation
   d. Directive Super ego
   e. Religious Inclination

9. *n Abasement*
   a. n Blame: Blame-acceptance
   b. n Def: Subservience
   c. n Harm or n Inf: Surrender

10. *n Passivity*
    a. n Inactivity
    b. n Aba: Acceptance

11. *n Seclusion*
    a. Isolation
    b. Reticence
    c. Inf. Shyness

12. *n Inviolacy*
    a. n Dfd: Vindication
    b. n Ach: Re-striving
    c. Agg: Retaliation
    d. n Auto: Resistance

13. *Negative Cathexis*
    a. Supra: a Mother
    b. Female
    c. Father
    d. Male
    e. Brother
    f. Sister

g. Contemporaries Infra:
h. Brother
i. Sister

14. *n Aggression*
    a. Temper
    b. Combativeness
    c. Sadism
    d. n Dom: Coercion
    e. n Auto: Rebellion
    f. n Sue: Plaintance
    g. Destruction

15. *n Autonomy*
    a. Freedom
    b. Defiance
    c. Inv: Resistance
    d. n Ach: Independence

16. *n Dominance*
    a. Leadership
    b. Inducement
    c. n Agg: Coercion

17. *n Rejection*
    a. Hypercriticalness
    b. n Inf: Narcisensitivity
    c. n Sec: Inaccessibility

18. *n Noxavoidance*
    a. Hypersensitivity, Gen.
    b. Food

19. *n Achievement*
    a. General
    b. Physical
    c. Intellectual
    d. Caste
    c. Father
    e. Rivalry
    f. Ego Ideal
    g. n Inv: Re-striving
    h. n Auto: Independence

20. *n Recognition*
    a. Recitals of Superiority
    b. Cathection of Praise
    c. n Exh: Public Performance

21. *n Exhibition*
    a. n Rec: Public Performance
    b. n Sex: Exhibitionism
22. *n Sex*
    a. Masturbation
    b. Precocious heterosexuality
    c. Homosexuality
    d. Bisexuality
23. *n Acquisition*
    a. Greediness
    b. Stealing
    c. Gambling
24. *n Cognizance*
    a. Curiosity, General
    b. Experimentation
    c. Intellectual
    d. Sexual, Birth
    e. Genitals
25. n Construction
    a. Mechanical
    b. Aesthetic
26. *n Order*

    a. Cleanliness
    b. Orderliness
    c. Finickiness about Details
27. *n Retention*
    a. Collectance
    b. Conservance
28. n Activity
    a. Physical
    b. Verbal
29. *Intensity*
30. *Emotionality*
31. *Persistence*
32. *Sameness*
    a. Constance of Cathexis
    b. Behavioural Rigidity
    c. Mental Rigidity
33. *Inhibition*
35. *Imaginality*
36. *Deceit*
34. *Elation*
35. *Imaginality*
36. *Deceit*

Factors of Personality

There are various factors which enter into the structure and functions of personality. Personality is influenced by: (1) Physical factor; (2) Chemical factor; (3) Glandular factor; (41 Social factor; and (5) Heredity factor.

1. *Physical Factor:* A physical factor of personality is the individual's physique. An individual's personality differs according to his physique. Tall and fair persons enjoy an advantage over their short and ugly associates. A bodily defect or deformity may, again, alter the whole personality. A blind man has to depend upon another person. A stutterer's speech is affected by his handicap. Fatty persons are often of an entertaining and ease-loving nature, while lean and thin persons are their opposite counterparts. Again, different organic states produce changes in personality. A fatigued and hungry man loses his temper for nothing. Persons whose blood-circulation is abnormal and whose oxygen supply runs short, lack encouragement to work. Again, application of drugs like alcohol produces bodily changes, which in their turn, alter personality. The excess or shortage of sugar in blood also affects personality. Factors like fasting and disease may also produce changes in it. Last but not the least, brain-disorders may cause remarkable changes in personality.

2. *Chemical Factor:* The chemistry of the humour or glandular secretion is an important factor of personality. Hippocrates, Galen and other scientists of Greece grouped

personality into four classes according to the predominance or subordination of the four great humours of the body. Persons in whom blood, yellow bile, black bile and phlegm predominate are respectively Sanguine, Choleric, Melancholic and Phlegmatic. This chemical theory of personality is now obsolete. But this theory draws attention to the important part that chemical action plays in the structure of personality and paves the ground for the glandular or hormone theory of the same put forward by the modern science of endocrinology. The Ayurvedic theory of the three *dhatus* or elements, viz., air (*Vayu*), bile (*Pitta*) and phlegm (*Kapha*) as determining different types of personality deserves mention here. The neuro-humoral theory of personality combines the physique of an individual with his chemique as factors determining personality. According to this theory, personality is determined by the interaction of the nervous state of the individual with his glandular secretions.

3. *Glandular Personality:* Glandular secretion determines personality. The glands are twofold, viz., duct and ductless ones. The substances secreted by the glands find their way out of the body through some duct or canal. Salivary, sweat, tear, urine and a part of sex are the main duct glands of the body. Saliva secreted by the salivary glands helps the assimilation of food. Sweat, tear and urine glands eliminate poisonous or waste products from the body. The excess or shortage of salivary secretion interferes with the digestion of food. Too much or too less perspiration, secretion of tears, urination or sex-secretion produce remarkable changes in personality. A person suffering from these disorders may, for example, flare up in anger, strike or insult a friend or lose his job by his rude behaviour with the authorities.

   As compared to the duct glands, the ductless glands exert a greater influence upon personality. The substances secreted by these glands find no outlet in the body and so get mixed with the blood to spread over its different parts. The influence of the thyroid, the adrenal and the pituitary among the ductless glands upon personality is great. Excessive or less secretion of thyroxin produces various distortions of personality. For example, hypothyroidism results in cretinism, while hyperthyroidism produces myxoedema. The adrenal or the suprarenal gland secretes adrenaline or epinephrine. It is also a powerful autacoid like thyroxin. The pituitary gland secretes pituitin, which exerts a great influence on personality, for which reason it is called the master gland. The pancreas, the thymus and the pineal glands also determine personality by their excessive or inadequate secretion.

4. *Social Factor:* Personality is not a passive entity but a pattern of different functions. An individual is born and nurtured in society. He acts in response to environmental stimuli. The social environment consists of social role of a person. He abides by the rules and prohibitions of his society and finds in it a place of his own. Social rules and prohibitions or taboos regulate the individual's customs, manners and conduct. The child, for example, has to court ridicule, punishment and even expulsion, if he violates the social code. So he deems it prudent to abide by it. Yet in spite of being regulated by it each individual develops in his own way. Personality is not merely a social product but also the product of an individual's nature. Again, nor is the society a creation of individuals. The social rebel, therefore, is taken to task, punished or even expelled by the society.

The social code is acquired by the individual in childhood. Even the child at play has to obey the rules of the game. If he tells a lie he is disbelieved. On reasonings of such a nature the child comes to learn that it is wise to obey rules and not to tell a lie. Again, every individual has to find his place and function in the society. In the drama of life one is a player, one is the stage-maker and another is the audience. On the play-ground, again, the place and function of each player as of every other person are fixed. In social life someone is the leader or social reformer, someone, again, is the follower. In family life also, one is the father, mother or the child. Thus, the same individual has to play different functions in different situations of life. So social life is a life of inter-personal relationship.

The place and role of the child in the family exerts a great influence upon his personality. These depend both upon the child's parents and the child himself. The main function of the child in the family is to grow. Many parents are unjust to their children and fail to afford them the scope for normal growth. Some are over-careful supervisors or over-zealous guardians and become a detriment to the child's growth into a self-reliant and responsible person. The place that the 'spoilt', 'pampered' and undesirable children find in the family leaves an indelible stamp upon their personality.

Adler has studied the order of birth of a child in relation to his personality growth. The place of the child in his family is distinct, for in spite of the parent's equal treatment to him he finds his companion in other child. For example, of two brothers the elder one is the companion of the younger and the latter of the former. Adler has attached much importance to the birth order of the child. The only child may grow into a hanger-on or a tyrant, for he has no partner in life to circumscribe his freedom. The eldest son assumes the position and plays the role of the only son for some time and may be dethroned by a new arrival. So he develops a jealous, conservative, authoritarian and power-loving personality. The second child is eager to catch or be equal to the first. So he tends to revolt against the accepted social code. The youngest child is forever the youngest. He wants to remain a pet and dependent. Except in a big family, the fate of every child is associated with some or other miserable place.

But Adler's view does not stand for the test of criticism. No birth order or place in the family is an absolute evil for the child. Besides, children of different birth order are found to have a similar personality. Birth order may be associated with some advantages and disadvantages. But these are not the final determinants of the child's personality. Home environment and the child's nature itself are also important determiners of it. To regard Adler as having considered order of birth as the only cause of personality development is, however, to misconstrue him. He has not ignored other factors of personality. The child's personality development, as he shows, depends also on how the mother accustoms him to social life. The mother should take proper care so that the child regards himself as one among other members of the family. Lacking such adjustment, the child is faced with various problems. For example, the pampered child wants to become the centre of attraction while the neglected child keeps himself away. Thus does a style of life develop in the child, which remains unchanged.

Freud also has laid emphasis on family and social place as influencing the structure of personality. The child interjects within himself the punishing authorities of the parents and develops the super-ego or the conscience which plays their role. Loyalty to the parents extends over the larger sphere of social life, so that the child learns to obey teachers, leaders and other father-surrogates. These processes, according to Freud, occur in the unconscious. The future personality development of the child depends upon how he absorbs his relation to the parents. The child in whom the hatred component of the ambivalent attitude to his parents is conscious, becomes anti-social. In criticism of this view it may be replied that notwithstanding the child's vital relation to the parents, the impact of the society upon him cannot also be denied. It is a fact that a child's personality changes in relation to his companions.

5. *Heredity Factor:* What the individual gets at birth from his ancestors is a great factor of personality. Heredity is the force by which some characters of the previous generation are transmitted to their descendants. The hereditary factors of personality are those that reside in the child from the moment of conception. On the other hand, the factors that work upon the child from the moment just after birth are those of the environment. That heredity greatly determines personality is certain. Like that of other higher animals, man's life also starts as a protoplasmic cell or as a zygote formed out of the union of two parental cells. His future is contained potentially in the zygote. The heredity of an individual is unchangeable. But the environment bears closely upon heredity in the development of the individual. Environment determines which heredity factor will develop to which extent. In the development of the individual heredity plays a definite, while environment an indefinite, role. Environment cannot originate an ability which was not transmitted by heredity. Its improvement only facilitates the development of the best among the hereditary factors. Again, environmental progress is confined to the individual, while heredity determines the progress of a species of individuals. Of two persons equally intelligent, one enjoying better environmental facilities makes more progress in education than the other with no such advantages. But the next generation of both these individuals starts where these two predecessors started, with no benefit accruing to the descendants of the more fortunate of them.

So heredity lies at the root of all the possibilities of personality development, environment being a means to the actualisation of these possibilities. An individual or a nation cannot be made highly intelligent by sheer training or practice, unless the factors of heredity are favourable. Social heritage also, like individual heritage, contributes to the development of personality. The child is born with a social heritage. The parents cannot transmit their acquired characters to other children at birth. Yet the accumulated wisdom and ethos of collective humanity pass over to the child. This acts as an environment stimulus to the development of the child's personality. Parental heredity is congenital. But the accumulated culture of the ancestors has got to be acquired by the individual anew.

Types of Personality

There are various types of personality. Different psychologists have given different types. A detailed description of the types is as follows:

Greek-type personality

Ancient Greek scientists like Hippocrates and Galen grouped personality into four temperamental types. According to them personality is: (1) Sanguine (2) Choleric (3) Melancholic (4) Phlegmatic.

Sanguine persons are always restless and spirited. Choleric individuals become short-tempered and active. Those who are melancholic are of morose temperament, and phlegmatic persons are dull and calculating.

Glandular-type personality

Berman has given a number of glandular personality types. They are as follows:

(a) Adrenal personality is determined by excesses or shortage of adrenal secretion. Hyper-adrenal personalities are of those who have excessive secretion of adrenal glands and are therefore vigorous, energetic and persistent. They have hair all over the body. Their skin is thick, hair dry and teeth large. They show qualities of physical and psychic vitality. Hypo-adrenal personalities are those who suffer from inadequate adrenal secretion. They are nervous people. Their blood pressure always goes down. They are full of indecision. They are also irritable and unbalanced.

(b) Pituitary type personalities are determined by an excess or shortage of pituitary secretion. Hyper-pituitary personalities are those who have brain power, physical development and muscular vigour. They are dull and have sensual potency. Hypo-pituitary personalities are those who are dull, dwarfish, sluggish and unbalanced. Napoleon, Darwin, Nietzsche and Julius Caesar had all pituitary personalities according to Berman.

(c) Thyroid personalities are those who have excessive or inadequate secretion of thyroid glands. Hyper-thyroids are those who have vitality and sexuality. Sometimes they lack emotional balance. Hypothyroidism leads to inadequate sexual impulse. Women who have hypothyroidism dress like men and men, likewise, dress like women.

Freud's type of personality

The following is the classification of personality according to Freud. Freud classification of the psychosexual stages of development correspond to the changes in personality, for example, the child at first derives pleasure from the stimulation of its oral orifice through sucking at the oral-erotic stage. It is in the beginning passive or masochistic, for at this stage the child wants to retain the mother's nipple in his mouth. Now the child's life is like that of the parasite, when he remains inert, dependent and optimistic. At the next stage the child's passive anal-erotism becomes active or sadistic. Now the child is aggressive in not merely retaining the mother's nipple in its mouth but also in biting it and entertaining an attitude of jealousy, ridicule and despair in relation to the mother. The second stage of the child's psychosexual development is anal-erotic. In it the centre from which the child derives pleasure shifts from the mouth to the anus. Here the child is at first active and later on passive. In the first stage the child derives pleasure from the contraction and the expansion of the anus and in the other it has it from the anus and faces themselves. Mentally the child at this stage grows awkward, obstinate, egotist and opportunist. At the third stage of its psychosexual development, the child becomes genital-erotic, which at first is phallic and then genital. The first is relatively vague and homogeneous in which the child thinks all individuals as possessed of the penis and derives sexual pleasure from the mouth, the anus and all parts of the body. So the child at this stage is called 'polymorphous perverse.' The genital phase is the normal stage of psychosexual development, in which the genital organ becomes the centre of sexual pleasure. At this stage the child is creative, adaptive, dependable and cooperative.

Spranger's philosophical types

Spranger's philosophical types of personality consist of the Theoretical, the Economic, the Aesthetic, the Social and Political and the Religious. The first is dedicated to philosophy and science. The second is materialistic, the third a lover of beauty, the fourth a philanthropist, the fifth a lover of power and the sixth an aspirant for the greatest good of life through the help of absolute force.

Sheldon personality types

W.H. Sheldon and S.S. Stevens have shown differences in temperament and mental structure corresponding to different bodily structures. They call predominance of bodily softness and roundness endomorphy. An endomorphic personality has a fatty and lax abdomen, undeveloped bones and the endomorphic person is viscerotonic. A viscerotonic personality pines for ease, rest, love, support, entertainment and help in danger. Second, Sheldon calls a bony and muscular body mesomorphic, which is neither fat nor thin but slim. From the side of temperament and mental structure, a mesomorphic person is somatotonic, who is active, reckless, aggressive, competitive and self-assertive. Third, the predominance of skin and nerves makes a body ectomorphic, which is weak and frail. From the side of temperament and mental structure, ectomorphic individuals are cerebrotonic, whose attitude and way of life are restrained and stiff. They suppress emotions, are afraid of people, lack self-confidence and seek solitude when in sorrow.

Eric Fromm personality types

Eric Fromm has grouped personality into five types, viz., receptive, exploitative, hoarding, marketing and productive. These correspond respectively to Freud's Passive Oral-erotic, Sadistic Oral-erotic, Passive Anal-erotic, Sadistic Anal-erotic and Phallic types.

Kretschmer's personality types

Kretschmer's personality types are based on the structure of the body and that of mind. Personalities from the standpoint of bodily structure are fourfold, viz., athletic, asthenic, pyknic, and dysplastic. An athletic personality has a strong-built body with firm muscles, wide chest and shoulders, large hands and feet. The asthenic personality is usually lean and tall with flat chest. The pyknic personality has a large head, chest and abdomen with large cavities. His body is plump, roundish and rich in fat. His face is soft and broad. He has small yet broad hands and legs. The secondary sexual characters of a dysplastic personality are undeveloped. His body is also undeveloped and unbalanced. From the side of mental structure, again, Kretschmer points out two types of abnormal personalities, viz., cyclothymic or manic-depressive and schizophrenic. The first manifests itself in extreme emotions changing repeatedly and rapidly. Sudden excitement and joy alternated with depression and melancholy are its characteristics. But in spite of such emotional disturbances, the cyclothymic personality maintains normal contact with the world. The schizophrenic personality lacks unity and splits up into many personalities. He is shut up within himself and loses contact with the world. Besides these two abnormal personalities, Kretschmer divides normal personality into two types, viz., cycloid and schizoid which are the normal counterparts of the cyclothymic and schizophrenic personalities. Jung's introvert and extrovert types correspond to the schizoid and the cycloid respectively. The schizoid is self-centred, given to imagination, unsocial, hot-tempered, unsympathetic, eccentric and often intelligent. The cycloid, on the other hand, is social, good-natured, active, sentimental, excitable and restless. The cycloid and the schizoid when abnormal become cyclothymic and schizophrenic.

Jaensch's personality types

According to Jaensch, personality is divided into 'T' type and 'B' type. There may be also mixed types like BT, TE, BH. These are based according to differences of susceptibility to the eidetic image.

Traits of Personality

Trait is usually an adjective like industrious, sad, cheerful, liberal and ease-loving. A trait of personality means such a distinctive character of a person's thoughts, feelings and actions as marks him off from other persons.

Cattell has done some good work on personality traits. He has distinguished between the surface traits of personality and source traits of personality. According to him, surface traits and source traits are 20 and 20. They are as follows:

The Main Surface Traits

1. Fineness of character	Versus	Moral defect, non-persistence.
(a) Integrity, altruism	Versus	Dishonesty undependability.
(b) Conscientious effort	Versus	Quitting, incoherence.
2. Realism, emotional integration	Versus	Neuroticism, evasion, infantilism.
(a) Realism, reliability	Versus	Neuroticism, changeability.
(b) Practicalness, determination	Versus	Day-dreaming, evasiveness,
(c) Neuroticism, self-deception, emotional intemperateness	Versus	Opposites of these.
(d) Infantile, demanding, self-centredness	Versus	Emotional maturity, frustration, tolerance.
3. Balance, frankness, optimism	Versus	Melancholy, agitation.
(a) Plasticity, social interest	Versus	Agitation, melancholy, obstinacy.
(b) Balance, frankness, sportsmanship	Versus	Pessimism, secretiveness, immoderateness.
4. Intelligence, disciplined mind, independence	Versus	Foolishness, undependableness, unreflectiveness.
(a) Emotional maturity, clarity of mind	Versus	Infantilism, dependence.
(b) Gentlemanliness, disciplined, thoughtfulness	Versus	Extroversion, foolishness, lack of will
(c) Creativity, self-determination, intelligence	Versus	Narrowness of interest, fogginess.

(d) Intelligence, penetration, general talent	Versus	Lack of general ability.
5. Egotism, assertions, stubbornness	Versus	Modesty, self-effacement, adaptability.
6. Boldness, independence, toughness	Versus	Timidity, inhibition, sensitivity.
7. Sociability	Versus	Timidity, hostility, gloominess.
8. General emotionality, high-strungness, instability	Versus	Placidity, deliberateness, reserve.

Primary Source Traits

1. Easygoing, genial, warm, generous	Versus	Inflexible, cold, timid, hostile, sky.
2. Intelligent, independent reliable	Versus	Foolish, unreflective, frivolous.
3. Emotionally stable, realistic steadfast	Versus	Neurotic, evasive, emotionally changeable.
4. Dominant, ascendant, self-assertive	Versus	Submissive, self-effacing.
5. Placid, cheerful, sociable, talkative	Versus	Sorrowful, depressed, seclusive, agitated.
6. Sensitive, tender-hearted, sympathetic	Versus	Hard-boiled, poised, frank, unemotional.
7. Trained and cultured mind, aesthetic	Versus	Boorish uncultured.
8. Conscientious, responsible, painstaking	Versus	Emotionally dependent, impulsive, irresponsible
9. Adventurous, care-free, kind	Versus	Inhibited, reserved, cautious, withdrawn.
10. Vigorous, energetic, persistent, quick	Versus	Languid, slack, day-dreaming.
11. Emotionally hypersensitive, high-strung, excitable.	Versus	Phlegmatic, tolerant.
12. Friendly, trustful	Versus	Suspicious, hostile.

Measurement of Personality

There are many instruments that have been developed to measure personality. Personality measurement may be divided into two sections. (1) Non-Projective Tests; and (2) Projective Tests. Besides this, the methods of measurement of personality can be classified as objective or subjective. The following is the description of the methods of personality measurements, (see Fig. 1)

Graduated Scale or Rating Scale

The measurement of personality with a graduated scale is also called the Rating Scale. The personality of a number of individuals can be measured in terms of ease-loving, industrious, etc.

This rating scale is marked into seven points, though there might be more points in it according to variation in the degree of a trait or quality. Of Rajesh, Krishan, Chuni, etc., it is found that two of them are placed at the mid-point of the ease-loving and industrious, while one each of the rest finds his place at the other points, (see Fig. 2 on page 332.)

Interviews

With the help of the interview technique we get information about an individual, but personal interview cannot be called an objective type of test. However, interviews lay scope for appreciating the individual's feelings and attitudes. In it is revealed how the subject speaks on a particular topic, where his voice changes and in what ways and where he gets stuck.

Observation

Observation is of great value in throwing some light on the personality of the boys, in gauging their different natures and in forming some idea about their work interests and work experiences; for example, the boy can be asked to recite a poem, to narrate a story or know incidence from their lives of their childhood days. The purpose of observation is to watch social behaviour, individual characteristics, likes and dislikes and leadership qualities.

Paper and Pencil Test

To test a number of persons simultaneously, a questionnaire consisting of a series of questions with 'yes' or 'no' written against them is supplied to the testees. The testee has to strike off one and retain the other of these answers. For example:

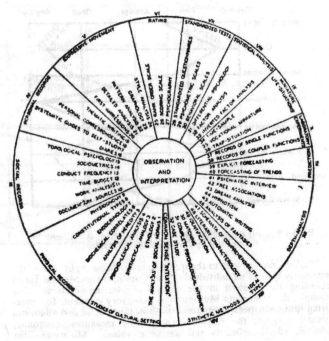

FIGURE 3

A survey of methods for studying personality. Since this listing was prepared some years ago, it does not place as much emphasis on the 'projective' methods as more recent developments would justify. However, this listing does reflect the diversity of personality approaches. (From Allport, G.W. Personality, New York, Henry Holt and Co., 1937).

Questionnaire

Do you feel shy?	Yes-No
Are you always in a hurry?	"
Do you arrive at your office on time?	"
Do you feel that time is passing away fast?	"
Do you have sound sleep?	"
Do you stand noise?	"
Can you stand noise?	"
Do you like to be let alone?	"
Do you join social functions?	"

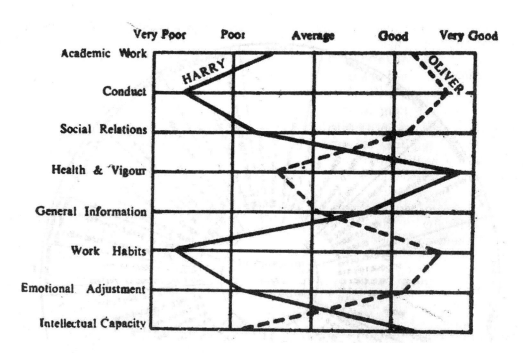

FIGURE 4

Profiles picturing the abilities and traits of two boys, as indicated by rating made by their homeroom teacher

'Yes' or 'no' answers to the questionnaire throw light upon the personality type of an individual. The Questionnaire Method varies according to variation in the method of selecting questions. For example, the Minnesota Multipurpose Inventory is meant for measuring different personality traits both in the normal and abnormal persons. Again, the Allport–Vernon Scale measures economic, political, social, religious and aesthetic values. Moreover, the Cattel–Luborsky Test tries to measure personality by examining individual tests and sentiments. The Questionnaire Method is, however, objectionable on the ground that it demands answers either in the affirmative or in the negative, while the vast majority of individuals would prefer an intermediate answer.

Situational Tests

The measurement of personality by observing how a person behaves in and faces different situations of life seems to be more satisfactory than by the Questionnaire Method. For example, to test the honesty of children, they may be placed in situations which enable them to deceive the psychologist. In one text, children may be given coins to be put into a box, so that the psychologist may see which of the coins have been left and which stolen. But such tests prove the child's honesty only in one situation.

Experimental Tests

Experiments may be made to measure personality. For example, it is experimentally determined how the perceptual process of college students is influenced by their interests. At first their scores are ascertained and a few words associated with their interests are selected. For example, economic interest is measured by showing them words like value, dollar, etc., religious interests by words like prayer, God, etc., and asking them what these words are. They are found to recognise these words in shorter or longer time according to their interests. Such experiments prove that interest in objects makes their recognition prompt.

Projective Methods

Projective methods aim at observing a person without giving him to understand that he is put to test. In projective method the individual may project his personality into what he does. The following are two important projective tests.

(a) Rorschach Test: This test is also called ink-blot test. The Rorschach ink-blot test is now quite generally accepted as a valid instrument in determining the dynamics of personality. The test is also a culture-free test because this test can be applied successfully on subjects from different cultures. Rorschach test consists of ten cards of blots.

  Of the ten ink-blots, five are black and grey, two black and red and the rest fully coloured. The testee is shown one blot after another and is asked what it might be or might suggest. It is tested whether (i) the whole or a part of the picture produces the reaction of the subject; (ii) the dark shade, colour, size or motion of the picture determines his reaction; and (iii) the subject discovers any man, beast, the limbs or some other object in the picture. Reaction upon the whole block indicates subtlety of thought or theoretical knowledge, while the same upon a part suggests compulsion neurosis. Second, the perception of movement suggests introversion, while that of animal shapes indicates narrow thinking. Thirdly, excessive reaction upon colour expresses the subject's impulsiveness. Again, reaction upon colour and shape as well indicates his spontaneity of emotional expression.

(b) Thematic Appreciation Test: Thematic Appreciation Test or TAT as devised by Murray and Morgan means the interpretation of a number of pictures. These pictures represent vague stories. So the subject gives vent to his mental attitude in explaining them variously. The subject is asked to narrate a story centred around the incident portrayed in the picture. He has also to say how the incident may have taken place and what might follow as a result thereof The fun is that the subject happens to identify himself with one or other character depicted in the picture and his narration becomes a sort of autobiography. Thus are expressed many feelings, emotions and motivations of the subject, which he would be reluctant to express voluntarily. In it, a well-built youth is seen by the side of an old woman. Personality of the interpreter is indicated by how he explains the attitude of the youth to the old woman and that of the latter to the former.

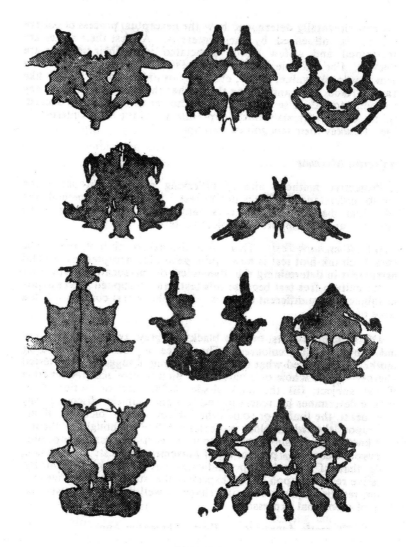

FIGURE 5

Rorschach Test (Ink-blot test)

Word Association Test

In this test, the subject is showed or told a number of personality-indicating words and is asked to say or write out the word suggested to him by them. Some responses come out promptly and others with delay. The latter indicates the subject's complexes or repressed wishes. On the basis of this test C.G. Jung has divided personality into introvert, extrovert and ambivert, among other types.

***

3
Bases of Personality

Heredity and Environment

The heredity and environment question (also named nature and nurture by Francis Galton) has been under scientific investigation since the year 1860. This subject has been discussed with much emotion in educational psychology. There has been a tendency on the part of a few psychologists to behave in an extreme partisanship either towards heredity or towards environment.

The Mechanism of Heredity

Germ Cells

The heredity of physical and anatomical characteristics has been well established — like begets like. The transmission of characteristics from one generation to another takes place by means of germ-cells of the parents. In the nucleus of the germ-cells, life chromosomes are the material basis of heredity. The chromosome is said to consist of genes that are not visible under the microscope. It has been said that they are usually arranged in the chromosomes in pairs of long strings. Many of these pairs are necessary to produce even the simplest physical characteristics of the animal. Unit characters are produced by various combinations of genes.

Modern science on genetics has thrown some light on the nature of heredity. Behaviour genetics have been investigated elaborately. It is observed that in modern genetics, science of heredity shows how physical characters of offspring are derived from the characteristics of parents. Behaviour genetics concern itself with the inheritance of behaviour rather than of physical structure. According to the latest information available on genetics which is reproduced later, an individual's heredity consists of specific genes which he receives from each parent at conception. Heredity implies, in the technical sense, the biological heredity. According to the present evidence, an individual's heredity is determined by the specific genes received by him from each parent at the time of conception (see Fig. 1).

To understand the mechanism of heredity, the concepts of phenotypes and genotypes have been introduced. Phenotypes explain the actual individual as we can understand him, such as,

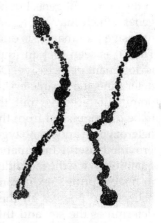

FIGURE 1

Chromosomes in elongated threadlike form showing genes arranged in linear order. (From L.P. Thorpe, *Child Psychology and Development*. Copyright, 1946, by the Ronald Press Company.)

a person who can see the colour normally. Genotypes explain the nature of the carrier or genetic qualities that may or may not be manifested by him, such as, a mother who may transmit colour blindness to her sons. For the understanding of the heredity unit of the chromosomes and genes, individual genotypes have to be understood. The genes, determinant of individuality, are grouped into chromosomes. These are coloured bodies. They become visible within the nucleus cell when the cell is stained with certain dyes for observation. It has now been observed that chromosomes occur in pairs, the two members of each pair being similar in appearance and functions. The number of chromosomes in each cell is, in general, constant within each species but differs from one species to another (see Fig, 2).

Each human cell contains 46 chromosomes, 23 from the father and 23 from the mother. Recent researches have led us to believe that the correct number of human chromosomes is 46 and 48 as thought previously. Chromosomes are visible under the microscope appearing as rod-like or V-shaped bodies. The genes with each chromosome, however, are so minute that it becomes sometimes difficult to see these with the high-powered microscope. At the time of conception every individual begins life as a single cell.

The determination of the traits in the individual is caused by the pairing of genes. If both members of a gene pair are dominant, the individual will show the trait determined by the gene. If one is the dominant and the other is recessive, the individual will show the trait of the dominant gene, but he will also carry the recessive genes which may show up in trait in his offspring. A recessive trait manifests only if both genes, are recessive. Thus it is seen that an important attribute of the gene is dominant or recessive. Dominant and recessive genes determine the characteristics in an individual. In the dominant–recessive trait, the heterozygote is, of course, to be distinguished from the homozygote. The study of heterozygote and homozygote and their conditions have provided useful information regarding the hereditary qualities which the individual is in a position to transmit

FIGURE 2

Chromosomes in pairs

to his offspring. Sex chromosomes determine the sex of an individual. Every individual is believed to possess all the genes necessary for both sexes. It is only the combination that determines the sex and this determination of sex is due to chance factors.

In the human race, as well as in lower animals, the characteristics are determined by genetic combination. As is obvious, the simple human characteristics generally depend upon the combined influence of a large number of genes.

Experiments by Mendel and Galton

In 1866, Mendel published the results of his experiments in the Hybridisation of peas. Mendel showed the difference between dominant and recessive traits. The dominant character, when present, always appears. The recessive character can appear only when the dominant is not present. The Mendelian Ratio (3:1) shows the expectation of the appearance of dominant and recessive character in the offspring of the second generation of two pure types. Only characteristics inherited by the parents are passed on to their offspring.

Characteristics acquired by the parents are not inherited by their children. This point has been discussed for a long time and the debate is still going on, but the evidence at present is against the possibility of the inheritance of acquired characteristics. Many of the physical characteristics of man are found to be inherited in the Mendelian fashion.

Francis Galton was the first person who stimulated interest in the inheritance of psychological traits. His first important contribution was *Hereditary Genius* published in 1869. He studied the family histories of many eminent men and found that a certain trait or ability appeared frequently in a family. He concluded that this trait was inherited. This way he began the family history method for studying the question of inheritance. Francis Galton recognised for the first time the importance of the study of twins. He gathered data by means of the questionnaire. By showing the greater similarity of more closely related individuals and by studying large numbers, Galton is said to have started the correlation method for the study of inheritance. These two methods are discussed as follows:

The Family History Method

The pioneer work here is Galton's family histories of eminent British men. In his study 'Wedgewood Darwin', Galton family had eminent scientists and scientifically inclined individuals. Karl Person later extended this family tree, tracing it back many hundred years and found individuals of outstanding ability all along the line. Dugdale (1877) did pioneering work in the study of inheritance of inferior mentality. Jukes family has become famous. In the Jukes family were found a number of prostitutes, criminals and paupers. The author comes to the conclusion that prostitution, criminality and pauperism are inherited traits.

This early work by Galton and Dugdale has stimulated a great many family history studies in recent times. Family showing feeble mindedness, superior mental ability, insanity and so on are considered as evidence for the inheritance of mental traits. Goddard's *Kallikak Family* is one of the best known. Here, we have two collateral lines, one highly intelligent and the other feeble-minded, both going back to the same progenitor at the time of the American Revolution. This man contracted two unions, one with a feeble woman from which a feeble-minded line descends and the other with an intelligent woman from which the superior individuals descend. Goddard has studied the family histories of 327 feeble-minded individuals. He came to the conclusion that feeble mindedness is inherited in about 54 per cent of these families.

Correlational Method

With the help of the correlational method we can find the correlation between measurements of mental traits of pairs of individuals and we can thus compare the degree of similarity in the case of individuals of different degrees of relationship. It has been found that among chance pairs of unrelated individuals we find positive correlation increasing in size according to increase in degree of relationship between paired individuals. Galton maintained that mental traits were inherited in the same manner of degree as physical traits. Person found a correlation of about 5 between siblings for such physical traits as height, colour of eyes and hair. He also found a correlation of about 5 for such traits as vivacity, self-assertiveness, temper ability or the like. He came to the conclusion that environment has no influence upon the height or colour of the eyes of siblings and hence the degree of resemblance is caused by heredity. In mental traits also we find the degree of resemblance. This can be illustrated by correlational studies done on twins and siblings.

Twins

Twins are of two kinds: identical and fraternal. Identical twins are the result of the germination of one ovum. Fraternal twins arise from the germination of two separate ova. The study of twins, especially identical twins, is, therefore, of great interest for heredity. In identical twins we have the closest possible relationship between two individuals. Thorndike, Merriman, Wingfield, and others have conducted many studies on twins. The correlations between pairs for intelligence range from .62 to .92 and correlations for identical twins cluster around .90 and around .75 for fraternal twins.

The question arises what happens to identical twins if they are separated at an early age and reared apart from each other for most of their lives. Newman and Muller have been gathering data about such cases. The results are as follows:

	Average I.Q. (Difference)
Identical twins reared together	5.3
Identical twins reared apart	7.7
Fraternal twins reared together	9.9
Re-tests of same individuals	6.8

Thus, it can be seen that identical twins who are reared apart, differ somewhat more than identical twins reared together, but they still remain more alike than fraternal twins reared together. Evidently here the potency of heredity is much more.

Siblings

The relationship between siblings is not as close as that of twins. What is the correlation? Many psychologists found some correlations and they ranged from .27 to .68. They cluster round 50. Hartsthorne and May find a similar correlation between the siblings in tests of honesty. In physical characteristics also the correlation is .50. Thus, we came to the conclusion that intelligence as well as physical characteristics are inherited. The summary of correlated results is shown as follows:

Identical twins	.90
Fraternal twins	.75
Mid-Parent and Child	.60
Siblings	.60
Single Parent and Child	.45
Cousins	.25
Unrelated children	.00

Hence, the growth of the personality of a child is determined by two factors—heredity and environment. The child inherits his bodily form and certain mental qualities from his parents. Education is the process by which these inborn and inherited tendencies are so developed and modified that he learns to adapt himself to the environment in which he has to live.

Hereditary Endowment

1. Every man and every woman at conception receives 23 chromosomes from each parent or 46 in all.
2. During mating each passes one half of his or her chromosomes to every child.
3. The father's role is that of passing one half of his chromosomes by way of a sperm.
4. The mother although she acts as incubator and nourishes the egg, also contributes no more to the child's heredity than does the father.
5. These 46 chromosomes comprise everything that determines the heredity of the child.

Heredity means the sum total of all traits which are present at the time of birth. It means likeness. The offspring of man is man and of monkey is monkey. All resemblances such as height, pointed features and similarity are considered due to heredity. Heredity includes all likeness and dislikeness between parents and off-springs. Reflex action, instincts and emotions are all inborn tendencies. They form the bases of human personality. Heredity forms a foundation. The whole of later behaviour depends on heredity. The main law of heredity is—like begets like. Cow gives birth to calves and human beings to human babies. Therefore, heredity is the sum total of all inborn individual traits. Heredity is the major factor, determining the development of the individual. Heredity puts the limits of growth and development. It is just like the raw material out of which objects are prepared, moulding it and treating it with a special process, but retaining the basic properties.

What the individual is and what physical and mental traits he possesses are determined by the type of parents, grandparents and other ancestors he had. What is transmitted from parents to offspring is not the brain itself but the gene which will determine the form that it will take in off-springs. To understand fully the role played by the gene in heredity, one must know what gene is, where it is located, and how it acts as transmitter of hereditary traits. According to Hurlock, man like all the higher animals starts life as a single cell. It is a fertilised ovum or egg cell which is technically known as zygote. The zygote is the most wonderful speck of matter in the whole universe for it contains potentially all the characters—mental, moral and physical that the adult human being will subsequently display. The zygote is formed by two cells—the male and the female.

The male generation cell is known as sperm or spermatozoon. The female cell is an egg which is known as ovum. The ovum is only 1/25 of an inch in its diameter and the spermatozoon is about 3,00,000 times smaller than the ovum. The combination of these, results into a fertilised egg or zygote. The sperm of every species of animal or plant carries a definite number of bodies called chromosomes. The egg also carries the same number. For human beings the number is twenty-three. Consequently, when the sperm unites with the egg, the fertilised egg will contain twenty-three pairs of chromosomes. Each chromosome bears a large number of genes. Genes are regarded as the carriers of heredity. So in one zygote, there can be thousands of possible combinations. On this combination of male and female genes depends the whole heredity. If the good genes from the male combine with the good genes of the female, the offspring will be poor for particular traits. Thus the ultimate genes are the seats of heredity. When the two cells unite (also their genes) it is then and there determined whether this resultant will be male or female, tall or short, blue eyed, or short eyed, clever or stupid. Every trait that the individual will later exhibit is potentially present; in other words, his or her heredity is fixed and nothing can possibly be added to it. If anything is added to, after the egg is fertilised that is not considered as heredity. Heredity, therefore, can be defined as the sum total of traits potentially present in the fertilised ovum, (see Fig. 3).

The fertilised egg or the zygote divides into two cells. One is known as germ-cell and the other as body-cell. The experiments of Galton and Weismann showed that the germ-cell is reserved unchanged for the formation of germ-cells of the following generations. As a matter of fact, the sex cells which form the generations are separated from the rest of the body at a very early period of embryological development. The second part of egg zygote known as body cell divides very quickly and differentiates to form the various parts of the body of the adult worm. This early segregation as has been observed in many animals, and presumably holds true for man. The child is, therefore, as old as the parent.

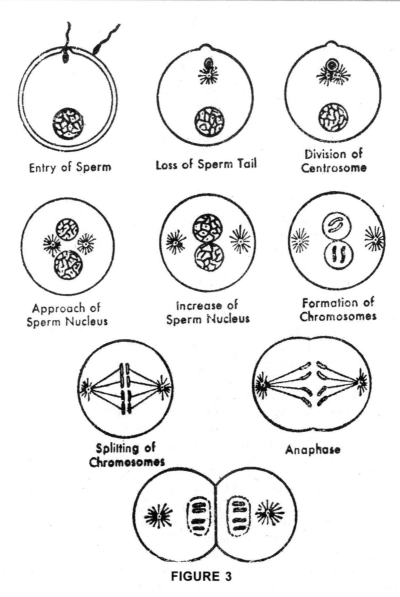

Entry of Sperm   Loss of Sperm Tail   Division of Centrosome

Approach of Sperm Nucleus   Increase of Sperm Nucleus   Formation of Chromosomes

Splitting of Chromosomes   Anaphase

FIGURE 3

The Process of Fertilisation
(Paternal chromosomes are represented as black; maternal chromosomes as white.)

It is extremely difficult, rather impossible, to control the human genes, though the investigators are doing research in this field. It is easy to do experiments on plants and animals than on human beings. In plants the cotarists are quite successful in producing the better seeds. Every day we find that new seeds of cotton, wheat and others have a better yield and are also more useful. This is known as the genetic field of research. Similarly, the breeder of animals gets better offspring from the selected parents. It may be pointed out that an intelligent parent may have dull genes also. A tall person may have genes for shortness. This is the reason why an intelligent person may give birth to a dull child or tall parents may have a short son. There is a great variety of genes.

Heredity does not depend on the immediate parents but it goes very far. It may go up to animal level. According to Galton, if heredity is considered as a unity, i.e., one half (½) is due to immediate parents, i.e., father and mother. One-fourth (¼) is due to grandparents, i.e., paternal grandfather and grandmother and maternal grandfather and grandmother. Similarly, one-eighth (1/8) of heredity depends on the father and mother of grandfathers and grandmothers. The same series goes on and its sum total is never equal to one or unity, and, therefore, heredity is very old.

Law of Inheritance

(a) Like tends to beget like; cats give birth to kittens, dogs to puppies, cows to calves and human beings to human babies. Further the kittens, puppies, calves and babies resemble their own particular parents rather than other species and their parents. Not only is this true in a general way but in every detail as well. Black-coloured parents generally have black children, tall parents have tall children and dull parents have dull children. That the clever children resemble their parents is due to the continuity of the germ-cell. The germ-cell is handed over from generation to generation, the individual being the custodian of it.

   Francis Galton and others made several statistical investigations on the inheritance. He studied the biographies of 977 fairly eminent men. He wanted to know whether 977 men under investigation had a greater or a smaller number of eminent relations than the general population. The result of his study showed that these men had relatives of the same or higher degree of eminence.

(b) *Law of Variation:* The second law of inheritance is the law of variation. It is true that although like birds beget like, yet there are always variations. Common observation shows that although like begets like, yet the resemblance of parents and offspring are never perfect. Babies are never exactly like their parents. Sometimes the difference is more marked, as for example, when a tall child is born to short parents, black-eyed children to brown-eyed parents.

   The cause of variation is still a mystery. There are two theories to explain it, i.e., the theory of Darwin and the theory of Lamarck, but so far this is a controversial point and there is no final universal acceptance of the earlier-mentioned theories. All that can be said about variation is that it is a fact of life that all living protoplasm has an inherent tendency to vary. Even two twins are not exactly alike. Without variation in plant and animal kingdom, there could be no evolution.

Recent Researches

Recent advances in research on genetics have thrown considerable light on the mechanisms of heredity. As already stated earlier, chromosomes form the genetic substance. It has been learnt that chromosomes, in germ-cells, have some contribution in providing limits to one's abilities and sets the seal of inheritance in a person. Researches in genetics have shown that 'gene' is the functional unit of heredity. It is very firmly asserted that chromosomes contain genes. Detailed studies of genes have revealed that they are formed of a special compound of an acid called amino acid. Molecular biologists are engaged in continuous research in studying the mysteries of 'genes' which are called as the secret of life.

The development of personality in a person is as much determined by forces of change in the environment as it is determined by gene which lays the basis of foundation for the personality structure of a person. A combination of dominant and recessive genes provide tendencies in the individual towards behaviour characteristics. The specific characteristics, carried by the genes, have not been identified in the human species clearly, although a lot of research has been done in this field.

Eysenck has given genetic orientation to personality. His works in the personality field is important. He has found and described three primary dimensions of personality – introversion versus extroversion, normality (stability) versus neuroticism (instability), and psychoticism. His researches have led him to believe that personality is genetically caused. He traces neuroticism to the autonomic nervous system and extroversion–introversion to the central nervous system.

That genes determine the hereditary features of an individual has been made clear enough by many experiments with mutations and it has induced changes in specific genes. Mutation changes have been found to change not only the structure of organisms but also their metabolic activities. The demonstration of this relationship between genes and metabolic activities has established that there is a close link between genes and enzymes. Genes may influence many hereditary characteristics by influencing enzyme systems. Although the relationship between genes and enzymes has been established, it has not yet been known for certain just what the link is between them.

Breakthrough in the researches on cytological genetics, including the work on the causes of cytological genetics and of mongolism, has thrown light on the working and nature of biochemical genetics. These studies have shown that there is a relationship between human genetics and intelligence. It has been observed, as stated earlier, that genes exert their influence on human behaviour through their effect at the molecular level of the organisation. It has been found that enzymes, hormones and neurons could be responsible for the sequence of path markers between the genes and intelligence behaviour.

It is important to make a distinction between the 'innate' and 'congenital' concept which are very often used while discussing heredity. The distinction between heredity and the innate qualities has to be likewise clear. Cattell has provided a diagram which tries to illustrate several commonly used terms in heredity. Cattell has commented that haemophilia, which affected several descendants of Queen Victoria, was innate but not hereditary since it has apparently appeared as a mutation and not as inherited from her ancestors. Cattell explains this distinction in Fig. 4.

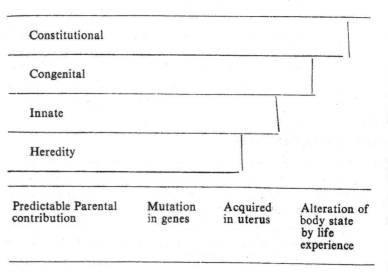

FIGURE 4

Environment

The earlier paragraphs give the viewpoint of genetics on the inheritance of traits in human beings. It is worthwhile to present the viewpoint of environmentalists on the role of environment in personality.

Environment has a broad significance. It is a comprehensive team. It has a dynamic connotation. Environment means social, moral, economic, political, physical and intellectual factors which influence the development of the individual. Environment is the aggregate of the total forces and stimulations which the individual receives from the conception until death. Environment also includes the pre-natal and post-natal environment. Food items, school, family and locality are also included in it. In short, the environment affects the behaviour of the individuals. The question that arises is which is important—heredity or environment? There is no doubt that the environmental factor also makes an important contribution to the development of the personality of the child. It is generally believed that the intra-uterine fluid constitutes the suitable environment upon which the embryo draws in order to mature. The embryo or the foetus depends on the mother for its blood and oxygen supply as for the supply of hormones, vitamins and the materials which make for the nutrition and the healthy growth of the child. The cells of the embryo also develop by the influence of the surrounding cells and cell-tissues acting upon one another chemically or electrically. Each neighbouring cell acts upon another like an environmental force. Third, whether exercise at the intra-uterine level helps the development of the embryo is open to doubt. Again, it is also uncertain whether any definite learning takes place during the pre-natal period. According to some competent authorities on the problem, the conditions for a simple type of learning are present and some genuine learning takes place before birth.

Watson, the behaviourist psychologist, believed that environment was important for a person and not the heredity. He asserted that environment rather than heredity determines human behaviour. His assertion is that the effect of the environment is chiefly brought through a definite process which he called the conditioning reflexes. He carried his theory to the extent where heredity was allowed no significant weight in determining behaviour. Watson said that science, being a public process, must ignore private awareness and deal with only that data which are available everywhere. The influence of environment has more importance in Watson's eye.

The quality of social environment, some authors think, therefore, determines the development in a person. If social environment is very stimulating and enriching, it will create favourable impressions in the person on his or her development, and if this environment is dull or insipid, the behaviour is likely to be shaped in an unhealthy way. The absence of adequate stimulation in the environment is liable to cause various emotional deficiencies. Continued living in this environment may lead to various emotional problems and emotional instabilities. Emotional immaturity and various personality disorders may also ensue in a social environment threatened by insecurity.

According to this school of thought, the social environment of the person at various stages of life—infancy, childhood, adolescence and even adulthood, are formative in character as it influences the maturation process with which heredity is closely connected. The type and quality of influence that is prevailing in the environment will shape the mind of the person. Social environment refers to all forces and influences that enumerate from the environment. It includes all types of activities, social, cultural, spiritual and economic which, in all their totality, affect development.

Children born in a 'free' environment or a 'restricted' environment follow a distinctive pattern of development. Experiments have been carried out on animals as well. It has been found that dogs brought up in a restricted environment showed a definite pattern of growth. This environment also creates a lot of 'fear' and 'anger' among them. They also showed little avoidance of noxious stimuli, i.e., the little pain. So, the restricted environment had prevented the normal development of the pain perception.

Complex development of adult emotions like fear and anxiety are also affected in a hostile or a restricted environment. Fear-like patterns of behaviour and experiences are also likely to be developed in a hostile environment.

Another leading support that an environmentalist can draw is from anthropological and cultural studies. The type of culture in the environment, they assert, shapes the personality of a person. If the culture is liberal and permissive, the type of personality that develops in it is different from the culture which is based on authoritarianism and regimentation. In both the types of cultures, there are standard ways of performing actions, of acting and working. Each culture has a particular essence in it and it emphasises a definite mode of personality and life. Accordingly, the system of beliefs, conventions, morals, sanctions, laws and conveniences can influence the capacities and abilities in persons who live in that culture. As culture tends to educate, it serves as a sort of social heritage to people. A rich cultural life produces a personality with rich experiences. And the environment where there are conflicting cultural forces, changes in personality of people may take place in an imperceptible manner; values and ideals are blurred.

An environment, characterised by superficial interests and ideals, is likely to create a sense of shallow outlook in people, with predominantly mundane attitudes. There has been concern for human values like truth, beauty and goodness in societies where the environment has been poor and unhealthy. A new brand of materially oriented generation is likely to be fostered in a sterile or uninspiring environment. Proper socialisation may not be possible in an environment where social interaction is not properly ensured. The form of behaviour and manner of thinking in students can be radically affected if the modes of behaviour are restricted. The following illustrations reveal that environment in all its manifestations – social, economic, cultural, political – has great potentialities in affecting a change in the behaviour of a person.

It has also been found that a poor environment can produce serious maladjustment in a person. Such characteristics like poor living conditions, fatherless families, ill-treated mothers and subjugation to cruel treatment are responsible for creating unhealthy trends in personality. If the wants and needs are not properly and judiciously gratified in the environment, the personality gets dominated by personal idiosyncrasies which later become responsible for developing maladjustment among victims. An impoverished environment tends to develop militancy in a child in later years which may foster such tendencies like that of destroying tendencies, participation in delinquency acts, etc. A poor environment tends to weaken the identity which may produce many difficulties in the personality of the person.

The influence that the environment can bear on the development of personality is given in the following quotation from Fredenburg:

"Obviously, this was 110 genetically based structures of personality but rather a dynamic formation growing out of environmental influences. Elkins (1959), an historian, sees slavery as exerting a crushing blow upon the personality not dissimilar in its effect from that of the concentration camps of Nazi Germany. He maintains that both were closed systems which produced profound personality changes in the individuals. A high degree of dependence was introduced in both systems. There was a total acceptance of the plantation owner as a father-figure among the Negro slaves in much the same way as prisoners of war accepted the Nazi SS guards."

Deprivation in the early years of childhood can have spurious repercussions on the development of the personality in later years. The studies, made by Bloom, were based on various subjects. He had taken identical twins who were reared apart in differential environments and educated in healthy and vitalising environments.

His studies were also based on Negro children; quoting results from Bloom, De Cecco quotes:

"You can see that one-half of the development of the intelligence occurs in the first four years. Early deprivation, therefore, can be much more serious than deprivation in the years from eight to seventeen...Bloom is hypothesising that a change from a deprived to an abundant environment can mean the gain of 20 I.Q. points. Such a change, in the realities of our occupational world, can mean the difference between a profession and a semi-skilled labouring job."

De Cecco concludes that studies by Bloom indicate that early home environment has a great influence on the child's development. As much of the child's intellectual development tends to occur in early years, elementary school years are the most crucial period of advancement. It is, thus, evident that environmental conditions, in which a child lives, has a positive bearing on the intellectual and educational development of a child. Environment, constructed by social class and occupational level of parents, plays a significant role in the development of personality and the intellect of children.

Environmental changes have brought changes in the I.Q. of children. Many studies have proved his hypotheses. De Cecco states:

"The most celebrated of these studies are the Scottish surveys of 1932 and 1947, as reported by the Scottish Council for Research in Education (1953). In 1932, intelligence tests were administered to nearly all eleven-year-old Scottish children (87.498). In 1947, the tests were given to children of the same age (70,809). The average scores showed a small but significant improvement over the fifteen-year period. In another study, Caster Lockceler (1942) compared the intelligence of East Tennessee children over a 10-year period. During that time the schools in the area had improved their circulating libraries, the training of their teachers, the availability of free textbooks, and so on. Wheeler found that the average mountain child had gained 10 points in I.Q. or nearly one point per year during the 10-year period. In a third study, Read Tuddenham (1948) compared a soldier's intelligence in World Wars I and II. The average I.Q. score for World War I soldiers was 62. For World War II soldiers the average score was 104. This is a highly significant observation as 83 per cent of World War I soldiers scored below the average of World War II soldiers. Tuddenham attributes these dramatic differences to the varying amount of education of the two groups. Soldiers in the first World War had an average of about eight years of education while those in the second World War had an average of ten years of education."

In psychology, the social environment has to be characterised in accordance with age, mental level and the individual needs of a person. The life-space of a person varies from time to time. As age advances, there has to be general extension and differentiation in the social environment of a person. An open environment has a different psychological significance than a restricted environment.

Psychologically, critical conditions like uncertainty and friendlessness in the social environment are likely to produce certain fundamental changes on the person. It may alter the intellectual appreciation of the problem on the part of the person. Quality of life-space in the social environment, develops various bonds in the mind of the person.

Social environment exerts considerable influence in the development of the personality of a person at all stages of life. Social environment may also include influence like average and individual milieu of the person. There is a fundamental dynamic relationship between the individual and the environment. The total situation develops concrete individuality. The forces in the social environment are important for the development of child behaviour. Human behaviour experiences intrinsic maturation in a rich environment. Social environment is not generally understood properly. Psychologically sometimes it is meant to mean the momentary situation in a child's life. But it refers to a milieu having some chief characteristics of a permanent situation.

The same physical object may have quite different sorts of psychological existence for different children and for the same child in different situations. It appears to be so as there is a direct relationship between the momentary state of the individual and the structure of his psychological environment.

The environment may have quasi-physical and quasi-social characteristics depending upon the needs, fantasies and necessities of a person. This provides dynamic meaning to the environment, which has its own functional possibilities and critical properties. The properties of the environment are determined by valences, strength and vectors. These factors, according to Gestalt psychology, determine the important properties of the environment.

Thus, environment means social, moral, economic, political, physical and intellectual factors which influence the development of the individual. All these factors mould and influence the behaviour of a person from time to time. Two individuals born with the same biological heritage differ because of differing environments. The environment is nothing but a process under suitable conditions to change the shape of a raw material just as a potter does while making toys of mud.

Heredity vs. Environment

As in most aspects of development, there is always the question of which is more important for personality — heredity or environment. According to traditional views, the personality of the individual was believed to be a direct result of his heredity. This is expressed in the saying, 'A chip off the old block.' Because people were so certain that the child was born with a personality trait. The child was permitted to grow up with such traits becoming stronger and the effort on the part of his parents being directed towards trying to discover which side of the family was responsible for these traits, instead of putting the same energy into an attempt to correct them.

Later, with the spread of the Freudian point of view concerning the growth of personality disorders as resulting from unhealthy environmental conditions, the pendulum swung to the opposite direction and major emphasis was placed on the role played by environment. Today, a middle-of-the-road interpretation is being accepted in place of the extreme view, which placed the whole emphasis either on heredity or on environment. It is now rather generally believed that the foundation of personality comes from the maturation of heredity traits, but that these are influenced, partly through learning in connection with direct social contacts and partly, through conditioning. This point of view is expressed by Landis who holds that personality is a dynamic and a growing entity. Psychologically, it is vested with the capacity for maturation. Except as mutilated by environment, physical traits follow their predestined course from childhood to maturity. Psychologically, it is plastic and is capable of an infinite number of modifications by external stimuli. Sociologically, it is dependent on the group to provide the patterns of development, because human nature is a group project.

Considering the bulk of evidence available, it may be stated that there is a definite operation between heredity and environment. Modern researches have shown that every trait of an individual and his every reaction depend both on the joint impact of the heredity and the environment. In no way can the environment and hereditary factors be sorted out in two exclusive categories. There is a constant interaction between the hereditary and environmental forces on an individual and they operate in an integrated and collective manner. Although the importance of the two may be relative only, it cannot be said that their operation is reclusive. The hereditary factor may operate differentially but this differentiation is determined by the environment. All said and done, the relative importance of the contribution of hereditary and environmental forces in the development of an individual depends on many factors and it would contain an infinite number of possible answers.

Viewing these factors in an objective manner, heredity and environment have a cumulative significance and they cannot be understood without proper qualifications. Heredity and environment imply many influences, specific in their own way and yet interactive and interdependent in their operation. In the process of development of an individual, interaction occurs within as well as between the specific factors in each of the two categories. Each gene has its specific chemical and other properties, but they ultimately operate into a field of total force that is an individual.

The importance of both nature and nurture for the development of the child is shown by many studies. The students of nature–nurture problem have tried to understand this question by studying the origin or differences in mental abilities, on the average, between various socio-economic groups, occupational groups, national groups, etc. Further, this controversy has also been tackled by studying children of identical genetic constitution or heredity, including children of identical multiple births and also on children whose genetic constitutions are known to be dissimilar. In various studies, nature has been kept constant and in others nurture. Studies conducted in the 1960s have shown that generally both nature and nurture are significant even though the importance of each in terms of percentages is now indeterminate and may continue to be so. Further, Blatz and Millichap studied the mental growth of the Dionne quintuplets. The report states that these individuals, presumably identical, manifest differences in emotional and intellectual traits which the authors conclude have been environmentally caused.

The controversy over nature–nurture will lose its colour once it is seen that mental development always takes place in some kinds of environment and is the result of an integrated action of nature and nurture. From the accounts of extremely deprived children, it is clear that mental development always requires cultural experiences within our society. Since mental ability is measured in terms of behaviour consistent with our culture concepts of intelligent activity, the impact of environment cannot be considered inconsiderable.

Mental abilities, according to the present research evidences, are seriously limited in its development in an environment which is markedly deficient. Variation in cultural environment, including schooling opportunities, are of great significance. Educationally, this fact cannot be ignored for it means that many children can, as a result of nursery-school experience, achieve a higher level of mental development that they could do without such opportunities. Improvement in the environment can improve a child and deficiencies in it would retard his many-sided growth and achievement. A recent publication by Schmidt has shown that many boys and girls can be spuriously classified as mentally deficient due to unfortunate and deeply rooted environment factors.

From the foregoing paragraphs, it would not be justified to conclude that one's personality is a product of heredity alone. Environment also plays an important part in the growth of a person. Development in a person is related both to heredity and environmental influences and both determine overall growth.

The hereditary–environment controversy is reflected in empiricist–rationalist controversy. Empiricists, who emphasise experience, tend to play down the influence of heredity by stressing the crucial importance of experience. They compare the mind at birth to a blank state. Ideas appear in the mind only when environmental impressions are received by it they assert that there are no innate or inborn notions or ideas. Everything is learnt by sense experiences.

But this is only a one-sided story. Adaptive reflexes and complex instincts suggest that there are some inborn tendencies which predispose a person to act to various stimulations in his own way. Infants and children leave individual ways of reacting to things. Talent is inborn. Training and special environment can develop it. Sense experiences cannot work independently of talent.

Butcher has summed up the problem in the following words:

"It should be realised at once that hardly any observable quality, physical or mental, can be ascribed to the influence of heredity alone or of environment alone. Even where a particular observable aspect of behaviour has been shown to be directly influenced by a gene or single genetic unit (such cases are rare in the study of human beings), this is no guarantee in itself that the behaviour is not also substantially dependent on variations in the environment. This principle is illustrated by a finding of Hogben about the fly Drosophila, in which he established that two distinct genetic mutations affect the number of facets in the fly's eye."

In short, it could be maintained that the effects of heredity and environment are interwoven from the time of birth and they cannot be isolated and studied in pure form. While the heredity determines the level, environment determines the functions of these abilities.

Educational Implications of Nature–Nurture Problem

In view of the considerable overlapping of mental abilities between children of several occupational levels, and in view of the fact that all levels of mentality are found among children of parents in each of the occupational levels, the point of educational significance is that the occupation and economic level of a family does not provide a basis upon which to evaluate the educational promise of any given child. With regard to this aspect of the nature–nurture problem, it is essential that for the sake of developing the child, total influence on the child must be conducive.

In the classroom the teacher should understand the nature mechanism of these two bases of behaviour. This can be so in order to diagnose and guide the growth and development of children. For instance, if a child is mischievous, it may be due to the fact that he comes from a home where good manners are not emphasised. Similarly, a child may fail to learn due to the vital deficiency in his physical condition, or because of insufficient motivation.

To enrich learning, the teacher should always stimulate the environment to the maximum. Without environment stimulation no organism could live or grow in a vacuum. Without stimulation, no modification or differentiation of behaviour is possible. As a few differences, existing between children have been traceable to the environmental differences, homes and schools should provide experiences to children which would help them to develop to their maximum.

Teachers should develop a realistic attitude in children. Further, teachers should also develop a fair and impartial attitude towards the potency of the organic and environmental forces in education, and they must endeavour to promote the growth of behaviour of each child under realistic and appropriate conditions. To understand the child, teachers must know him as a biological organism with needs and goals and must know his social and psychological environment of which he is a part.

In view of the background and evidence produced in the preceding pages, it is evident that the separation of developmental factors into heredity and environment is not sound. Both the factors operate together and one is inconceivable without the other. The level of mental development depends on the innate potentialities and also upon the quality of environment during the developmental period. To stimulate a pupil fully, enlightened, democratic, social and educational practices will have to be made available to him at school.

An average teacher needs to realise the tremendous significance of environmental, hereditary and cultural factors for the child's development. Attitudes, adjustments and behaviour patterns have to be structural to suit the child's ability and development.

Education means the modification of the behaviour of the child. Thus heredity and environment are two great forces, responsible for human behaviour and personality and both these should be studied by the teacher and parent. Nature and nurture are both potent factors in the development of the child. One is seed and the other is soil. One is spirit and the other is body. A successful teacher must know all about this.

The truth lies in the fact that both environment and heredity are needed for the development of an individual. An experienced gardener knows that both the seed and the soil are necessary for the proper growth of a plant. He could never grow a good crop from a poor seed, no matter how rich the soil, nor even from the best of seeds sown in poor soil. Just as the development of a plant depends upon the heredity present in the seed as much as on the environmental stimuli of soil, moisture and sunlight, etc., much similarly the growth and development of the individual personality is the outcome of both these factors. In other words the growth of the individual is a product of environment and heredity and not merely a sum of the two. The relation of heredity and environment is more like multiplication than like addition. Just as the area of the rectangle is not equal to the base and the altitude, but is equal to the product of the base and the altitude, similarly the individual development is not equal to the heredity and environment but it equals the product of the two. Just as we cannot say that the area of a triangle depends more on the base or more on the altitude, for if either of them is zero there will be no rectangle and hence no area whatsoever, similarly we cannot say that an individual depends more on the heredity or more upon the environment, for if any of them is absent there will be no individual whatsoever. Without heredity, the individual will not come into existence at all and without environment it will not grow; it may result in still birth. All development, therefore, depends upon both heredity and environment.

***

4

Personality Tests and Testing

T he profound learning on a wholesome personality is the learning on what personality testing can say on potential wholesomeness of personality in a child. A negation gives widespread misery which could be due to indifference on personality tests and indifference in teachers to know personality tests.

The contribution of teachers in building personality and attitudes of their students and wards is monumental. In fact, a teacher is the originator of change and growth in the affairs of a student, and a teacher, who helps the growth and development of a student's personality is the constructor who constructs for the society. The scrupulous role of teacher in shaping the personality of his students his been emphasised time and again in all educational reports and commissions.

The interest in personality tests, available in the market, can be both educational and vocational for teachers. Use of psychological tests by teachers can help them not only in providing competent guidance in growth of personality but also in evaluation of pupils in a proper and balanced way. Development of a pupil is a struggle of conscience to provide the best to the deserving pupils and to help the backward and the claim to realise his potential for full development of the self and self-realisation. Pupil is a resource, a test on personality is a measurement tool to evaluate the resource, and teachers who can evaluate their pupils can as well help in shaping the resource properly. The knowledge of personality tests is, therefore, very much an index of efficiency on what teachers can do for their students.

During the last 25 years, at least, a few thousand research tests on personality have been prepared and some have proved to be of outstanding help to teachers in their profession. Some outstanding tests on personality are outstanding forever and have been in use for the last 30 years without exception to their value for the general good of the students and for man and the patient. If on a view that information is power, correct use of information is wisdom and in that sense plans to think on how to use information reliably and wisely, is the plan to study what personality tests can let us know of a student, of a teacher, of a patient etc.

Personality tests, described in this chapter, are some of the useful tests which teachers may use on students for proper evaluation for the sake of proper educational development of students. Every year, a few million copies of tests of personality, all together, are used by psychologists and educationists to gather information, or data on pupils, patients, retarded children, gifted children, etc. Regardless of the country of origin, the tests, described in this chapter, are used as tools all over the world for programmes which are thoughtful and useful for several specific teaching objectives, and knowledge of these tests by teachers would enable them to use tools for testing scores which provides impetus for higher quality of growth in pupils through proper teaching services.

Personality tests are not drives by themselves, but are the driving force behind a decision, a development or instruction on what a teacher could achieve for a pupil after the pupil is evaluated on his personality quality and resource.

The genius in the work of classroom teaching dates back to days when personality was taken as the size of scope which highly skilled teachers could get out of pupils through knowledge on complex aspects of personality that pupils had. It is, therefore, open to argument that some of the personality tests do provide enthusiasm to teaching.

California Psychological Inventory (514)

This personality tool has been used by knowledgeable practitioners for assessing clinical information on psychological aspects of behaviour. In the 1956 edition of the test, there were 480 items in the test. Long form has added predilection and expectations too. The emphasis of the test is to study interpersonal behaviour and dispositions relevant to social interaction. Dominance, sociability, tolerance, etc., are emphasised in the inventory. The tool is valid for ages 13 and over.

The types of qualities measured by the tool are dominance (Do), capacity for status (Cs), sociability (Sy), social presence (Sp), self-acceptance (Sa), sense of well-being (Wb), responsibility (Re), socialisation (So), self-control (Sc), tolerance (To), good impression (Gi), communality (Cm), achievement via conformance (Ac), achievement of independence (Ai), intellectual efficiency (le), psychological mindedness (Pm), flexibility (Fx), femininity (Fe).

There are 18 scores and the scores are used in the profile type.

It is claimed by the makers of inventory that CPI is universally meaningful and relevant. The scores of the CPI are used as an index for decision-making processes.

The inventory validates usefully with various clinical samples, Examination of the 42 cross-validation correlation coefficients depict relationships between the CPI scores and various criteria (range: 0.21 to 0.60). The CPI scores correlates well with college attendance.

Burger has produced 240 item version of the inventory. Correlation between shorter and standard scale ranges from 0.78 to 0.93.

It is reported that CPI would fare well, given sharply defined criteria. For counselling, it gives some positive results.

Researchers have shown that data can help select talented youth and predict delinquent behaviour. It can also be used to assess moral development.

The inventory is also used for selection situations.

The CPI acquired its 1000 reference in 1972. Wide usage of this test in a great variety of situations is a scientific curiosity to test its clinical and psychological role. Test is seen to predict some useful information on behaviour.

Educational Apperception Test (541)

The principle of apperception is widely used in psychology and educational apperception test is a valuable tool to study the feelings and attitudes of children towards various educational settings. The test is usually meant for pre-school age children but can be extended up to elementary school. The use of the modified version of test for a higher age group is anticipated.

Educational Apperception Test or EAT has 18 photographs attempting to evoke fantasy in 4 areas namely, reaction towards learning, peer relationship and attitude towards school, etc.

There are separate forms for boys and girls. There are eight pictures for each gender and two pictures are common. In all 10 pictures are administered for complete administration. The photographs or pictures depict scenes in which children appear in various educational settings. The purpose is to elicit stories which reflect underlying feelings and attitude about schooling.

The test procedures are very delicate. Methodological procedures are to be carefully followed, psychological sensitivity of the situation is to be carefully observed and sense of 'timelessness' is to be kept to keep attitudes and feelings available for psychological analysis.

It is reported that the EAT evokes many of the images, emotions, thoughts and swells associated with school experiences. It is considered useful as an assessment tool or technique for school children. Interpretation of stories is to be done carefully and in a correct way so as to avoid an incorrect sense in the substance of the stories. This can add diagnostic relevance and maximise correct information and minimise errors of interpretation.

Though there can also be low correlation between the fantasies and behaviour, learning problems, attitudes, schooling ethos, etc., do get manifested. Perceptions of school and educational processes do have investigative relationship.

Validity and reliability data are not fully available. But the tool is of useful design to teachers.

Eysenck's Personality Inventory (553)

Eysenck's Personality Inventory is the revision of the Maudsley Personality Inventory. It also is drawn from the Eysenck Personality Questionnaire. The inventory is standardised on grades 9-16 and adults. The EPI remains the best known self-report tool. It assesses two major dimensions of personality. These two dimensions of personality were obtained from analysis of questionnaires and ratings. Eysenck's theories of personality have played a dominant role for 3 decades now. Data were obtained from MPI and later the EPI.

As per the reports on the inventory, the EPI was first published in 1963 and then replaced the MPI.

The test has 3 forms: A, B and A-I; forms A and B are parallel tools. Form A-I is the industrial version.

Three scores are obtained from the inventory namely extra-version, neuroticism and lie. They represent the Eysenckian dimensions.

Each form consists of 57 yes–no questions. The N and E scales consist of 24 items each. Items, numbering 9 are lie score items. Lie scores tend to identify the 'faking good'.

Both the N and the E scales encompass a wide variety of context.

Manual reports that high N scores indicate irritability, easily hurt, nervous, worrying, moody, feelings of unfit state, sleeplessness, dissatisfied and guilty. Of the 24 N items, 21 indicate negative or unpleasant experiences of some kind.

Eysenck has started neuroticism as general emotional over-responsiveness or over-activity. The trait was obtained after lengthy and repeated factor analysis.

Eysenck describes the dual nature of extraversion which includes sociability and impulsiveness components. It is stated that a unitary sociability–impulsiveness dimension is not strong.

EPI information is available against trade and occupational groups. It is also available for the abnormal groups. Information is given in terms of mean and SD values. It is seen that N and E scores are related to work adjustment, academic achievement and also to psychopathology.

As already said, the N scale consists of 23 items, all keyed for a 'yes' response. N scale appears to be very successful in discriminating between normal adults and neurotics.

E scores describe playfulness, seeking excitement, carefree attitude, fast moving, impulsive, lively, talkative and gregarious. The E scale consists of 21 items, 18 of them keyed for a 'yes' response.

The L scale consists of 21 items, 6 of which are scored for a 'yes' keyed response.

Lie scale reveals untruthfulness. Lie scores measure same 'approval motive'.

Each items for N, E and L scores were retained on the basis of actual validation data of the final product.

P scale consists of 25 items, 14 of them keyed for a 'yes' response. Test and re-test correlations have been worked out and also parallel-form correlations. Test–retest correlations range between 0.81 and 0.85 for each scale. The parallel-form correlation in a sample of 1 to 55 normals was found to be 0.80 for N and 0.75 for E scales. The internal consistency reliability of N scale is quite satisfactory being around 0.80. The internal-consistency reliability of E scale is around 0.80 in a number of samples.

It is reported that like MMPI, CPI can play a very useful role in clinical and counselling settings, and in research design it can play a useful role on assessing personality.

In summing up, there was the first Maudsley Medial Questionnaire which was a measure of neuroticism (N) dimension only. It was succeeded by the Maudsley Personality Inventory which measured N and extraversion–introversion (E) dimension. Then followed the Eysenck Personality Inventory which measures the N, E and L scores.

Holtzman Inkblot Technique (578)

Holtzman Inkblot Technique (HIT) is generally a clinical and general tool to measure as many traits as 20–22 in all. The tool is meant for ages 5 and over. Compared to the Rorschach, the HIT is not very popular as it is time-consuming and takes a lot of time to administer and to score.

However, better prediction of personality is expected when the tool is combined with another personality test. The test has also been used to study personality theory.

Qualities, or traits, that the test measures are rejection, reaction time, location, space, form definiteness, form appropriateness, colour, shading, movement, pathognomonic, verbalisation, integration, content (animal, anatomy, sex), anxiety, hostility, barrier, penetration, balance etc.

The test appears to be related to body awareness and muscle awareness feelings among females. This sex effect is further being investigated.

All details on the validity and the reliability of the test are not fully known.

IPAT Anxiety Scale Questionnaire (582)

This test is generally used as a measure for anxiety. It is applicable from age 14 upwards. There are 40 items each requiring endorsement of one of three alternatives. The items are classified into 20-item sub-scales. One scale measures covert anxiety. Second measures overt anxiety. The scale measures apprehension, tension, low self-control, emotional instability, suspicion. The items are simple such as:

I seem to tremble or perspire when I think of a difficult task ahead, (a) yes, (b) in between (c) No. Subject has to select one answer. Answers are keyed as 2, 1, or 0.

Overt refers to manifest indication of anxiety Covert refers to less obvious signs of anxiety. It gives 5 scores separately for 5 components of anxiety.

Norms are prepared separately for the sexes.

The scale correlates 0.70 with Taylor scale. With Eysenck and Maudsley scales it correlates up to 0.73.

It is reported that school dropout proneness and ASQ rule show high relationship.

Administration and scoring of the test is simple. The reliability of the test is 0.82 to 0.93 (test–re-test). Validity of the tool is also worked out against standard anxiety scales as quoted earlier.

Minnesota Multiphasic Personality Inventory (616)

The MMPI has been used widely all over the world. It has 6000 citations to its credit. Meehl, a clinical psychologist, argues that personality assessment should be considered in the light of Einstein's judgment concerning the state of physics. The test has been used on more than 50,000 patients. The MMPI remains a matchless tool as the objective instrument for the assessment of psychopathology.

It is reported that score categories may not give pure trait, or, absolute discrete entities. Generally, most of the patients show a mixture of symptoms. Further, scores are also not highly stable over a long period of time. It is reported that symptoms of pathology go and regress as the patient progresses in his or her psychotherapy. The individual form of the test, when used on a person, consists of 550 cards each with a question.

The scores are available in F score, L score (lie), K score (for discrimination on normal vs. abnormal conditions).

It is composed of 550 items. Answers are Yes, No and Cannot say.

The MMPI yields 14 scores. But the following 9 are most frequently used: Hypochondriasis (unwanted concern with bodily health); Depression (pessimism and low morale); Hysteria (dodging duty or problems through physical symptoms); psychopathic deviate (delinquency); paranoia (superior); psychasthenia (beset with doubts and fears); schizophrenia (disorganised thinking and behaviour); hypomania (excitement); masculinity-femininity.

The MMPI has been used extensively to find out conditions of drug abuse, alcoholism, motor disturbances, therapy, and predicting brain damage cases and emotional disturbances; it is also used sometimes for employment screening; for military screening and civil screening; professional activities; discipline and order; fire fighting jobs, etc.

Computerised scoring and interpretation sources are available for automatic psychological assessment. The programme on interpretation is written and data collected. But information are often chiselled for objective and critical evaluation and for overall accuracy to avoid prejudicing data.

Omnibus Personality Inventory (634)

The inventory tends to measure social attitudes, intellectual values and social adjustment and emotional characteristics. These values are ascribed to the forward-looking disposition of a person besides his potential to meet life objectively and with flexibility. The organising capacity in personality is the focus of attention. The inventory tries to study or predict college achievement, besides intellectual efficiency, responsibility, self-control, etc.

The OPI is a self-reporting inventory designed for use with college students which measures personality dimension associated with effective functioning in college settings besides surveying other attitudes.

Considerable work was done to evolve theoretical and empirical aspects on theory of the test. The theory emphasises and assumes that a human being is the possibility of his remote past, present background and future to design. For homogeneity and separation, the development nature of man is explained in terms of social context, and current behaviour is the call for the necessity to better the future which is amount of change.

The test yields 15 scores: thinking introversion; theoretical orientation; aestheticism; complexity; autonomy; religious orientation; social extroversion; impulsive expression; personal integration; anxiety level; altruism; practical outlook; masculinity–feminity; response bias; and intellectual disposition.

The scale tries to give a matrix of relationship between various sub-scales. It also measures the attitudinal and interest aspects of the person and includes the personality aspect in the contextual-behavioural terms.

The OPI tends to emphasise intellectual values and interests, liberal attitudes (vs. lack of them), social-emotional adjustment characteristics. But the qualities are not fully psychometrically defined in terms of fact or development.

The inventory is difficult to score. Even the computer work is cumbersome.

In brief, assessment on attitudinal values can be easily supplemented with OPI to add information to conventional trait inventories.

The validity and reliability of the inventory are not consistently high.

Rorschach

McArthur, in the 7th MMY, describes Rorschach, as the 'only game in town' by which to know the idiosyncratic laws of the personal mind. The game that Rorschach sounds is the game of responses to document blowout and apparently bizarre behaviour. The Rorschach is still one of the most popular and frequently used clinical procedure for assessing emotional disturbances of the psyche. It offers a psychodynamic theory on psychopathology of the personality and to fathom the complex personality structures. Even anxiety complexes are studied from test protocols.

It can be used on ages 3 and above. The material is composed of 10 cards each with a complex ink blot. The blot or picture is bilaterally symmetrical. Some blots are in black, some white and grey, and some in two or more chromatic colours.

It is reported that Rorschach provides some long-range prediction information on the generalisation of cause of disturbance and the ability of the person to cope with present and future stresses. It has been used to study sexual problems, to study 'school readiness', to predict success, to predict suicide, delinquency, de-personalisation, well-being, growth and change.

The concepts like movement, colour, anatomy, etc., have been used to analyse data. More details on this aspect of testing have been discussed in the previous chapter.

Very elaborate scoring systems are developed to analyse data. Data are analysed into intellectual qualities, and into temperamental and motivational qualities.

The data from the test have been used for studying the disposition and treatment of individuals. Test responses and personality characteristics seem to provide a predictable relationship regarding psychopathology, ego strength, somatic illness, contamination and confabulation of thought processes.

Rorschach method, Rorschach Test, Rorschach INK Blot Test, Rorschach psychodiagnostic test, etc., are titles under which the test is known. Herman Rorschach revolutionised projective technique procedures. The test is an unstructured task and structure is dynamic. The nature of projection is expressive in form.

Barclay Classroom Climate Inventory (502)

This Inventory is the first of its type to measure social interaction and group expectations. It consists of three major parts The first part is made up of 163 items with three parts: there is a 72-item section on vocational activities, on sports, on radio, news or weather; 40 items on personal competence; and 51 items on behavioural interest.

The second part is made of 28 peer nomination items which provides information on likes and dislikes.

The third part has 63 items which are adjectives or items on social adjustment, personal adjustment, motivation and diligence. The teacher rates the adjustments.

The self-reporting section provides three scales: self-competence, vocational interests and behavioural interest scales.

The validation data on BCCI gives highest correction of 0.33 and the minimum correlation of 0.13 to 0.17 with different tools.

The reliability of various BCCI scales ranges from 0.50 to 0.90.

The BCCI is regarded as an instrument which is still in a developmental stage.

Bradfield Classroom Interaction Analysis

Classroom interaction phases involve teacher–pupil bi-polar process or pupil–pupil interaction behaviour. Classroom dynamics is the process of operation of essential teacher ambitions and goals on change in behaviour of pupils. Teachers follow democratic or authoritarian attitudes or conditions on justice and use which are dimensions of learning process.

The tool can be used on children kindergarten to 12. It is made of three parts which can be used together or separately or in combination. The academic therapy models are described in the tool. The scale has teacher-style scale and pupil–pupil or pupil–teacher interactional scale. It also has another scale called the teacher-attention and pupil-behaviour scale.

The three scales deal with warm, cold personality classroom environment, authoritarian-democratic attitude items, etc.

The reliability and validity of the scale are in progress. There are biases and subjective feelings that enter into the working of the instrument and tend to influence scoring of the scales.

Rosenzweig Picture-Frustration Test (662)

Rosenzweig Picture-Frustration Test was developed by Saul Rosenzweig in 1944–1948. It is a set of cartoons in which one figure is shown to thwart another. The subject is shown as talking to the second person and the picture demands a reply. It is a sort of a self-reporting test using the fantasies of the persons. The subject has not to draw any drawing but to interpret them carefully.

The concept of projective technique is generally applied for use of the test. It is basically a clinical tool which requires minimum of instruction, and is considered promising and useful.

The ambiguity of the task and undefined nature of the material gives better scope, expressive activity and the projective technique reactions are emphasised and fantasy activised. The subjective appeal of pictures is very interesting.

The test is used on ages 4 to 12, 13 to 18, and 18 and over.

The items in the test are cartoon-like and drawings show two people in conversation. The situations are varied and each situation tends to involve person in a designed way through identification and projection mechanism.

The test gives 15 scores such as direction of aggression, (extrapunitive, intropunitive, impunitive), type of aggression (obstacle-dominance, ego-defence, need-persistence), and nine combinations of the preceding categories.

The P.F. test was designed to measure primarily three different kinds of reactions to frustration:

Extrapunitive (E attacks his environment)

Intropunitive (E turns his aggression on himself)

Impunitive (E glosses over the problems and tries to minimise the frustration).

The test is available for children and for adolescents. The revised form is available for adults too.

According to information available on test reliability, it is seen that it is moderate i.e., 0.4 to 0.8.

Validity data are also low. The test material needs to be used judiciously for interpretation. While in theory or practice, the test has lots of potential; the need for proper validation is still there for useful prediction.

Sixteen Personality Factor Questionnaire

R.B. Cattell has attempted to define and refine conception on personality on the basis of 16 traits. Cattell's traits of personality are based on the factor–analysis method and underlies the trait theory on personality. Cattell was educated at London University and worked at University of Illinois as the Research Professor of Psychology. According to him, personality is a structure of traits which are both surface traits and source traits. The traits emphasised in the inventory are source traits.

The 16 PF is an inventory consisting of 15 self-report personality scales and one general intelligence scale. The scales assess a variety of traits and are non-homogeneous in content. The scales are collected on the basis of some prior premise and there is no apparent theoretical basis for the selection of traits. However, certain criterion observations have been used to build the test on 16 factor base. The PF was constructed and refined through scores of factor–analytic studies. Cattell had categorically stated that the factor–analysis procedure could isolate underlying causal influences in human personality. The trait concept was studied by him under discriminant validity, convergent validity, and factor validity.

The intelligence scale is designed to assess a combination of what Cattell called 'fluid' and 'crystallised' intelligence. The primary purpose of reviving intelligence into fluid and crystallised dimensions was to make the concept more pragmatic.

As per the information available on the tool, data is used in 22 scores.

The primary 16 factor scores are: reserved vs. outgoing (A); less intelligent vs. more intelligent (B); affected by feelings vs. emotionally stable (C); humble vs. assertive (E); sober vs. happy-go-lucky (F); expedient vs. consciousness (G); Shy vs. venturesome (H); tough minded vs. tender-minded (I); Trusting vs. suspicious (L); practical vs. imaginative (M); forthright vs. shrewd (N); self-assured vs. apprehensive (O); conservative vs. experimenting (Qt); group-dependent vs. self-sufficient (Q2); undisciplined self-conflict vs. controlled (Q3); relaxed vs. tense (Q4).

There are six second-order factor scores that are obtained from the test:

Introversion vs. extroversion (I); low anxiety and high anxiety (II); tender-minded emotionally vs. tough poise (III); subduedness vs. independence (IV); naturalness vs. discreetness (V); cool realism vs. prodigal subjectivity.

The information on test reports that the 16 PF possesses a number of positive features. Each pole of the 16 bipolar scales is defined into 3 to 17 adjectives or descriptive phrases. This description renders clinical reporting on the person more precise and simplified. No one has ever taken a more vigorous and ambitious research for the fundamental dimensions of human behaviour as Cattell. Accordingly, the factors which 16 PF purports to scale range from intellectual ability to affective states, ego-functioning, coping, style and group orientation.

The applications of the test are widely discussed. It is said that the test can be used for assessing school achievement, creativity, leadership, delinquency, vocational guidance, clinical diagnosis and, above all, for research. Some of the 16 PF scale's have acceptable levels of stability.

Reliability of the test is also discussed in positive language. The traditional test–retest reliabilities for the 16 scales average to 0.705.

Validity of the source traits is discussed indirectly. Validity co-efficients range up to 0.50 are quoted. Also validity is discussed in terms of its prediction towards school success and job satisfaction.

Norms for forms A, B, C & D of the 16 PF are based on a large sample of high-school students and college students. Form 'E' of the scale is based on culturally disadvantaged subjects.

Test is available in forms like A, B, C, D and E. Forms A and B have 374 items and forms C & D have 174 items.

Thematic Apperception Test

Thematic Apperception Test belongs to a thematic projective class of techniques. TAT belongs to type and tools in which the subject is asked to handle a problem in his own style. In a way, TAT is a class of stylistic tests in which thoughts and fantasies of the subject are stimulated through appropriate stimuli. Thematic categories are not mutually barren but full of symbolism; the style of information gives sources to come closer to personality and to the whole man, as the psychological nature of emotions, attitudes, feelings, fears anxieties and cognitive processes. To Murray, the brain is the seat of power and personality is anchored to the brain.

The author, H.A. Murray, was born in New York City on May 13, 1893. He graduated from Harvard College and later also graduated from Columbia College of Physicians and Surgeons. He got his Ph.D. in biochemistry from Cambridge in 1927 and it was at that University that he turned to psychology.

In 1943, Murray joined the Army Medical Corps and directed an assessment service for the office of strategic services. He was given the task of screening candidates for complex, secret and dangerous missions.

This work on TAT grew at the Harvard Psychological clinic. The role of the author with Morgan was to build TAT but not on purely orthodox Freudian or psychoanalytical review. But the basic emphasis was very close to the Freudian school and the concept of identification as the mechanism was employed to build testing theory.

The test is used to study the patients or subject's needs, motives, values and basic attitudes. The pictures consist of characters representing various moods, situations, needs, motives and responses. The pictures are vague, sometimes even the gender of the characters is not revealed, and the characters are unclear and blurred.

The TAT consists of 20 pictures and one blank card which are given to a subject. Total content of the protocol are the aids to the exploration of personality. Contemporary psychology is a relationship between mind and body or study of both and TAT has given thought to know that psychology tends to win.

The subject is instructed to tell or write a story about each picture. The subject is told that the test is a test of 'powers of imagination'. The story is to be given in a sequence of past, present and future goals on the probe of the psyche of the subject. The needs and presses of the subject are regularly examined and his anxieties and interests are explored in terms of test theory as advocated by Murray. The clinical psychologist's goal is to get the basic personality details of the patient.

Time limits are imposed and it depends upon the job, and 10 pictures are used for all subjects and 10 more pictures are selected from 20 others. Each picture is coded for age and sex. A blank card is also shown. The total number of pictures are 31. Each story is coded for needs (inner states that can be expressed) and for press (inner states that involve a perception of some external force acting upon the subject).

Reliability of TAT assessments states that various interpreters vary and agreement is not close always. A general idea prevails that agreement tends to increase when interpreters have shared similar experiences. It is quoted that retest reliabilities have been generally moderate to low. Values have been 0.80 after 2 months; 0.60 after 6 months and 0.50 after 10 months.

Validity of the TAT assessments provides various data. The conditions of the ranking of the items by the 17 experts with this criterion ranged from 0 22 to 0.76 with an average of 0.60. Variations in validity index are due to quality of criteria used to validate it.

Adaptations of the TAT have grown since years. To meet the problems of clinical significance, sounds and visual design, and even high stimuli intensities in sound ranges have been tested whether the subject could give data on anxieties, fears, emotions, exhibitions and attitudes. McClell has used TAT principles to study the need for achievement and achievement motivation. Some have used high sounds to leak the brain.

TAT is described as a viable assessment tool. Morgan and Murray have shaped the test and let others shape the skills to use the test properly.

Concept-specific Anxiety Scale (528)

The concept-specific anxiety scale is a tool used generally for research purposes. After extensive and proper researches, it may be useful for clinical studies and diagnosis particularly in studying anxiety states. This scale has a unique background in its development in the score that it had attempted to quantify the amount of anxiety elicited when the same specific concepts are used as stimuli. It is differential, in the sense that anxiety is measured with respect to a specific stimuli or concept.

The scale has some resemblance to Osgood's semantic differential.

Stimuli is presented in either verbal or pictorial form and it is used both for adult patient and non-patient population.

The scale gives factor I which measures the physiological responsivity dimension or state-anxiety factor. The factor second score measures enduring mood or trait anxiety.

The reliability of scale is 0.79. It is not sufficiently validated.

Kerontological Apperception Test (566)

This test is specifically designed for the elderly population. The Kerontological title suggests so. Elderly persons have minds which have stereotypes of older people who generally are depressed, decrepit and too aged to assent to personal liberty, a way of life which is unlifelike, a support in home which is unworthy in terms of ego and self-respect, and a mind which is called dumpy and clothed with no style.

The test is used for ages 66 and over. There are 14 cards. Out of 14, 11 cards show the final expressions of the older figures as very distraught, a sort of negative stereotype which is associated with that age level.

The test has a sort of therapeutic effect on the person being examined. The cards tend to neutralise the negative identity of self-image imposed on elders.

This is the only projective test available for the elderly. The validity and reliability needs to be verified with the pathological aging for the manifest age.

Dynamic Personality Inventory (539)

This is one of the unique tests in the sense that the test is only for those who are 15 or 17 and over and ones who have an I.Q. of 80 and over. In a way, the scale does not give a distorted picture in the sense that it demands certain basic ability quota. The emphasis throughout given by the test is on psychological meaningfulness rather than on mathematical purity or rigidity. The study of the specific group is the important feature of the test. The test is, therefore, based on empirical data on personality testing. The dynamics in a way present some data basically psychoanalytic in bias.

The test is based on the Freudian model of personality, but it also adopts a few changes based on clinical and statistic experiences. But, the authors generally try to use psychoanalytic analysis and experience as the subject theme on presentation of view.

The test measures hypocrisy, passivity, seclusion–introspection, morality, oral aggression, verbal aggression, emotional dependence, emotional independence, boarding, attention to details, conservatism, submissiveness, law-and-order attitudes, insularity, drive for achievement and adventure, sexuality, tackle impression enjoyment, creative interests, masculine interests, feminine interests, social role seeking, social activity interest, need to give affection, ego defence persistence initiative.

It is a self-administered test and consists of 325 items to be marked as liked or disliked. The test is not suited to a psychotic patient. The use of mental level, as considered basic to test norm, is to see that those whose mental ability are low or impaired, are not allowed to subdue the data due to their organic or psychic pathologies.

Reliability co-efficients fall between 0.23 to 0.90. A sample of 103 British neurotics gave higher co-efficients in the range of 0.51 to 0.91. Some of the scales only reach a reliability of 0.75.

Validity of the test, tested against several criteria, gives various results. Validity data are generally used in a psychoanalytic context. The work on validity needs to be undertaken.

Indian Tests Related to Adjustment, Anxiety, Attitudes, etc.

The Agra Psychological Research Cell has issued information on a catalogue of psychological and educational tests produced, adapted and standardised by Indians. Following are the details on titles of some of the personality tests.

A. 1. Multivariate Personality Inventory (MPI)
   2. Personality Adjustment Inventory
   3. Personality Need Inventory
   4. Humour Test

  5. Sentence Completion Test
  6. Moral Judgment Test
  7. Children Personality Questionnaire
B. 8. Security Insecurity Inventory,
  9. Behaviour Deviance Scale
  10. Youth Problem Inventory
  11. Liar and Criminal Detection Test
  12. Problem check test
C. 13. Socio-economic Scale
  14. Study Habit Inventory
  15. Teacher's Job Satisfaction Questionnaire
  16. Teachers Proficiency Scale
  17. Test of Democratic Values

Details regarding authors and publishers of the earlier tests are available with Agra Psychological Research Cell, Belaneani, Agra-282004.

The Mirror-Tracing Test

The Mirror-tracing Test is about to complete nine decades of its existence in psychology. Ninety years is a big span of life for any psychological tool to show its worthwhileness as a multivariate tool. There appears to be no other tool which has been introduced in the field of psychology with so little fanfare as the Mirror-tracing Test. Introduced by Buckwald (1948) of Berlin in 1878, the test has lived a long period of existence, and, since its introduction, has suffered from the vicissitudes of fortune from time to time. Its popularity has varied from university to university and from one psychological laboratory to another. Beginning its role as a tool for studying the relationship between visual perception and motor movements, the mirror-drawing technique has entrenched itself variedly in different universities and psychological laboratories of the East and the West, and has been employed in studying various problems, beginning from learning and extending to the study of problems on trial and error transfer of training, delinquency, pilot selection, and psychodiagnosis and psychotherapy. There is also an interesting application of the test in the field of clinical psychology as demonstrated by a research study by Tutoo (1968). As the researches on the Mirror-tracing Test are numerous, it is worthwhile to assess the potentialities of the test in diverse fields so as to arrive at an objective assessment on the assets and liabilities of the test in psychological and educational research.

In the initial stages of work, the Mirror-tracing Test was employed by research workers as an experimental tool in analysing and observing the nature of the learning process and in studying the relationship between visual perception and motor learning. Henri (1948) and Dearborn (1910) employed the test in studying the mechanism of learning in a human situation. They found that there was alteration of established customary visual-motor behaviour among experimental subjects because of the mirror which rendered performance difficult to execute. The subjects in the experiment were required to master the task of tracing by re-establishing the customary coordination in their visuo-perceptual movements in their successive trials on the Mirror-tracing Test.

In the wake of the first publication of the results on the Mirror-tracing Test, there followed a series of other publications emanating from experiments conducted in various psychological laboratories of the world in both the East and the West. Though all the results on the test did not find their way to journals, a large number of studies were mainly devoted to the learning process among subjects. Clinton (1930) explored the nature of the mirror-drawing ability by studying the norms on mirror-drawing for white and black children by age and sex. In his investigation, the investigator obtained data on 1903 unselected students in four school systems, who were allowed to work for a period of five minutes on the mirror-drawing pattern sheet. On the basis of trials, the investigator found that mirror-drawing was essentially a trial-and-error motor-learning process, that mirror-drawing performance developed from year to year, that there was a positive relationship between mirror-drawing ability and general intelligence, and that there was a positive relationship between mirror-drawing ability and simple motor speed-marking and making letters. Studies published by other investigators supported some of the finding of Clinton (1936), and Yoakum and Calfee (1913), found that the subjects, on the basis of performance on the Mirror-tracing Test, could be classified into fast, slow and irregular groups. Extending this aspect of research further, Cook (1914) employed the test in studying the prospects of positive and negative transfer in learning among subjects from time to time. He gave 100 trials to (subjects, involving various parts of the body such as the left and right hands and left and right feet, which were tested for transfer. His results indicated that there was some transfer to all muscle groups and that transfer was the greatest to the symmetrical muscle group on the opposite side of the body and least to the muscle group opposite to the unsymmetrical parts of the body. Similar types of studies followed. Valentine (1954) considered mirror-drawing as a crude and primitive method of learning in which movements were learnt and remembered through kinesthetic cues. Burt (1938) had also employed the test for examining the motor-habit formation in children. In the studies, Burt found that the skill acquired with the right hand was transferred to a considerable extent to the left hand among normal children but not among the dull children. Collins and Drever (1956) employed the test in studying the mechanism of coordination of movements between the hand and the eye during trial-and-error learning. They had drawn a curve of learning based on the time taken for the respective tracings. Postman and Egan (1958) also utilised the Mirror-tracing Test for studying cross-education and bilateral transfer. The authors, through their experiments, had found that most of the subjects start at a low level of skill but improve considerably after practice. They found that transfer effects were the result of the method of 'attack' and 'attitudes' which transferred from one situation to another. Kuppuswamy (1947) and Scheldemann (1948), through various experiments, found that the new coordination among subjects between their motor and perceptual processes was a result of trial-and-error learning and not imitation or ideational control. Scheldemann's experiment had yielded learning curves which bore similarity to Starch's one hundred records and were typical of all learning curves. Scheldemann had found that the effect of practice of the right hand upon the left hand was quite considerable.

Other investigators employed the Mirror-tracing Test as a tool for studying the problems of habit formation. Notable studies of this type were undertaken by Dashiell (1948), Grings (1952), Stevens (1951) and Woodworth (1947). These investigators studied the characteristics of the learning curves by studying time-and-error scores of subjects. They also studied qualitative changes in the performance of subjects by examining the turns and curvatures of the learning curves.

The contribution of the Mirror-tracing Test in helping to understand the learning process is manifold. Experiments carried out with the help of this test have helped in understanding the types of changes brought about by the practice in learning curves. Notable investigations in this direction are those of Woodworth. In part, his studies had examined the extent of transfer that was maximally possible from one hand to another and from one foot to another. But his later experiments with the test showed that other factors like nervousness and self-consciousness also affected performance of subject irrespective of their age at the time of testing.

In an educational situation, the mechanism of 'acquisitive' process in learning is important to know. It is, therefore, imperative to understand the psychology of this process. The Mirror-tracing Test has helped considerably in unravelling this process. The findings from mirror-drawing studies have shown that the role of cognition in a behaviour-like learning is not mechanical but pervasive. Relevant studies, throwing light on this aspect of learning, are those of Trow (1950), Bugelski (1950), Guilford (1947), Gagne (1952), Sartin (1958) and Shaffer (1956). These mirror-drawing studies have not only explained the principle of trial-and-error learning scientifically, but have also enlarged the concept of learning process from the mere 'substitution' process to a dynamic one. Thus, these experiments have shed considerable light on trial-and-error learning. They have also simplified the principle underlying 'positive', 'negative' and 'zero' transfer that occurs in various learning situations.

Perceiving the fact that the Mirror-tracing Test had the genius to explain the learning process in detail and depth, many alterations were made in its constructions to study other problems pertaining to learning behaviour. Important studies in this direction are those of Whipple (1948), Calfee (1913), Wells (1918), Pyle (1923), Ewerts (1926), Starch (1948), Lachman Witty (1948), Higginson (1938), Weber (1938), Cook (1941), Lasterback (1927), Suoddy (1948) and others. The important observation emerging from the aforesaid studies is that Mirror-tracing Test has diverse uses in a laboratory.

However, modification in the design of the test was not only necessitated by the difficulty faced in counting errors but also in motivating subjects to respond favourably towards the test. The structural changes in the design were as diverse as there were innovators. Dearborn came out with "a single-line star whereas Whipple devised a concentric double-lined figure (Star) which has, in fact, remained a standard figure since then. However, due to limitations, which the star pattern has posed—that the learning process could be memorised and might therefore facilitate learning without complete mastery of the visuo-motor relationship— Calfee and Yoakum devised a circular design about 16 centimetres in diameter, around which were marked 12 equally spaced points. The centre of the circle was marked with '0' and its circumference was labelled with figures from 1 to 12 in random order to avoid memorisation. The advantage claimed in this design was that it eliminated practically all automatic behaviour and demanded attention and ingenuity on the part of the subject.

Since these innovations in design changed the character of experiments on the Mirror-tracing Test from time to time, many new explanations were advanced by various investigators regarding the learning process. The purpose behind each change was to understand the trial-and-error phenomenon if learning on a more scientific basis. The intention while changing the design was not only to render a systematic account of errors but also to remove the possibility of learning by mechanical means alone. Keeping these prerequisites in view, Well (1918) introduced another change by employing electric devices for counting errors. In his apparatus, electric connections were tied to a metallic start which was connected to a counter and also to a power source. A metallic stylus connected to electric connections, completed the circuit. This arrangement enabled the experimenter to count errors easily for each trial separately.

In the wake of changes in the design of the test, experiments carried out with the help of the Mirror-tracing Test exposed many interesting changes in the learner's behaviour. However, each modification in design was introduced with a specific purpose in view. Pyle (1923), for example, employed concentric circles, fortified by electric connections with numerical numbers from 1–24 placed around the circumference of two circles. With a view to make the learning process more complicated, subjects were asked to place a dot on each number and thus to draw a continuous line cutting these dots again in numerical order. This device helped in reducing the scope of memorisation in a subject at the time of working on the test.

As each change in the design of the test was accompanied by a spate of new findings on the mechanism of learning, many more changes were registered in the test. The main motivation behind each change was to study the learning process in detail and depth. It would therefore be pertinent to briefly describe the other changes that were brought about in the designs of the test, besides those already mentioned earlier.

Lachman and Witty brought a change of an altogether different type in the Mirror-tracing Test. He contrived the design out of three leaf-metal frames. The top leaf covered the window and was held in place by a wire hinge. The middle-leaf was of polished metal which operated as the mirror. The slug across the bottom of the leaf was made to rest against the third leaf which formed the base and the platform for the entire pattern. All the three leaves were collapsible so as to form a compact unit for storing. Another modification of importance was that made by Starch (1948). He used simple hooks to support the mirror in place and used a cardboard screen which was clamped to a tripod. This arrangement had the claim of simplicity and economy over the equipment illustrated by Pyle. Another change introduced by Higginson (1938) in the design was motivated by the idea of introducing illumination which was found helpful in eliminating shadows which had affected the performance in earlier studies.

However, a significant change in the test was introduced by Weber (1939). He replaced the simple mirror by convex and concave, and later by parabolic mirrors. These mirrors created many distortions in the object. Such distortions made the mirror-drawing performance even more difficult for all subjects to perform.

Despite these changes in the design of the test, the test continued to remain simple and economical and enjoyed immense popularity due to its simplicity and versatility. Because of these advantages in the test, many investigators were eager to do more studies with the help of the Mirror-tracing Test. These investigations belonged not only to the realm of learning but also to other areas of the educational process. It would be profitable to dilate on these mirror-drawing experiments as they would help in throwing light on their mechanisms of the learning process in detail.

Holsopple (1932) found that in a classroom where different types of subjects are studied, the teaching process had to be differential and unique. The investigator based his conclusions on the fact that emotionally disturbed pupils were unable to control or inhibit their habituated responses. He concluded that mirror-drawing could serve as a helpful tool to counsellors for diagnosing important behaviour characteristics in the case of emotionally disturbed pupil. His experiments on the learning behaviour of emotionally disturbed pupils had also shown that their performance was slow and their lines were very light or very heavy. Their digressions from the correct path were numerous and wide. They were unable to control their movements which moved in many pointless ways. They even laughed and sighed. In the case of emotionally adjusted pupils, the drawings were drawn early and quickly and were characterised by uniformity, energy and by persistent performance. Similar prognostic experiments were conducted on other types of pupils belonging to various clinical groups and diverse socio-economic levels.

To verify the findings of Holsopple's experiments, Weidensall used the mirror-drawing technique in studying the learning behaviour of normal pupils and compared it with that of the pupils who were studying in various classes lodged in different reformatories and in schools functioning in villages. He confirmed Holsopple's observation that emotionally disturbed pupils were incapable of sustained effort stress. The findings bore an important bearing on the teaching practices followed in the classroom. The educational implications of these studies are that because pupils in a class come from diverse background their progress in learning is not only to be reviewed from the intellectual angle but also from the emotional angle, as is evident from the aforesaid studies. Laiprade (1948) also suggested a specialised curriculum for children who are not too well emotionally. He suggested separate classes and a separate set of instructions for various groups of pupils. He found that children suffering from various emotional problems tend to invert their writing when using a mirror. Vogt (1948) also advocated a separate curriculum and special teaching methods for children with definite emotional problems. Bois (1948) and Ball (1928) were also able to use the mirror-drawing technique for differentiating the more stable pupils in the classroom from unstable pupils.

Cook, while investigating the studies in cross-education, used the Mirror-tracing Test as the instrument of study. After 100 trials of practice with their right hand in mirror-drawing and using a star-shaped maze as the tracing object, the left foot, the right and the left hand were tested for transfer. Similarly, after 100 practice trials with the left foot and the right hand, the left hand and the right foot were tested. The author reported that:

1. There was some transfer to all muscle groups.
2. The transfer was greatest to the symmetrical muscle group on the opposite side of the body, next to the muscle group on the same side and least to the muscle group which is both unsymmetrical and opposite of the practised hand or foot. The percentage of transfer varied with the measure used.
3. There was no difference between the amount of transfer from hand to foot and from foot to hand.

Burt, in his investigation, reported a correlation of 0.67 between speed in mirror drawing and intelligence as estimated by teachers. Clinton, however, found no correlation between mirror-drawing and the scores made on intelligence tests. Comparing the two results Clinton argued that, after all, the teacher estimated highly the intelligence of that child who quickly and easily inhibited those bits of behaviours that were not approved by the teacher. The results obtained by Burt, obviously, appear to be circumstantial.

The mirror-drawing technique was used by Hartog (1948) for studying anxiety provoked during examination in students. He called this technique as the 'Kotaphograph'. In his tentative work, he compared the mirror-drawing performance against the criterion of number of affirmative answers given by pupils on a questionnaire of 25 items pertaining to examination anxiety.

Later Abt and Bellak (1952) employed the Mirror-tracing Test for studying pupil behaviour in the classroom under stress as introduced by teachers. In their various experiments they found that this device was a visuo-motor expressive technique which functioned as a projective device. The investigators found that the following essential factors were partially measured by this device:

1. Speed and accuracy of performance
2. Marked agitation and disorientation
3. Degree of endurance under stress
4. Adaptability to novel situations

From the studies reviewed earlier, it is evident that the Mirror-tracing Test has many uses in educational practice. Further research is required to explore the full potentialities of the test in educational and vocational guidance.

***

5

Personality: Motivation, Needs and Leadership

Motivation is the driving force that causes the flux from desire to will in life. Motivation has been shown to have roots in physiological, behavioural, cognitive and social areas. Motivation may be rooted in a basic impulse to optimise well-being, minimise physical pain and maximise pleasure. It can also originate from specific physical needs such as eating, sleeping or resting, and sex.

Motivation is an inner drive to behave or act in a certain manner. These inner conditions such as wishes, desires and goals activate to move in a particular direction in behaviour.

Problems of motivation are a very important subject in educational psychology. Learning or perceptual processes are very much related to the motivational process and its principles. The knowledge about process and nature of motivation on the part of teachers and parents will enable them to control the behaviour of pupils and wards respectively in an effective manner. This understanding is necessary because human organism is a complex system, and this understanding will enable us to understand complexities of behaviour in a better fashion. Changes in human behaviour can be easily brought if mechanisms of motivation are fully understood. Studying of motivation has, therefore, significant importance for everyone who is interested in human beings.

Motivation is a dynamic and purposive process. It is a positive process. Activity or behaviour in life cannot be ensured satisfactorily in the absence of an adequate environment if it is not properly charged with motivation. Conflicts and frustrations are a part of motivational process and they form inevitable units of social environment. They generate affective disturbances in a human being and affect his pattern of life and sources of thinking. Motivation is, therefore, instrumental in a behaviour process. The identification of motivational properties of human behaviour have to be fully grasped in order to serve organism better and on proper considerations.

Motivation of behaviour is the crux of human problems as all behaviour stages of life in human beings. It includes a wide set of factors which try to stir up various drives and hungers in human beings. Without the proper motivational level, the actual conception and scope of behaviour in human beings is difficult to comprehend. Sympathetic and adequate attention to the underlying mechanisms and principles, which induce persons and individuals to strive and act, cannot be obtained without proper evaluation of the theory of motivation. The present-day behaviour in society has become all the more motivation oriented. Achievement motivation has become the principal source of investigation in society in order to explore underlying dynamics of motivational process and to understand various factors which try to condition it. As human behaviour is not sustained by dry laws, the importance of studying the dynamics of human behaviour has become all the more clear.

Society is under constant flux and change. There are many wanton forces that want to change it and drift it away from the main current of national life. There are many individual influences which are constantly struggling to bring social, cultural and economic forces in their fold. In this process, all human beings are involved, and social organs of society and cultural units of the country are regularly registering changes in their structure. In order to ensure an orderly change in society and vouchsafe peaceful construction in society and in the country at large, the psychology of motivation of various forces, operating in society, have to be carefully known and understood. Without properly understanding these processes of motivation, it will be difficult to ensure desirable changes in society in a predicated manner. The boundaries and direction of changes in human beings can be better ensured, when motivational forces are allowed to operate in the society in a pre-determined manner. Proper control over motivational factors will ensure "regulated change in the apparatus of society. Similarly, adequate stimulation in known directions will help foster desirable changes in the people. Change and progress cannot be purposive without regulating the factors that govern the motivation process.

Motivation among human beings cannot be purely organic. A human being is not animal alone by nature. He has spiritual, cultural, ethical and ideological sparks in him also. For a human being to orientate himself properly to other 'quests' of nature, he must explore their native nature also. It again becomes a question on the philosophy and motivation, and this then adds importance to the process of motivation in the human context. Man has no doubt a biological tradition. But he has a philosophic and religious tradition as well. He has to know the process that sustains him towards them. He has to learn how others behave towards these values of life. This personal or non-personal experience cannot be visualised in totality without fully grasping the essence and psychology of motivation. The problems of instincts, hedonism, nationalism, determinism and unconscious mechanism cannot be fully evaluated without proper knowledge of the motivational process.

Some Definitions of Motivation

Motivation, as a term, has proved to be a very illusive concept. It has been studied at great length by psychologists and they have arrived at different definitions on it. Young has defined motivation in his book entitled *Motivation and Emotion* in the following manner:

"The concept of motivation is exceedingly broad—so broad, in fact, that psychologists have attempted to narrow it . . . singling out one aspect or another of the complex process of determination. The two most important aspects are the energetic aspect and . . . regulation and direction . . . we may . . . define the study of motivation broadly as a research for determinants—all determinants—of human and animal activity."

Motivation has also been defined by hedonists. It has also been defined in terms of imaginative responses. Definitions given by McClelland, Atkinson, Clark and Lowell belong to this category. The authors use the word motive to design learned anticipations (expectations of rewards) or punishment. An individual has a fear motive or an anxiety motive if and when he is exposed to cues that have previously been followed by punishment. Murphy (1947) has tried to define motivation in the following fashion. "It is a general name for the fact that an organism acts are partly determined by its own stature or internal structure."

Motivation has been defined also by Dececco as referring to those factors which tend to increase or decrease the virus in an individual. It determines the level of activity in him. It imitates and directs the activity.

Hebb has emphasised that in the motivation process, pattern and direction and not the arousal of activity have been taken into account. He states:

". . . motivation then refers (1) to the existence of an organised phase sequence, (2) to its direction or content and (3) to its persistence in a given direction."

Theories of Motivation

Considerable research has been done in theory and research of motivation. The overriding concern with motivational theories is due to the interest in behavioural sciences. The works of Darwin and Freud, it is felt, have given fillip to this field of psychology. Since nature and motives of men have been described variously from time to time, it has given rise to various theories of motivation. Investigations like Machiavelli, Hobbes, Shaftesbury, Rousseau, McDougall, Darwin, Freud, Pavlov, Thorndike, etc., have added a lot of information to this field. Developments in depth and comparative psychology have provided further data for analysis on such human functions such as consciousness, reasoning, memory, learning, skills, emotions, affections and the like and these works have tried to view motivational theories from various vantage points. Research has proved to be useful in investigating the nature of motivation in their respective ways. Different authors have tried to develop various models on the theory of motivation, and each model has tried to represent a major view in its own prominent way. As it is not possible to describe all the theories in detail, some of the important theories of motivation are stated briefly as follows:

Biological Motives and Motivation

Biological and instinctive theory on motivation has been advanced long time ago. The history of the instinctual concept of motivation is ancient, and in early years this psychological thinking had dominated the field of psychology for quite some time. The advocates of this theory are called instinctivists. However, the inadequacy of this theory was soon discovered and new concepts and notions like drive, reflex, habit and native response were introduced. Experimentalists in psychology were not happy with the instinct theory. This unhappiness, among other things, was due to the fact that 'instinctive' behaviour had several thousand sources of arousal in human beings. McDougall used instincts in a classical concept. Biologists also used the term in their own manner. Instinctive activity was supposed to involve many arousal behaviours. By way of definition, the instinct was considered as an inherited, specific, stereo-typed pattern of behaviour which was said to have its own energy and to be released, rather than guided by particular environmental stimuli. The school of thought advocated that the most elementary form of energy mobilisation arose from definite biological needs of the organism. Conditions in the human body like hunger, thirst, escape from pain, etc., give rise to motivated behaviour. Biological motives involve internal conditions in the individual. Instincts basically involve certain basic wants, needs and biological motives in a human system.

The intensity of an instinctive or a biological motive is expected to enhance with time. Extensive and prolonged absence, deprivation of instincts and biological needs may develop a state of restlessness or disturbance in a person and it may create conditions that will disturb the minor physiological homeostasis in the person. In order to preserve the essential equilibrium in the body, human behaviour is likely to develop a certain sequence. According to this principle, an active urge will start in the human beings which will compel them to mobilise their energy so as to restore inner equilibrium and this activity will persist till equilibrium is re-established in the body.

Emotion and Motivation

Although psychologists have defined emotion in various ways, it is undoubtedly very clear that emotional processes are basic to motivational behaviour. The psychologists who have given hedonistic interpretation to emotions are Young, McClelland and Helen Peak. All of them have used affect as an important aspect of the theory of motivation. According to Young, motivational state is sustained in animals and human beings by palatability and affect of the situation. His theory of motivation underlines the tension as the basis of drive which organises or disorganises behaviour. McClelland and associates emphasise the need for achievement and other needs in human beings as pivotal to motivational behaviour. According to this theory, all motives are treated as acquired and can be learnt. McClelland has defined a motive as "a strong affective association, characterised by an anticipating goal reaction and based on part association of certain cues with pleasure or pain." This theory conceives affective processes as fundamental to motivation. It asserts that direction, not arousal, of behaviour is to be the proper function of motivation. This system treats motives in terms of the expectations and secondarily in terms of the results of action. McClelland regards all motives as learned approach–avoidance tendencies.

Hedonistic theories of motivation underline the role of emotion and feelings as sources that organise, direct and energise behaviour. Motives may cultivate approach–avoidance tendencies. Unpleasantness will induce approach tendency. Peak, another hedonist, uses affect as a force that gives direction to behaviour and this direction may not be necessarily motivational in form.

Emotion is also considered to affect the behaviour of a person and motivate him in a variety of ways. Although a human being inherits bodily structures, glands and a nervous system which to a certain extent determine his emotional behaviour and his personality, it is again said that other behaviour tendencies like timidity, fear, aggressiveness or excitability can also be fostered by environmental conditions. Reactions of fear, love and energy can motivate behaviour in many ways. Learning to be afraid, fearful or happy can be acquired and these reactions can be transferable to other situations. Functionally acquired fears can inhibit or retard behaviour or may give various complexes to a person by way of generating worries and anxieties in him.

Within the context of motivational theory based on emotions, the role played by frustration, conflict and stress in motivating a person cannot be ignored. Extreme conditions in environment may activate or depress a person. They may generate a series of physiological, psychological, social and related behaviour actions in human beings. Behaviour can be motivated by a frustrating condition in the environment. If a person fails to materialise his ambition, he will become more activated and will be motivated to try again and again depending on the degree of fascination that he has for the object. His repeated attempts will depend on his frustration tolerance level. Chronic and prolonged frustration is also liable to break him down. Similarly, presence of conflict in a person has motivational elements. Conflict can be temporary or situational or they may be permanent. It may activate progress or it may retard progress by producing barriers before goals. Sources of frustration and conflict can serve as strong drives in persons.

The emotional states, which are characterised by such attributes like frustration, conflict, stress, can promote or impede human activities. They may contribute and arouse a variety of responses in human beings and they, in turn, will develop tendencies in behaviour which can be motivational in behaviour. Any system of motivational theory cannot ignore their influence in affecting psychological growth and development in a person.

Social Motives in Motivational Theory

Some psychologists have explained the motivation theory on the basis of social motives. These theorists feel that people are not driven by biological needs alone. Hunger and thirst are not the only bases of activating a person. They also assert that emotions alone do not activate a human being always. In human life, social values play a considerable role in arousing energy and directing a person to behave in a particular way. It is asserted by them that social values play an important part in behaviour. Social motives in human beings are treated as sources of activity in human beings. In this context, the values and incentives may be formed in terms of rewards, or praise or it may be administered in terms of praise. Knowledge of results and overall performance may also release a motivational state in a person. Type and nature of motives may also set up a level of social aspiration in a person. Varieties of motives may influence the behaviour of persons. Motives are determined by the nature of home and the culture in which a person lives. Vocational needs, cultural aspirations and religious inclinations also may constitute essential ingredients of social motives. A particular person will become devoted to any one of the aforesaid motives depending upon his needs, values and philosophy of life. Beliefs will also determine his attitudes which can consequently influence his behaviour. As the type and quality of motives can be large in number, they will vary from country to country and society to society in which a person lives. However, there are certain general motives which can influence people's behaviour irrespective of class, culture and society in which he lives. Among such motives, acquisitiveness is one of them. A person strives to acquire more and more wealth or more and more property.

Another social motive, which dominates the life of a person is the love for his country. It is generally expressed in terms of patriotic feelings towards his country. It may associate itself with such feelings as national security, dedication and love for the country. This motive exerts strong influence in the lives of people who try to identify themselves with the values and aspirations of the country. A national leader can also give direction to this social motive. Development of patriotism is a psychological and educational process. It is the feeling of love from persons towards nation in general. Feelings of patriotism may also generate aggression if this motive is thwarted or locked. Similarly, religious, cultural and social motives can equally be strong factors in motivating a person as is the case with patriotism. In all these motives, there is identification with the ideal or ideals and there is general mobilisation of energy of a person towards this end. Goal and ideology are set by the person, and the perception and realisation of them become the main concern of his achievement and aspiration.

Psychoanalytical Motivation Theory

The psychoanalytical theory, advanced by Freud, has also been used to explain motivational behaviour among individuals. Freud developed his theory of psychoanalysis on the basis of study of mental cases. He derived his inspiration partly from Darwinian theory of evolution of species. It gives, in a sense, emphasis on biological needs and environmental conditions in which a person lives. One of the bases of this motivation theory is the importance that is given to the unconscious. The nature of the unconscious part of the mind of the person has been elaborately described by Freud. He assumed that the vast part of the mental process is in the unconscious portion. In this assumption, he believed that behaviour is caused through unconscious strings. He also assumed that all behaviour is to a considerable extent, determined by the unconscious processes. These processes gave motivational import to the behaviour of persons in their own fashion.

Energy provided to the motivational behaviour in persons, according to the psychoanalytical theory of motivation is provided by psychic energy. This energy is drawn from the libido. Its source is also attributed to metabolic energy. Sometimes it is also associated with nervous energy. There were other implications applied to this energy. But Freud was not very explicit about its real import and at the same time he did not give any mystical or supernatural significance to it. He felt that it was only vitality in form.

Psychoanalytical theory of motivation draws, inspiration from biological and instinctive force of human system. Instincts are treated as a type of inner force which sustains life. It may have both bodily and clinical manifestations. The human system has motivational characteristics and that being so, instincts seek for gratification and hence, instincts are, according to Freud, the sources of all activity in a human being.

Psychoanalytical theory, has, among other concepts, emphasised two basic instincts which constantly influence a person. The two instincts are: the life instinct and the death instinct. Life instinct works in the preservation of life and death instinct in the destruction of life. Preservation also leads to reproductive activities and to preservation of life. Death instinct involves destructive instincts in which aggression becomes part of this energy. There is, however, a close relation between the two courses of energy and mind is a constant process of adjustment.

The psychoanalytical theory also emphasises that behaviour is psychodynamic and purposive in nature. It has a sense of fulfilment. Mental processes like perceiving, judging, generalising and activities are determined by this dynamic process. The organism, therefore, is original in its demands, and decides and selects things for itself depending on the inner needs and compulsions of the person. The effectiveness of action will depend on the quality of energy available. The higher levels of functioning in the human beings are also determined by this level of dynamism. Mental mechanisms like identification, displacement and sublimation become part of determining progress in human behaviour.

Adler and Jung who also belonged to this category of class of psychoanalysis initially, later developed their own respective schools and gave different explanations to the mechanism of human behaviour and motivation.

It would be, however, fit to remark that psychoanalytical theory of motivation has definitely contributed in explaining certain important aspects of human motivation. It has not definitely exhausted the whole truth about it. This fact has to be kept in view without losing sight of essentials on the theory.

A Critical View of the Theories of Motivation

It would be pertinent to remark that the theories discussed so far on motivation have their own merits and they may be valid in their own respective ways but they are not adequate all by themselves. Each of the motivational theory has made a contribution of its own but it would be unjustified to overlook the contributions made by other theories. Concepts like drive, needs, motives, emotions, etc., have their own use in explaining motivational behaviour but they cannot explain everything about human motivation. Similarly, social motives and the unconscious process may have to say things about motivational behaviour among human beings but those explanations are not the last words on the motivational process. This position has to be fully realised so that one does not take a partisan view on any one of the theories discussed earlier.

Motivation is a very important determinant in human behaviour. The understanding of these determinants is very essential so that it is possible to evaluate behaviour in an objective manner. Enquiry into the role of motivation is essential in order to understand the invigorating mechanism in human beings. Motivation theory cannot be without utility. It has to reinforce and provide some fundamental interpretation about the basic nature of human energies. As motivation is a central topic in psychology and education, its entire meaning and grasp has to be fully understood. It is due to this reason that sufficient attention has been given by scientists and researchers on understanding this aspect of behaviour. While one cannot quarrel with concepts used for motivation, one should not be in a mood to overdo things and support one school of motivation at the expense of the other. The precaution has to be kept in view and it has to be studied in a scientific way.

Factors Affecting Motivation

As motivation is a complex process factors that can motivate the behaviour in a person can be many. Many research studies have been undertaken to examine this problem scientifically. Results from such studies are diverse. In the background of those diverse results, it is necessary to have dispassionate, careful understanding on essential factors that affect motivation in human beings as without such an attitude one is liable to be carried out by many biases and influences on the subject. Organisms have their own ways of reacting to various stimuli, and responses of an organism may be different to the same situation from time to time. These difficulties are bound to exist in view of the complex nervous system that human beings have inherited. However, in spite of difficulties stated earlier, it is not out of the way to identify some of the prominent factors that arouse a motivational state in a human being.

Goals affect motivation. Goals may vary from person to person and the intensity to reach a goal may vary from time to time in the same person or from person to person. It is very difficult to establish a well-confirmed empirical law on the relation of goals to human motivation. Even speculation about the subject may be difficult to make. Goals may be aroused but in accordance to one's needs, drives and aspirations that an individual has for him. And since behaviour is molar in nature, the process of motivation may become integrative in character. Similarly, motivational behaviour can restrict goals only for some time and later the behaviour may work independently of the goal. A man may set his goal to become rich. After he has become rich, he continues to hoard money although his original goal of becoming rich has been reached. Allport has explained this phenomenon in terms of autonomy of motives. It may be said that any goal that appeals to man, may arouse him and cause his behaviour to get motivated. Goals will vary and they have no end.

Incentives may also motivate the behaviour of an organism. Incentives of all types influence behaviour and motivate the person to work better and harder. A person may have abilities and those abilities he may employ as tools to fulfil his ambitions but incentives will determine the extent to which he gets motivated towards the work. Incentives try to change, as has been found, the capacity of a person to work. By virtue of better incentives, the level and amount of effort in the person will increase or decrease. Incentives can be tangible as well as intangible. Praise from teacher may serve as an incentive for a student, but for a worker better wages may encourage him to work better and harder. Similarly, incentives may be given in various forms and shapes. They may fall in the category of biological, social or ideological spheres. Other incentives like better income, better home, better social group and better opportunities for promotion may also motivate a person in various ways. The categories of incentives, which can have influence on the behaviour of an individual and motivate him, may be diverse and large. Participation in work depends on the quality of incentives offered to a person.

Vim and vigour in a human being can also be enhanced by teachers, parents, friends and members. The quality of influence on a person by them will depend on the type of attitudes that the aforesaid influences will show towards him. The attitudes, values, personality and understanding on the part of elders can serve as motivating agents for a person. These conditions and encouragements in the environment will foster habits, abilities and interests in him which can score as incentives for him. Elders may develop and encourage curiosity and goal-seeking behaviour which may activate the person to learn, explore or initiate. These persons may serve as mediums that will arouse behaviour and activity in them. It is generally seen that caretakers, feeders, presidents, tutors, mentors, etc., have influenced and affected behaviour in human beings in a variety of ways in the history of human civilisation.

Mobilising the will-to-work is another factor that affects motivation. The human resources can be geared up to top efficiency through proper level of will on the part of the workers and the people. Proper volition will also affect the capacity to work. It will also affect the drive to work more. Morale can affect the motivation. Morale can give an attitude in a person towards the work and the quality will determine the motivation in a person or of an organisation. A good morale will also increase the willingness in a person to strive for the goal. Morale will provide a sense of feeling and well-being which is so essential not only for energy and enthusiasm but also for self-discipline. Morale can also stimulate a feeling of 'togetherness' which can work as an assertion in a big organisation. Employee morale is important for reducing industrial conflict. Morale increases capacity for making an effort and it gives a boost to the philosophy and psychology of a worker. These conditions affect motivation.

The quality of environment, in which a person lives and works, may serve as an important source of motivation. If the environment is stimulating, a person can acquire dynamic living, growing, developing and maturing his personality. It will foster maturation and well-being in the individual and this state is psychologically a motivating state for better performance. A good and stimulating environment may appeal to the ego of the person, and the ego can motivate a person to push forward. The environment, if good, can secure the attention of the person and enable him to develop interest and enthusiasm in his surroundings. They may arouse his motivation and affect his behaviour in a number of ways. It may also develop his attitudes and attitudes have a significant relationship with motivation. Thus it may be concluded that the quality of environment, in which the person lives, may become a strong factor in determining and sustaining motivation in a person.

The drive for self-actualisation may also set a condition of motivation in a person. Allport, Forman Maslow and Rogers have demonstrated the relationship between the state of motivation in a person and his drive for self-actualisation. An individual has his own uniqueness and he has his own experiences which determine his conduct. An individual wants to discover his real self and in the process for his discovery he may have to undergo a lot of trials and tribulations. A helpful environment may assist him in this pursuit and it may enhance his curiosity to work till his selfhood is fully unfolded. This quest for identification of individuality serves as a strong force in a person to explore. The character and implication of this inner need in a person is deep, and this depth adds intensity and reputation to his eagerness to place himself in the environment in which he is born. The quest for self-actualisation is therefore, motivational in character in persons.

Anxiety can be served as a motivating source in the sense that it can arouse and determine the activity and the ability of a student to learn.

The child is an aspiring, dynamic and a thrilling individual. He has a total personality. Care has to be taken that he is not ignored as a non-entity. Experiences given to children should be relevant to his maturation level, should deal with his interests, should appeal to his sense of well-being and ego and should appeal to his attitudes. Tasks given to children should be within his grasp and it should be coordinated with his total social, emotional, mental and psychological development. Learning among students cannot take place without proper motivation. Mental activity on the part of the learner is essentially a motivational problem. Level of the mental activity is best ensured through a strong level of motivation. Motivation is a gateway to learning.

There can be a number of factors which may arouse motivation in a person. Biological, social and emotional needs have already been explained. Supervision, teamwork, pay and security may also affect motivation. Guidance, personality of elders and teachers, abilities and disabilities in a person may also influence motivation. Unconscious factors, anxiety, fears, failures, successes, ego-involvement, social rewards, experience, frustration and conflicts can also be factors that influence the behaviour and can affect the motivational state of persons. Dynamics of behaviour is deep and the human organisation may react to various factors in a characteristic way. Emotions can be swayed in a person through a series of factors. This being so, there are very large number of factors that affect the motivational process in a person and that being so, the actual factors that may affect behaviour in human beings can be large and diverse.

Motives Underlying Child's Behaviour

It is very important for the teacher and parents to know exactly which main motives underlie the child's behaviour. The following motives are very important from various points of view:

Curiosity or exploratory motive

From an early age the child is attracted towards the objects around him. At the age of about four he begins to ask: "What is this?" "What is that?" The father or mother gets annoyed when their children ask curious questions too often and parents generally evade the answer by rebuking them severely. This is the stage when the child is acquiring a vocabulary of new words and terms and must be given as much help as possible. The names of birds, animals, trees, fruits, etc., may be learnt by him if parents answer in an encouraging manner. The child of six years is very curious. He asks "What is this?" "How is that?" and his attention is easily diverted to moving and living objects. Teachers and parents can guide children in acquiring correct knowledge by answering these questions correctly and sympathetically. The child from 6 to 7 years of age is very eager to find out the 'why' of things. "Why does the sun rise?" "Why does an aeroplane fly?" By asking these questions the child is increasing his range of knowledge and trying to satisfy his craving for further enlightenment. Teachers and parents should not only give the answers themselves but encourage children to search for proper answers to their questions in books. Curiosity is an indication of knowledge and the more it is stimulated by teachers in classroom lessons, the more chances the child has of grasping the subject matter taught. Curiosity becomes more reflective after the age of ten when the child begins to think and ponder deeply. This type of curiosity should be stimulated and satisfied. Lessons in social studies and other subjects must give scope for its free play. Some of the world's greatest people like Christopher Columbus, Newton, Marconi and others were possessed of great curiosity which impelled them to go forth in search of truth and to give knowledge and enlightenment to generations after them. The old school of teaching discouraged children from asking questions.

Acquisitive motive

It is from a very early age that this motive shows itself. It may become the basis of selfishness, cheating and greed if left to itself, but through processes of training may become very useful and a cause of good work. The child exhibits this motive by beginning to collect little pieces of paper, tiny sticks, stones, feathers, etc. Some of the greatest treasures of art in the world are a result of the sublimation of this motive and through it much valuable services maybe done not to the individual alone, but also towards the welfare of the group.

Constructive motives

A four-year-old child who sees an object near him tries to handle it and throws it about here and there. As he grows older he likes to make and break things, to tear paper, to make paper boats, to transform and change things to his own liking. Parents and teachers are very upset by the child who is constantly fidgeting with things and trying to make something or the other. Actually this is a very useful motive. It is a part of the creative desire in human beings which leads them to make new things. Activities like clay modelling, paper tearing, paper cutting, paper folding, wood work, basket making, needle work, satisfy this motive in the child. The dullest of the lessons become very easy and interesting if it is followed by some constructive work related to it.

Self-display motive

Consciousness of his physical and mental abilities leads a child to display himself. He wants to attract the attention of others to himself, and is eager to win their praise. Children may be provided with suitable occasions of self-display, otherwise they try to attract attention of others by undesirable acts. Whenever they do good work, it should be properly appreciated.

Self-abasement motive

This motive is at work when the child is in the presence of superior persons. It makes the child submit to authority. When used with caution, this motive is very useful in making the child orderly and obedient, but it must not be used to create fear or inferiority in the mind of child. Very little use should be made of punishment in the school, as it creates negative feelings or acquire the combat motive.

Combat motive

It is stimulated when some strong impulse of the child is thwarted. It shows itself in very considerable forms at times and teachers, therefore, try to repress it. This repression is harmful. Under proper direction this can be of great help in the education of the child. The child should learn to fight against what is wrong and untruthful and to overcome them.

Needs

According to psychologists there are a number of needs and motives that underlie the feelings, thinking and overt behaviour of children. These needs, urges and the drives are the basis of personal adjustment and are the forces which cause children to learn and to work.

These terms belong to the same family because their meanings are closely related. They are mutually dependent on each other and have a cause and effect relationship.

Need indicates a lack of something which is useful or desired. A person has a need for food when he is hungry, water when he is thirsty, clothing when he feels cold and medical care when he is in pain. A person has need for company when he is lonesome, entertainment and excitement when bored by monotony, praise and success when he feels inadequate and activity when he has been sedentary in his living.

What is very closely related to need and indicates the state of having need or desire for something? An individual has want for safety, income, friendship, importance, variety, rest or freedom in order to be healthy and happy. These are his wants because of his need for them. According to the individual's physical and psychological conditions, he will have the drive or urge for eating, sexual activity, achieving distinction, gaining liberty, taking a brisk walk, becoming wealthy, or being very careful to avoid accidents. Motive is thought, feeling or condition that causes one to act. It is a need or organic state that prompts us to action. We think motive as a condition or a state which functions as a prevailing force for more than just a short time. For example a person is motivated to practise singing and to try to become an excellent singer because he feels that he can make a good living as a singer. A young man works hard to achieve economic status because he was poor as a boy and he does not want to remain in that condition.

Our thoughts, feelings and conditions will at certain times cause us to lie down and rest, at other times to drink a few cold drinks so that we can feel refreshed, or to work overtime to earn some extra money, to invite friends over to dinner, or to try to become wealthy, write a book, give a speech, or do something that will attract favourable attention and thus give us recognition and prestige. We have the urge or drive to do these things.

The human organism has various needs and wants and motives. They are not separate or distinct but closely inter-related and interdependent. They are dynamic forces. These are discussed in detail as follows:

The Need to Live

It means food, clothing and shelter. It also means struggle against disease. Everyone wants to live. We are terribly afraid when our lives are threatened. When seriously ill, we are greatly concerned about getting well because we do not want to die.

This strong urge to live has been called the instinct of self-preservation—the instinct to preserve oneself or to keep on living.

If we want to live, we must be free from illness. Children must keep clean in order to avoid infection, eat healthy food because they will feel better and live longer and avoid the use of liquor and other narcotics because they can cause illness and shorten life. Everybody has a desire for long life.

The Need for Economic Security

This means the avoidance of poverty. It also means:

1. A job and income.
2. Life free from poverty.
3. Building, land, equipment, animals, trees, etc.
4. Money in the bank.

People desire to earn good wages and have adequate income so that they will be secure economically. They want enough money so that they can have good clothing and shelter. They save money in order to have security in their old age, when their earning power has been lost. In order to satisfy the want for economic security, they are acquisitive. When children are asked as to why they go to school and why they want to get good marks in school, they say that an education will help them in getting better jobs and that if their marks are good they will get better recommendation from their teachers and principals. Economic security makes people better and happier, and has a positive influence on their personalities.

The Need for Social Security

This means the avoidance of solitude and lonesomeness. It also means:

1. Belongingness.
2. Social acceptance.
3. Friendship.
4. Love.
5. Affection.
6. Companionship.

Some of the organisations for obtaining social security are:

1. The family.
2. Teams.
3. Clubs.
4. Unions.
5. Congregations.
6. The school.
7. Gangs.

By the need for social security we mean the need for friends and companionship, and the desire to be with other people. This desire to be and the practice of being in a circle of friends or in a group, audience or crowd is called gregariousness.

Connected with this is our desire to be liked by others. We want to be thought well of and we are deeply concerned about what others think of us. Children want to be known.

Those pupils who are socially secure in their family because of harmonious living and because they get love, generosity and justice are likely to be emotionally healthy. Those, however, who are insecure in their family life because of parental dissension, over-severity, poverty, and parental neglect may be shy, fearful, depressed and troublesome. Security or insecurity in home has a very strong bearing on a child's personality.

Pupils want to be respected members of their classes. They want the approval and friendship of their teacher and also the approval and friendship of their classmates. Each pupil wants the feeling of security, of being an active and successful member of his class.

The teacher too should want the friendship and approval of his pupils. His or her personal relationship with his or her pupils should be so successful that she has their goodwill and confidence. Such a relationship gives the teacher a feeling of social security and this is conducive to good teaching and happy living.

Before going on to a statement and explanation of the other needs and drives, it must be pointed out and emphasised that all of them are closely related and similar in many ways. The needs and urges have common elements and are similar in several respects, as has already been made clear in the discussion of the various aspects of security and as will be more evident in what follows.

The Need for Personal Worth and Superiority

This means the avoidance of shame and inferiority. This also means:

1. Success.
2. Leadership.
3. Mastery and power.

4. Favourable attention or recognition.
5. Prestige—good status.
6. High standing self-enhancement.
7. Approval.
8. Importance.
9. Self-respect and esteem.
10. Worthiness.
11. Self-satisfaction.
12. Honour.

Every human being wants to have a feeling of personal worth; he wants to have recognition, to be well thought of and to have standing and status in society.

When a person buys a large expensive car, he does so not only for the extra riding comfort that such a car gives him. He wants the admiring attention of the people who see him in the car. He wants the prestige and the attention that the ownership of a big expensive car gives. The child in the cradle wants attention. If attention is given to someone else in his presence, the young child will feel insecure. When children go to school they seek the appreciation of their teachers and fellow pupils. They like to have their work displayed and achieve recognition.

All through life, people seek rewards, prizes and recognitions. Many want to be leaders because leadership has ego value. We like praise and recognition that enhances our value of self-esteem.

A feeling of value and importance makes us feel happy and a feeling of unworthiness and inferiority makes us unhappy. Just as in the physical world, nature abhors a vacuum, so in the psychological world human beings abhor a feeling of inferiority. We are willing to work hard to achieve a feeling of worth, but often we engage in tricks and dodges in trying to achieve it.

The teachers and schools use means such as prizes distribution, praise, school marks, honour rolls, selecting a leader, choosing a head of the class, picking a team for extracurricular activities and other such recognitions to appeal to their students' feeling of personal worth and superiority. Such things also give a feeling of security, which in turn contributes to a feeling of worth, but the important problem is to have all pupils achieve enough recognition and success.

Care needs to be exercised in any appeal to the feeling of worth, lest a child become egoistic or conceited. It is well to achieve a healthy feeling of worth or importance but such a feeling, if too strong, invades the feelings of other people and generates antagonism. Everyone should feel worthy, but accompanying this should be modesty that invites the goodwill of others.

The development of feelings of personal worth and superiority has more to do with personality and emotional health than anything else.

The Need for Health, Comfort and Feeling of Well-being (the avoidance of illness, discomfort and pain)

This also means:

1. Body needs and processes.
2. Healthy breathing.

3. Food digestion and elimination.
4. Liquids – absorption and elimination.
5. Rest and sleep.
6. Healthy, comfortable surroundings.
7. Clothing.
8. Equipment – beds, chairs, tables, etc.
9. Climate – humidity and temperature.
10. Sanitation and medical care.
11. Protection and safety.
12. Mental and emotional health needs.

So uppermost is the idea of health and one of the most common questions is "How are you feeling?" Health, comfort and feeling of well-being are important both psychologically and physically. The mind and body are not separate in this respect, although one may be more involved in illness.

It is common for us to think of health and feelings of well-being largely in terms of the avoidance of fevers, colds and pains. A good state of health, that everyone seeks, is accompanied by a feeling of well-being. A poor state of health is accompanied by pains.

Thus, two factors that influence behaviour a great deal are a feeling of well-being on the one hand and pain on the other. One is positive and the other is negative.

Life is controlled to a great extent by a feeling of well-being or satisfaction, and avoiding experiences which give us dissatisfaction or pain. Satisfactory experiences are healthful and, of course, healthful experiences are satisfactory. Correspondingly, unsatisfactory and painful experiences are usually not healthful.

The need and want for a healthy painless life is strong. Every school should offer adequate health service so that the students can have attention to the following:

1. Mental and emotional problems.
2. Sensory defects – eyes, ears, nose, etc.
3. Nutrition.
4. Healthful exercise.
5. Skin diseases.
6. Headaches and their causes.
7. Fatigue.
8. Other health needs.

In the classroom the teacher should be alert to lighting, seating, ventilation and other conditions that contribute to the comfort of the surroundings. Parents should study health education and should acquire the attitudes and knowledge which will enable them to take care of the health needs of their children.

The Need For Stimulation, Activity, Enjoyment and Satisfaction (the avoidance of monotony and boredom)

This also means the act of:
1. Work.
2. Play.
3. Reading.

4. Music.
5. Painting.
6. Travel.
7. Visiting.
8. Oral expression—speaking, singing and shouting.
9. Drinking and Eating.
10. Manipulation.

An individual wants to be stimulated interestingly and satisfyingly and, therefore, he tries to engage in and to watch enjoyable activities. Much happiness is obtained when a person places himself in situations which are stimulating and satisfying. Monotony and boredom are depressing.

The human organism with its eyes, ears, nose, taste buds and skin craves a variety of pleasing stimulation. People spend almost limitless amount of money on movies, on concerts, the theatre, ball games, horse racing, motoring and travelling—all in the pursuit of pleasure and excitement. We want variety in our lives to prevent monotony and boredom. In order to be healthy, we must engage in many pleasant activities.

We like to be in a situation where there is 'something doing' as we say. We like to be stimulated, to see people, things and interesting actions, such as races and games. To hear music, speeches and conversations, to feel the presence of others, to feel the warm sun and soothing breeze and to taste, to eat and to drink.

We not only want to be stimulated pleasantly through our senses, we want to be in action ourselves. We crave to be up and doing. We want to be with people and to talk to them. We want to play games and to dance. We want to be on the move, walking or riding.

In the growth and development of a person, learning is a major contributor and it is controlled by satisfaction and dissatisfaction. We are attracted to and tend to learn that which gives us satisfaction and avoid learning that which is unsatisfying.

The human organism grows and develops through stimulation and action. We learn by doing but we also learn because of what we see, feel, taste and so on.

Children have more urge for stimulation and action than those of any other age group. This urge or drive cannot be suppressed. The parents should utilise it and work with it rather than against it. If teaching is reasonably interesting, children will pay attention. If, what they are doing stimulate them, they are going to be completely absorbed in the lessons, projects or activities.

In the school, children have a tremendous urge for action and for doing and they should not be expected to sit rigidly in their seats for long periods. The time table should be organised so that they can work in groups, so that there is educational handwork, so that they can talk, participate in discussions, play games and work at the blackboard.

In old schools of India, an attempt was made to repress this craving for activity. The result was that the children were always annoying the teacher with their restlessness and would often break out into the more dramatic forms of pranks and mischief. The fact is that children cannot be repressed. This means that they cannot or should not be controlled but that it is best to utilise their want to be stimulated and to be doing. In the typical modern schools, games, sports, athletics, dramas, parties, and fun-filled activities are enjoyed by most of the students of all ages and grades. In stimulating them, visual aids make an appeal. The uses of films, both sound and silent, slides, radio, photographs, demonstration, apparatus, objects, tools and materials satisfy the natural want of children and contributes to effective teaching.

The Need for Freedom and Liberty—Individuality

This means the avoidance of regimentation, control and imprisonment. This also means:

1. To think.
2. To create.
3. To do.
4. To express oneself.
5. To make a decision.
6. To determine one's course of action.
7. To be free, to go about.
8. Self-government.
9. Equality of the individual.

We always see that when an infant or young child is held firmly and he cannot move, he will cry and struggle to be freed. He resists restraint.

Thus, in school, children want the right to do their own thinking and express themselves freely. They do not like to be governed by rules and regulations whose purpose they do not understand. But fundamentally they do not enjoy in a school where there is too much freedom or when there is disorder. Children find fault with a teacher in whose room they can behave in a disorderly fashion. The diagram on the right side implies that certain objectives of education will vary according to the child's stage of development. It also implies that at each stage certain objectives will be central and others peripheral and that there will be changes in the central objective of education according to the level of development the child has reached.

Running through Maslow's higher needs there is a considerable emphasis upon what Murray had earlier called the need for achievement. Murray (1938) and McClelland et al. (1953) had stressed the need for children to achieve in skills and

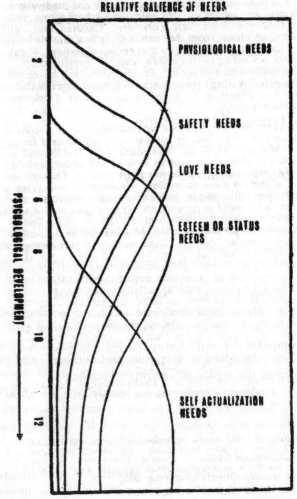

FIGURE 1

activities held in esteem by the peer group and by the adult groups. Through achievements, especially those in reading, arithmetic, spelling (the school subjects generally) and in play and sporting activities, the child comes to a feeling of inner strength. The acquisition of skills aids the child's personality development and adjustment. Usually total personality development is regarded as one of the overall aims of education, and the claim advanced here is that achievements in valued activities and skills promote this end. Skills are thought of as complex patterns of highly efficient behaviour which may be physical, social, verbal, scientific, mathematical and above all that most complex and all-embracing activity which we call thinking. It remains to determine that skills that are acquired are those that have social and psychological significance which will cause them to be valued by the community. The acquisition of skills implies careful and painstaking teaching and learning. This does not rule out the possibility of high interest level and even of an inspirational handling of skills—indeed both are highly desirable—but it does point to the need for patient careful work and to the necessity to judge and reward teacher effort in terms of fundamental and lasting contributions to development, rather than in things that are showy and ephemeral.

The needs of primary school children were examined by Lobdell and Van Ness (1962). They point out the need for children to have access to and association with their peers in achievement, not just their peers in age. This gives recognition to the established facts of individual differences in achievement (and therefore in needs) and the possibility of these differences being met, at least in part, by techniques of organisation such as non-grading, cross-grading, subject grading and schemes for individual progression.

Types of Leadership

Leaders can be broadly classified into the following types:

Authoritarian Leadership

The authoritarian leader is one who exercises more or less absolute power than the democratic leader. The authoritarian leader is more powerful and has a strong way in determining policies of the group. He may consult others in day-to-day activities, but he alone will shape the goals and aspirations of the group. He advises from first stage to the last stage when an activity is in progress. He directs the activities of the group. He can be extremely punitive and accept or reject contributions of a member according to his own fancies and wishes. His say in matters may be final.

The authoritarian leadership is one-sided and arbitrary at times. The leader deliberately develops the absolute authority in him so that others may not become contenders of his powers. He does not allow the change in a group for the sake of change. He imposes his own discipline in the group, and reinforces and protects the leadership from being destroyed from the onslaughts of other members.

In the authoritarian leadership, an individual's contribution is little. A member cannot set goals for the group. His advice may or may not be accepted by the leader. An authoritarian leader tries to impose his views, his ideology and his personality on the group. It has been found that work morale of the group under authoritarian leadership gets dwindled in due course of time.

As authoritarian leadership is self-directed, the leadership does not encourage intercommunication among the group members. The leadership tries to filter down the instructions and ideas to people down below. The group is conditioned to look at the leader always with the result that he increases the dependence round him which promotes a sense of indispensability in him. The leader develops his own style of leadership and he breeds it in the group.

As authoritarian leadership is one-sided, it ensures little changes for the individual's development or for each member in the group. There is less opportunity for the development of close interpersonal relations among all group members.

From the spirit of this leadership, there is a definite hierarchical organisation in an authoritarian leadership. The leader is at the helm of affairs and various stages of authority are looking at him in support of approval and approbation. If the atmosphere becomes too individual and personal, the group morale in the organisation may become too dismal and disappointing.

Democratic Leadership

Democratic leadership does not revolve round a single individual. It draws strength from the group as a whole. The democratic leadership can also enjoy the same degree of power as is enjoyed by the authoritarian type. But the nature of role of a leader in a democratic leadership changes a lot. Moreover, the group structure in a democratic leadership is also different.

In a democratic leadership, the group follows a democratic philosophy. The dignity of the personality of each member is respected. Individual contributions are incorporated in group goals and each member of the group tries to work in harmony with members. The leader in a democratic setting tries to accomplish his political ideas through group effort. Everyone in the group considers himself as good as the next man. There is no power of force. Each member is given claims and prerogatives in the group. He is treated as free and equal. The unique worth of each personality is taken for granted. There is essentially a spiritual equality in the group. Democratic leadership stresses upon the individual personality as the ultimate seat of all values.

In the midst of democratic leadership, there is fear of one possibility, the prevalence and danger of mediocrity and uniformity. It may not cultivate persons in the direction of selfhood, vision and achievement.

Krech and Crutchfield[6] have made the following distinction between authoritarian and democratic leaders:

Authoritarian	Democratic
1. All determination of policy by the leader	1. All policies a matter of group determination, encouraged and drawn out by the leader.
2. Techniques and steps of attaining the goal dictated by the leader once at a time.	2. Activity perspective given by an explanation of the general steps of the process during discussion at first meeting. Where technical advice is needed, the leader tries to point out two or three alternative procedures from which a choice could be made.
3. The leader usually dictated the particular work task and work companions of each member.	3. The members were free to work with whomsoever they choose, and the division of tasks was left up to the group.
4. The leader was 'Personal' in his praise and criticism of the work of each member, without giving objective reasons. He remained aloof from active group participation except when demonstrating.	4. The leader was 'objective' or 'fact-minded' in his praise and criticism and tried to be a regular group member in spirit without doing too much of the active work.

Laissez Faire Leadership

Here, the leader is only a stimulator and provides mainly materials and information. The leader tries to exercise a minimum of control. It is stated that under this type of leadership more successful results will be produced.

This leadership does not mean absence of leadership. It implies a person who stimulates every one and involves everyone in the group task. It is generally seen that in *laissez faire* leadership, the group works progressively but slowly. There is considerable activity much of which can prove ultimately unproductive. As there is no precision in activity, time is lost in this process of leadership. The group members are generally on their own initiative and they tend to go backward and forward in the midst of flow of ideas and suggestions till a correct solution is hit upon. Consultations and exchange of thoughts take a lot of time in this activity.

The growth of the group is more due to the individual activity of the group members than by the exclusive efforts of the leader. There is more a feeling of unity and harmony within the group. This feeling is also seen in members in a democratic leadership. This leadership ensures personal growth and does not block personal development. As there are no sharp boundaries in the group, uncertainties from the outside may influence the behaviour of group members. A united front may not emerge in the beginning, but as the discussion goes on and members start arriving at the goal, the front becomes more cohesive and determined, and the individual needs become integrated with the organisational goals. The quality and superiority does not remain the same from time to time as the solution is obtained through trial and error. This leadership is evident in very common and workable ways where the person directs the group goal in an undetermined fashion.

Personality Attributes of Leadership

In leadership behaviour, personality of the leader is important. Gibb is of the opinion that there are indications that certain traits are frequently found to characterise leaders of various types in a variety of situations. Leadership is correlated with the personal attributes of the leader as perceived by the followers. Some studies have emphasised generalisation of attributes in leadership. Studies were undertaken to study various leadership roles under eleven traits such as: order, ideas, smart, friendly, liked, empathy, books, sports, swimming, good influence and bad influence. The results of the study suggest that different roles required different personality attributes. Personality attributes may play a part in understanding leadership. Some writers, after doing some research, concluded that there is no reliable evidence concerning the existence of universal leadership traits. Trait approach has not been very much liked by some psychologists for measurement of personality traits of leaders. Stogdill,[7] after examining a large number of leadership studies aimed at isolating the traits of effective leaders, comes to the following conclusion: "The qualities, characteristics and skills required in a leader are determined to a large extent by the demands of the situation in which he is to function as a leader."[8] This is called the situationist approach to leadership behaviour. Other studies have also been undertaken to evaluate this problem from time to time. Tead reports a study on leadership qualities that are necessary for leaders. He has, for convenience, classified the qualities into various headings such as:

1) Physical and nervous energy
2) A sense of purpose and direction
3) Enthusiasm
4) Friendliness and affection

5) Integrity
6) Technical mastery
7) Decisiveness
8) Intelligence
9) Teaching skill
10) Faith

Krech and Crutchfield have also mentioned the following personality characteristics in leaders:

1) Resonant voice.

   The voice must reveal sincerity, goodwill and kindness, determination, conviction, strength, courage and abounding happiness.

2) Leaders must have an insistent need for dominance, power and prestige.
3) Leaders must have skills in interpersonal relationships.
4) Leaders must have high intellectual abilities and fund of expert information and technical competence.
5) Leaders must have techniques of handling people.

Other studies have also been done from time to time, which have been surveyed by Stogdill. He reports that leaders have personality attributes which distinguish them from non-leaders. He found leaders to be taller in height. Goldwell and Wellman found girl leaders average in height. Among leaders, they were bigger and heavier. Studies by Bellingrath, Gowin and Partridge and Zeleny also support the same view. Bellingrath has found that leaders had better health. Partridge found boy-scout leaders better in appearance. Regarding intelligence, it has been found that leaders are more intelligent. It has been reported that leaders and prospective leaders have higher intelligence scores than non-leaders. There are other significant studies on the subject too. Leaders have been found to be better adjusted, have higher will-control, are more dominant, are more talkative, more humorous, have more knowledge and better institutional adjustment.

U.S. Army has carried out a number of studies on leadership qualities. They have come to the conclusion that leaders should have the following characteristics:

1. Perform professional and technical speciality
2. Know subordinates and show consideration for them
3. Keep channels of communication open
4. Accept personal responsibility and setting an example
5. Initiate and direct action
6. Train men and a team
7. Make decisions

Other studies carried out by the American Institute for Research have discovered the following qualities in a leader:

1. Should have supervising personnel
2. Should have planning, initiating and directing action
3. Should handle administrative details
4. Should accept personal responsibility
5. Should show group belongings and loyalty to the organisation
6. Should perform professional or technical speciality

A number of studies on leadership qualities have been conducted. From the studies undertaken, three factors have been identified:

   i) Intellectual penetration

  ii) Strength of will

 iii) Soundness of feeling

In other words, the old threefold functions of the mind namely cognition, conation and affect have been deducted.

The Components of Leadership

Leadership is supposed to be associated with the following components.

   i) Interpersonal influence

  ii) The communication process

 iii) The situational dynamics

Boring has described the following attributes that a leader should possess. These attributes have been discussed in the special context of military leadership. These qualities may hold good in civilian life as well, at times. These attributes are:

1) Authority

2) Personal characteristics and attitudes. It includes:

   i) Competence.   v) Self--possession

  ii) Industry   vi) Integrity

 iii) Responsibility   vii) Teaching ability

 iv) Decision-making

A leader is expected to discharge certain roles towards his men. Leader's personal qualities produce a great impact on the follower's behaviour. A leader should look into the following requirements if he wants to obtain loyalty from his men.

   i) The leader should give personal recognition to every person who works under him

  ii) The leader should praise the work done by the follower

 iii) The leader should encourage rather than criticise

 iv) The leader should be emphatic and clear in his views and instructions

  v) The leader should convince his men by reason rather than by power and authority

 vi) The leader should train his men to expect surprises and reverses

 vii) The leader should adequately protect his men from overstrain and over-fatigue

viii) The leader should inculcate a right attitude towards success and defeat, life and death and health and ill-health

 ix) The leader should plan the goals for his men and introduce activity which will be useful for group morale and group goal

  x) A good leader should adapt himself to circumstances of a situation and train his men to do so

From the earlier-mentioned description of the qualities of leadership, the leader should, it becomes obvious, be a symbol of hope and strength, and he should lead his men to higher accomplishments. The leader has to look after his men and they will be loyal to him and will give their best to him and to the organisation which they are serving.

Selection of Leaders

Various methods of selecting leaders have been devised in various countries. It is felt that no rigid system of selection of leaders can be suggested as the essential characteristics of leadership have to vary from one situation to another, and in each situation the pattern of personality make-up may be different. The qualities of a good leader will vary to some extent with the character of the men to be led, and the nature of the job. The particular situation in which leadership is wanted has to be kept in mind. It is not possible to get a versatile leader who will be able to do all jobs for all men. Army General Classification tests have been devised in USA to select leaders from the general population. These tests emphasise that leaders should be intelligent and alert.

Qualities like initiative and responsibilities have been tried and utilised by German psychologists for identifying leadership traits. There are possibilities in such a method but leadership has to be considered as something greater than ingenuity in meeting emergencies.

Auren Uris has described a method of leadership assessment by emphasising certain qualities which the author thinks correspond to leadership qualities. The tests, developed in this process, measure the following qualities:

1. Objectivity
2. Understanding of people
3. Communication-mindedness
4. Use of Authority

Questionnaires, having the aforesaid qualities, are given to people and their suitability as leaders is evaluated on the basis of the score obtained by them on the questionnaires. High, low or medium scores provide an index of the measure of leadership qualities in the person.

Fiedler has described sociometric tests as tools for leadership measurement. Sociometric studies have made important contributions in studying the problem of leadership. The predictions on leadership are based on rating of men who perform highly similar tasks and are assessed on their behaviour by their peers. Ratings of these types have been useful for various purposes.

A good executive skill is not identical with leadership. Management is more than leadership. It may include non-imaginative tasks like routine administration, etc.

Terman's studies on leadership assessment have made significant contribution on selection problems of leaders. Terman is believed to have observed that strength and clarity of leadership increase as 'group spirit' increases and group goals had greater clarity. He pointed out that it was absolutely necessary to ascertain the criteria of leadership first before any careful attempt is made to identify leadership qualities.

In the measurement of leadership qualities, some psychologists have emphasised situational determinants. Work of Gibb is of particular importance. The assessment of leadership qualities has become particularly useful and purposive due to advance of personality research. It has now become possible to use measures of meaningful, factorially independent personality traits.

Other measures of leadership assessment have also been tried by other psychologists. Bass (1919) has found a correlation of 0.93 between ratings on leadership and the amount of participation in groups. Borgatta and Bales report (1956) that high ratings on leadership by group members tend to be associated with high rates of interaction initiation.

Some studies have shown that in the reason task, leaders ask for information or facts significantly more often than non-leaders. Further, Shaw and Gilchrist (1956) found that leader rank and the number of written communications sent were positively related and that the major source or the difference for leaders was communication about organising the group and giving factual information.

Leaders have been found to display such behaviour characteristics like organise the group, solicit and integrate contributions, and propose courses of action. A high rate of participation would not be necessarily associated with these behaviours.

A leader tends to have a high rate of participation in the discussion, he is task-oriented, attempts to specify the problem, to suggest courses of action, to seek out the members' contributions, to integrate these and to propose solution in the attempt to secure consensus in the group.

In various countries, a lot of research has been done on the subject of assessment of leadership qualities. Methods adopted by these countries can be classified broadly into two:

1) Projective methods
2) Non-projective methods

Projective Methods

In projective methods, non-structured psychological tests are used for assessing the qualities of leaders. Tests are projected on the screen and the candidates are required to give their responses to situations which are shown to them. Pictures are shown to them and they are required to construct stories. Personality qualities are ascertained from them.

Non-Projective Methods

In this method, intelligence, aptitude and personality tests are given to candidates. These tests may be either verbal or non-verbal. A battery of tests, which have been standardised on the given sample, is used on a group and on the basis of performance on these tests, a performance profile is obtained for each candidate and the suitability of the candidate for leadership roles is ascertained.

Biographical questionnaires have also been used for assessing some leadership qualities. Interviews are also used for assessing leadership qualities in candidates. The validity and reliability of interview technique would depend on the degree of experience and objectivity with which the interviews are conducted by people.

Training of Leaders

Leadership training is an important task in any society. There are a lot of theories and controversies in leadership training and management theory. The orthodox training doctrine holds that the leader must be the brain of the group. He is expected to plan, direct, coordinate, supervise and evaluate work done by members of his group. This theory emphasises that a leader must be able to self-direct group effort which will help the members to contribute creatively and constructively to the task. The two theories emphasise two philosophies of training programmes on leadership.

Learning theory on leadership training has been advocated by some psychologists. Leaders are taught what they can learn and there is special emphasis on the problems of learning directly from experience, from knowledge of acquaintance which is in contrast to more intellectual kinds of learning.

A few leadership training studies have been undertaken by psychologists. In these studies, the problem was to tap different aspects of group creativity. In these studies it was found that the relationship-oriented leaders tended to perform better in groups which they describe as pleasant and relaxed. The task-oriented leaders had to perform better in groups which they describe as relatively tense and unpleasant.

Some leadership training programmes give instruction in administrative procedures, in organisational policy and such various other fields as accounting, cost control and legal responsibilities of the organisation. These programmes are primarily designed to increase the individual's leadership skills.

Various methods of leadership training have been developed. One method is called sensitivity or laboratory training method. In this method, opportunity is given to members to explore their own motivations and reactions. Laboratory training methods potentially provide one important avenue for introducing the individual to leadership situations in which he can perform well and to those in which he is likely to fail.

Leaders in training programmes are expected to modify some behavioural and attitudinal aspects of personality. Organisational climate has to be conducive to new behaviours and attitudes. Laboratory training may assist the leader in developing a more favourable group climate and more positive attitudes. Trainee has, therefore, some effect on other trainees and on his group.

Leadership training programmes can either be designed to change the trainee's attitude and behaviour in the direction which will make him more task-oriented, managing and directive or in the direction which will make him more human relations-oriented permissive and non-directive.

Leadership training is an important activity in a democratic setup. In democracy, one does not believe in the statement blindly that leaders are born and not made. People have to be trained for leadership in government, in business, in education and in all sorts of organisational activity. However, success of a person in a leadership role and capacity would depend upon the inherent capacity that the person has. It is believed that every person has some capacity which can be harnessed in one way or the other in a group activity of various sorts and types. Every normal person has some inherent features of his personality upon which skills and attitudes can be built up.

Leadership training is very important in an industrialised society. Industry has to face and meet the problems of foremen and supervisors. Business has the problems of executives and office managers. Similarly, government has the problem of having administrators in offices. Universities and colleges similarly need leaders who can run them.

There are a few obstacles in the training of leaders. They are:

1. Leader may not be well disposed to training.
2. Leader's attitudes may not be oriented to additional training.
3. Leader's personality may not be amenable to training.
4. A leader may fail to adjust himself in a new leadership role.

Leadership training experiments have revealed much significant information. Bavelas has found that personality traits of leadership are not the most significant determining factors in how successful the leader is. In a period of three weeks, leaders who had been poor leaders for years were converted into good leaders.

In leadership training, role playing has been emphasised as a method in leadership training. Skills are developed by learning through doing. The trainee is asked to act out a role which stimulates to a real leadership situation. This technique has certain advantages. It gives the leader a new perspective on his roles. It also enables the leader to have better insight into his leadership roles.

In a military organisation, the training of leaders becomes all the more important. A person who has ability and ambition can become a leader. It is also felt that leadership improves with experience and as such it can be learned if the person has required aptitude and enough motivation. Leadership competence can be acquired with intelligence, motivation and practice and this competence can be a function of leadership training.

Thus it can be concluded that training for leadership is an accomplished fact. The objective of most of the leadership training programmes is to stress technical mastery and executive skill. It is generally felt that the common task in all training situations on leadership is to vitalise and harmonise the desires and motives of the led.

For achieving the objectives of leadership training Tead[9] emphasises the inclusion of five elements:

1. Knowledge of the general characteristics of human nature.
2. Self-knowledge of one's own unique combination of qualities with their varying degrees of strength and weakness.
3. A working grasp of the right attitude to possess in dealing with people.
4. An ability to apply all of this knowledge to the mobilising of energy and enthusiasm for the special objectives of the organisation.
5. Deliberate efforts at broadening of the total personality in a cultural direction.

In the end, it would be appropriate to state that there is a demand for leaders in modern society. It is said that people have a desire to be led. It is this earnestness of people to be led that adds responsibility of leading. Keeping this in view, it has become necessary to be precise about what is leadership. Activity of leading can be better understood only when conception on leadership is clear. The problem of exercising leadership in various walks of life has to be dealt with in full earnestness. The type of influence that the leader has to exert on others is equally to be defined and leadership calibre has to be fully appreciated.

Leadership is supposed to have certain objectives, and the success of a leader will depend on the type of such objectives. Leadership is not a matter of hypnosis, blandishment or salesmanship. It requires definite motives, impulses and efforts which the leader has to cultivate in himself. Leadership is known by personalities it enriches. The qualities, necessary in leaders, have been stated in numerous ways, and the achievement and cultivation of those objectives become the sole purpose of any leadership programme. Physical qualities are as important in leadership behaviour as are mental and personality qualities. The leader has to be an executive. He must possess technical excellence, must be sharp and decisive, imaginative and must have a sense of humour.

Leaders are meant to lead the followers and their methods and manners of leading have to be precise and appropriate. They must have the capacity to project themselves in action with competence and confidence. They must free their followers from the feelings of emotional instability, fear and inferiority.

In a democracy the need for leaders becomes all the more necessary. No democracy can live without leaders, and no leader can be truly great without democratic principles. Leadership in democracy has to supply excitement and exhilaration. It is vital to a democratic society. This being so, training of leaders becomes an important commitment on the part of society. Society cannot attain emotional stability without training leaders in a proper way because it is these leaders who give stability to society.

Implications for Education

1. The first step in school learning is to meet the school emotional needs of the child.

2. This accomplished, the task of greatest importance is then to develop in children the skills and competence which are valued by the children and by the community.

3. Throughout this learning it must always be remembered that the social-emotional factors can quickly disrupt learning, while a good adjustment permits learning to proceed. It is equally true that good progress in learning makes for a good adjustment. Because social, emotional and learning factors interlock the school course and should be such as to promote satisfactory adjustment in both of these areas. This means that 'dead-wood' should be cut away so that the school course is essentially interesting, realistic, related to felt social needs and oriented to practical everyday problems.

4. Proper socialisation of the child means:

   (a) that he learns social skills and forms social relationships; and

   (b) that he learns to achieve a degree of freedom and independence from group domination which we call inner-directedness.

   The school course and organisation should be such as to facilitate these ends by providing opportunity for group activities and for individual progression.

5. The human behaviour is dynamic and it is impelled by certain energies and forces. What people do can be explained and understood best in terms of needs and motives. The teacher can understand the responses of his pupils and how to teach them most effectively when he knows their needs and motives.

6. In the field of education, the area of emotional health and learning is of greatest importance. Understanding our basic wants and needs helps us to improve our learning and mental health. In a general sense, if we can gratify our needs and motives, we shall be emotionally healthy and happy. In order to understand why and how we learn, we need to understand the fundamental motives that underlie learning.

7. People have a need and want for economic security. Therefore, they work and save so that they will have the means for acquiring the food, shelter and clothing and other things that they need. A shortage threatens life and being without it, brings death. Thus, economic security and security of life are closely related. If a person builds up his economic security he gains a standing and prestige. Consequently, he develops a higher self-esteem and feeling of greater personal worth. Similarly, the urge and want for companionship and friendship results in a feeling of belonging and enhances the sense of importance. In similar ways, the needs and wants for stimulating activities, health and comfort, freedom and liberty can also be shown to be related with the other needs and drives. Without the basic needs there would be no human beings for there would be no forces to keep them in existence. If we get along well with people, have good jobs and make plenty of money, are married to the right person, have a variety of interesting experiences, are in good health and are free from undue restraint, we are likely to be happy and wholesome. Our wants, urges and drives will be satisfied. We shall have a feeling of security and life will not be dull. There will be comparatively little pain, life will be comfortable and freedom will be enjoyed. And with all these satisfactions will go the feeling of personal worth—or satisfactory ego value.

***

6

Personality Diagnostics

Diagnosis as an Aid to Adjustment

The recent trend in psychology is the use of diagnosis as an aid to adjustment. Diagnosis of an individual's traits and potentialities is essential to the selection of adequate material for effective adjustment. Diagnostic and remedial techniques are important as the basis of improved techniques of teaching and guidance. The pupil who is physically strong and healthy, who is mentally alert, who is emotionally stable, and whose home and school environments are well fitted to his needs and interests is usually a well-adjusted and successful learner. If he lacks anything in his environment or in himself the result may be maladjustment. The deficiencies of adjustment require remedial techniques. Redirection and readjustment are not possible, unless the source of difficulty is discovered. The task of discovering such difficulties, in other words, diagnosis is the function of educational leaders.

The scientific approach to an understanding of the nature of the individual's disordered behaviour requires objective study before any treatment is suggested. Diagnosis reveals the existing disorder. Ideal diagnosis on disordered behaviour must take into account the whole person, keeping in view the interaction between soma and psyche or body and mind. Diagnosis embodies as detailed a study as is possible of all the factors that may facilitate or retard an individual's progress in any form of activity. It includes an analysis of personal factors such as physical constitution, general learning ability, special abilities or disabilities, degree of emotional or social adjustment, work habits and achievements, and environmental influences. In simple words, diagnosis combines three things: (i) causal factors of discard; (ii) estimate of the prognosis; (iii) identification of the patient's conditions in terms of one of the accepted clinical entities. In other words, diagnosis requires the combined efforts of doctor, psychologist, social worker and psychiatrist. All of them work as a team. This is also called the interdisciplinary approach.

Interdisciplinary Approach

In the interdisciplinary approach the patient is studied through individual and family interviews, psychological examinations, laboratory reports, school records, and social investigations. In short, a complete picture of the background of disturbances is obtained.

The doctor conducts a physical examination in order to find out the organic factors which may be the cause of the patient's trouble. Examples are injury to the brain or spinal cord, stomach upset, headache and glandular imbalance.

The psychologist conducts interviews with the disordered patient, administers psychological and intelligence tests, and evaluates the existing abilities of the patient.

The psychiatric social worker prepares a life history of the patient which includes economic adjustment, social adjustment and school adjustment of the patient and other related factors.

The psychiatrist studies the mental status of the patient in relation to all other findings. It is the responsibility of the psychiatrist to diagnose the trouble.

Diagnostic Techniques

The techniques implied in diagnosis of behaviour and personality disorders are many. A detailed description is given as follows:

Medical Examination

In this technique a general medical history of the patient is taken. The functioning of the various organs of the body are investigated. A physician wants to study the presence of any physical condition having a bearing on the personality disorder. In diagnosis the physician studies the history of metabolic and endocrine functions, cardiac activity, blood and urine chemistry, and gastro-intestinal and genito-urinary functions.

Case Study

The case history is usually obtained by a psychiatric social worker from the patient or a close relative. Coville and others have included the following data in case history.

1. Identifying data (name, address, age).
2. Statement of the presenting problem (symptoms, complaints).
3. Health history (illness, serious disease, surgical operations).
4. Developmental history (course of growth through infancy, childhood, and maturation).
5. Family history (description of the family constellation, its health history and interpersonal relationships).
6. Educational history (school and college progress).
7. Work history (record of occupations, length of service, general occupational adjustment).
8. Patient's interpersonal relationships (patient's attitude and behaviour toward others in various aspects of his life experience):
9. Psychosexual history (sexual habits and attitudes of patient).
10. Marital history (statement of marital status and description of marital adjustment).
11. Special personal habits and interests (talents, skills, hobbies).
12. Personality traits (description of mannerisms, reactions, moods and emotional patterns of the patient).

The Psychological Examination

The psychological examination is conducted by a clinical psychologist. Although he also uses the interview technique, his principal function in the diagnostic team is the administration and interpretation of a battery of psychological tests which may vary in content from one type of diagnostic problem to another. It is the psychologist's responsibility to select the test battery to be employed with the particular patient. He may include tests of intelligence, aptitude, special functions, interests and personality. The personality tests constitute the significant core of the typical test battery.

Intelligence Tests

In clinical practice intelligence tests are used to gauge the patient's mental ability, to distinguish between his potential and his functioning level, and to aid in the process of differential diagnosis group tests of intelligence are used, but rarely in the clinical setting. The principal individual tests are the Wechsler-Bellevue Intelligence Scales and the 1937 revision of the Stanford-Binet Intelligence Scale (recently revised and now available as the 1963 L-M Revision). Where a language handicap exists, intelligence is measured by one of the non-verbal performance scales.

Since their publication in 1939, the Wechsler-Bellevue Intelligence Scales Form I and Form II have been the preferred instrument for evaluating the intelligence of patients in the adolescent and adult age range. The scales comprise five verbal sub-tests (information, comprehension, digit-span, arithmetic and similarities) and five performance sub-tests (picture completion, picture arrangement, object assembly block design and digit symbol substitution). An additional vocabulary sub-test may be included. A revision designated the Wechsler Adult Intelligence scale (WAIS) was published in 1955 and a scale for children (WISC) in 1949. The Wechsler scales afford much material for qualitative diagnostic evaluation and they give a highly valid quantitative measure of mental capacity.

Tests of Concept Formation, Aptitude and Interest

For some special diagnostic problems, the Goldstein-Scheerer or the Haufmann-Kasnin tests may be used. These tests reveal weaknesses in concept formation and abstract thinking, and are useful in work with patients in whom brain damage is suspected, as well as with schizophrenics. Other useful tests of special function are the Bender Visual Motor Gestalt, the Porteus Maze, and the Lowenfeld Mosaics tests. Tests measuring various aptitudes may be used in cases where vocational adjustment is indicated to be a problem. Tests of interest, such as the Strong Vocational Interest Inventory or the Kuder Preference Record, are similarly useful.

Personality Tests

Without question the major contribution of the clinical psychologist in the diagnostic process is his skill in the administration and interpretation of various personality tests. These may be grouped into projective techniques and personality inventories. Although the latter are occasionally used for clinical work, most psychologists have found the projective techniques more sensitive and of greater diagnostic value.

Projective Techniques

Under this heading is grouped a large number of methods for the development of insight into the functioning of the personality. These methods have in common the following characteristics:

(1) They evaluate the total personality instead of merely providing scores on a series of discrete traits.

(2) The stimulus situations that are used call forth a broad range of individual responses so that a pattern of responses uniquely characteristic of the individual under study will be revealed.

(3) The subject is asked to respond to, interpret, or complete a relatively unstructured stimulus (for example, an ink-blot). In doing so he projects his conscious and unconscious needs, wishes and fears. These projections provide the raw data for analysis by the clinical psychologist.

(4) The individual's behaviour (beyond his verbal responses) is noted and interpreted under relatively standardised conditions.

The most widely used projective techniques are the Rorschach Examination, the Thematic Apperception Test (TAT), the Draw-a Person Test, the Make-a-Picture Story Test (MAPS), the Sentence Completion Test, and the Word Association Test.

The Rorschach Examination, devised by the Swiss psychiatrist Herman Rorschach (1884–1922), and published in 1921, is the most widely used projective technique for testing the personality of adults and children. It consists of ten ink-blots presented to the subject in a standardised sequence for his interpretation and association. His responses are analysed on the basis of his use of form, colour, texture, movement, content, conventionality, originality and speed of response. Normative data are available in psychological literature, but not the validity of the clinician. While the Rorschach test is an aid in diagnostic classification, its principal value is to shed light on the structure and dynamics of the personality. The test reveals aspects of the personality such as contact with reality, richness of mental life, defence mechanisms, anxiety, depression and other aspects of interpersonal adjustment. The Rorschach Examination also lends itself to a qualitative evaluation of the patient's behaviour in the test situation. As is the case with all psychological tests, it is most valuable when used as a part of a battery of tests.

The Thematic Apperception Test (TAT), devised by Morgan and Murray in 1935, consists of a series of pictures of somewhat indefinite content. These are presented to the subject with instructions to make up a story for each picture. The stories are then analysed according to the predominant themes, mood or emotions attributed to the characters in each story. The underlying hypothesis is that by a process of identification, which may be unconscious, the patient projects his own drives and conflicts. This test has greater value for uncovering personality dynamics than it has for establishing diagnostic classification. The patterns it reveals are more likely to be related to the life experience of the individual than are those uncovered to the Rorschach. The pictures are also used to stimulate association in therapeutic sessions. For use with children, a variation, the Children's Apperception Test (CAT) has been developed.

The technique used in the TAT lends itself to the development of a special series of pictures for particular diagnostic purposes (for example, predication of delinquency, or measurement of prejudice).

The Draw-a-Person Test requires that the patient draw a person as well as he can. Upon completion of the first drawing, he is asked to draw a person of the opposite sex. The analysis takes into consideration such factors as size and placement of figures, relationships between the male and female figures, type of lines, distortions, omissions, measures, and bizarre treatment of various parts of the human figure. The basic assumption is that the drawing represents the patient's body image and that attitudes, impulses and conflicts are reflected in his drawing. Problems in psychosexual adjustment are frequently revealed by this technique. The drawings must be interpreted with caution and require a high level of clinical skill. One of the values of this test is its brevity and the ease of administration. A variant of this test is the House-Tree-Person (HTP) drawing test.

The Make-a-Picture Story Test (MAPS) consists of a large number of cut-out figures and various backdrops. The patient is asked to select figures and arrange them before a selected backdrop. He is then asked to tell a story about the arrangement he has made. It is assumed that the patient will select, arrange and tell stories about the figures in accordance with his own conscious needs and feelings.

The Sentence Completion *Test* consists of a series of incomplete sentences which the subject is asked to complete with his first spontaneous association. The content of the stimulus phrases is arranged to elicit reactions to principal conflict areas. The hypothesis underlying the technique is that in completing the sentences the patient will reveal his own attitudes toward the areas touched upon. Although standard sentence completion forms are available, interpretation is largely dependent on the ingenuity and clinical skill of the examiner.

The Word Association *Test*, probably the oldest of all projective techniques, was originally described by Carl Jung. Since his time psychiatrists and psychologists have used lists of words to elicit spontaneous associations from their patients with a view to uncovering conflict areas. Diagnostic indicators of conflict are said to be characterised by lengthy reaction time, odd or bizarre associations, stammering, or other signs of tension. Clinicians vary in the way in which they analyse the association processes revealed by the test.

There are other projective techniques. The Szondi Test utilises a series of portraits of psychiatric patients, which the subject is asked to arrange according to preference. His choice is said to reveal material or diagnostic value. The Rosenzweig Picture Frustration Test utilises a series of action pictures which the patient is required to identify with one of the figures and express his verbalisation of the described frustrating situation. The Rosenzweig test provides normative data on the basis of which various ways of handling aggression may be determined.

Handwriting analysis is another projective method in which detailed, painstaking study is made of the patient's handwriting on the assumption that it is an expression of personality.

Play techniques, although principally used as a therapeutic vehicle for children, may also be used in the diagnostic process. Dolls, puppets and playhouses are utilised to elicit emotional attitudes and conflicts.

Art analysis utilises finger painting or more formal means of art expression to reveal patterns of emotional reaction in both adults and children.

Personality Inventories: In these objective standardised tests, the patient is required to answer specific questions about his own behaviour or attitudes. The patient's responses are usually restricted to indicating whether or not a given statement is pertinent. Some of the tests are relatively simple, calling for only a Yes or No response; others require comparisons and selections among several items. Generally speaking, personality inventories have a limited application in clinical practice: they are used mainly with groups, for purposes of preliminary screenings.

Although there are numerous published inventories, the Minnesota Multiphasic Personality Inventory (MMPI) is the preferred test of this type. It consists of 550 items which have been gathered from the case records of patients having various psychiatric disorders. The degree to which the subject's answers correspond to items normally found in particular types of psychiatric history suggests his tendencies in that direction. Scores are expressed in psychiatric terms and provide measures of tendencies toward the following types of disorders: hypochondriasis, depression, hysteria, psychopathic deviation, paranoia, psychasthenia, schizophrenia and hypomania. The test also purports to measure masculinity, femininity and sociability. Extensive research has been done with this test, and it stands along the inventories with respect to its usefulness in clinical practice.

The Psychiatric Examination

The psychiatric examination utilises an interview with the patient to observe and evaluate significant aspects of his behaviour. Exaggerations, distortions and the absence of expected responses or the presence of abnormal responses are recorded. The traditional psychiatric examination includes statements on the following:

Appearance and general behaviour. This statement usually describes general health and appearance, habits of dressing, personal habits, speech, moods and sociability.

Attitude and behaviour during the interview. This statement describes the patient's attitude towards the interviewer (expressive movements as revealed by manner, voice, posture, facial expressions and motor activity.

Stream of mental activity. The data recorded here concerns verbal productivity, spontaneity of stream of thought, distracting language deviations and reaction time.

Emotional reactions. These are related to the patient's general activity, his mental trend or thought content. Generally, the emotional reactions observed by the interviewer and what the patient says about his feelings are recorded. Thus, the interviewer may note whether the emotional reactions are appropriate or not, whether the patient is composed, suspicious, depressed, indifferent, angry, elated, etc.

Mental trends. The statement with regard to mental trends or thought content describes persecutory trends, hypochondriacal ideas, ideas of unreality, nihilistic ideas, depressive trends, and grandiose ideas or hallucinatory experiences.

Sensorium, mental grasp and capacity. This statement estimates the patient's intellectual capacities and resources. The estimate is based on the patient's responses to questions that measure his orientation as to time, place and person, his memory for the remote and recent past, his powers of retention and immediate recall, his abilities in counting, calculation and writing, and his school and general knowledge.

Summary of psychiatric examination. The main findings are summarised and a statement is made concerning the patient's intellectual capacities, evenness of performance, deteriorative trends and self-evaluation.

Diagnosis of Pupil Difficulty

Unless careful diagnosis is done, the underlying causes of maladjusted behaviour can be misinterpreted. Every pupil is entitled to receive careful study from his teachers and other school leaders. Young pupil's attitude and behaviour needs to be evaluated. Individual or group difficulties should be recognised and their causes discovered. Remedial techniques should be established and steps taken to prevent the occurrence or reoccurrence of such difficulties. Since the human personality is extremely complex, any attempt at the discovery of basic causes of maladjustment is a difficult and painstaking process. Hildreth suggests that the following five areas of investigation are important.

Mental Equipment of the Learner

This includes aptitude for academic school work, learning capacity, readiness for learning habitual modes of response, judgment, reasoning ability, insight memory, association, perception, attention span, ability to see relationships, creative ability, intellectual interest and habits, command of mother-tongue, vocabulary, and matter composition.

Personality, Temperament and Dynamic Equipment

This includes the following:

Self-control, affability, desirable and undesirable inhibitions, attitudes, drive stability, responsiveness, shyness, day-dreaming, fear, sex interest, manners, attitude towards failure, (school disability, play interest, worries, ability to get along with other children, delinquent and anti-social activity, and degree of normal adjustment.

Physical Status

This includes the following:

Physical status, sensory and motor equipment, physical conditions, sensory activity, constitutional defects, physical maturation, disease history, glandular balance, condition of teeth, aetiology of illness, posture accidents, psychomotor status, muscular strength or weakness, handedness, steadiness and coordination.

Environment and Home History

This includes the following:

Economic factors, literacy of parents, number of siblings, marital status of parents, evidence of culture, harmony in home adjustment, attitude of home towards school, neighbourhood environment, association with other children, and full time activities of the child.

Child's Daily Schedule

This includes the following:

Child's daily schedule – nursing, eating, sleeping, playing, school work at home, and regularity or irregularity in home programme.

School Situation, History and Present Status

This includes the following:

Method of instruction, size, capability of class groups, school work, school progress, etc.

The function of diagnosis or evaluation is limited to the prevention of possible academic difficulties and to the guidance of the pupil into desirable present and future activities.

Method of Pupil Evaluation

The following are the diagnostic techniques for pupil evaluation:

1. Trained observation
2. Physical examination
3. Classroom and school tests and examinations
4. Standardised tests, scales and inventories including intelligence tests, aptitude tests, achievement tests, interest inventories, personality scales and inventories
5. Case study techniques (this has already been discussed in the preceding pages)
6. Interview

Each of these techniques is limited in its usefulness because the total personality is something more than the sum of its factors. No one technique can measure adequately the inter-relation of the various phases of individuality. Moreover, the personality of the tester or evaluator may affect the results of the diagnosis. For example, personal prejudices, degree of facility in handing, measuring techniques or the adequacy of testing conditions and of the tests may seriously affect the actual measuring process and the interpretation of the results. All the results of the measurement need to be recorded accurately and the recommendations followed carefully if diagnostic procedures are to be effective.

Observation as a Diagnostic Technique

Pupil maladjustment may be brought to the attention of the teacher as a result of observation of behaviour. The child who has difficulty in sitting in a correct posture, who cannot read material on the blackboard, who holds his book close to his eyes, who stammers or shows other signs of distress when called upon to recite, or who is generally uncooperative, displays to the observant teacher the presence of characteristics that need attention.

The value of observation as a tool of diagnosis depends upon the ability of the observer to make accurate and objective observations. The observer must be an emotionally well-balanced person, his training and experience should be such that he is able to recognise the presence and possible causes of deviations from normal behaviour. He should be alert and objective in his comparisons of normal behaviour with abnormal reactions

Diagnostic Techniques for Difficult Pupils

Physical Examination: Physical health is the foundation of mental health. The school should prevent undesirable health activities and physical examination should be made available as far as possible. A record of all physical examinations should be kept.

Classroom and School Tests and Examinations

This includes the following:

Daily, weekly, monthly, mid-term, and end-of-term tests. These are generally accepted as essential to teaching and learning.

Short-term test questions such as true–false, completion, multi-choice and matching of carefully constructive and based upon worthwhile material give opportunity for a comprehensive diagnosis of the specific difficulties associated with any learning situation.

Standardised Evaluation Techniques

For the comparison of the behaviour of any one individual or group of individuals with more trustworthy norms of performance, it is desirable to administer measuring techniques that have been standardised carefully through application and large number of subjects, under controlled testing conditions.

Measurement of Intelligence

Mental competence is an essential factor of mental health. It is the duty of school leaders to obtain as accurate a knowledge as is possible of the mental ability of their students and then to adjust the learning process and teaching technique to the respective levels of ability. The importance of mental tests has already been discussed in the Chapter *Intelligence*.

Measurement of Specific Aptitudes

Aptitude is a present condition which is indicative of an individual's potentialities for the future. Individual tests are designed to measure the degree of general alertness without emphasis upon any specific form of ability. An individual may be slow in general but may be better in one particular form of response. In order to determine the kind or extent of an individual's potentiality for success apart from training in one field, a specific form of measurement known as aptitude test must be administered. As occupational competition is keen, young people should be assisted in discovering their vocational field.

Measurement of Achievement

The techniques which have been discussed so far test inherent ability apart from directed and conscious training. Achievement tests differ from these in that all achievement tests have for their purpose the measurement of results of teaching and learning. An achievement test presupposes instruction in the definite field for which the tests have been constructed. Such tests may be either survey tests for the measurement of the outcome of teaching techniques or diagnostic measures of pupil difficulties.

Utilisation of the Case Study

For areas of pupil difficulty, the case study can be done by the following:

1. Physical, mental, and personality evaluation techniques.
2. Record of school progress.
3. Health norms and charts.
4. Interview with the subject, his family members, parents, etc. Case histories of pupils include:
   (a) Identification
   (b) Family background
   (c) Health history
   (d) Home and neighbourhood environment
   (e) Social and economic status
   (f) Intelligence
   (g) Social progress
   (h) Work history
   (i) Social behaviour and interests
   (j) Sex deviation.
   (k) Interpretation of data
   (l) Recommendation
   (m) Progress

Interview as a Technique of Diagnosis

Problems arise in the lives of most individuals that demand intimate personal constitution with other persons who are qualified to assist in the solution of the difficulties. The attitude should be sympathetic, tactful understanding and objective. Rambling should be discouraged. Frankness should prevail.

The Teacher's Role in Pupil Diagnosis

Remedial teaching is impossible without knowledge of the factors that influence human behaviour. The teacher should become acquainted with the previous diagnosis. The teacher should use informal techniques of evaluation which include classroom behaviour, oral recitation and written test responses. These usually give an indication about the emotional disorder of pupils. The teacher should also use standardised measuring techniques.

***

7

Personality Therapies

Psychotherapy

Psychotherapy is the most important and adequate from of health care available for psychologically distressed individuals. This is a method of treatment which aims at helping distressed individuals by influencing and stimulating their emotional process, their evaluation of themselves and others, and their method and manner of coping with problems of life. Therapies influence and change the patient's environment and increase his potentialities of mastery and integration. Therapies are required for disturbances which are emotional in origin and which contain a large emotional factor.

Therapies represent a fusion of the immediate needs of the patient and the demands of society. Therapies have two aims: (i) clinical aims and (ii) dynamic aims.

Clinical Aims

   (a) Relieving symptoms (suffering)
   (b) Increasing the ability to be happy
   (c) Increasing efficiency
   (d) Aiding in social adaptation
   (e) Increasing spontaneity
   (f) Adjusting bodily functions, i.e., eating and sleeping

Dynamic Aims

   (a) Increase in the patient's feelings of self-esteem and security
   (b) Release of forbidden and repressed impulses
   (c) Increase of insight in patient
   (d) To increase self-acceptance, i.e., the patient accepts himself as an individual
   (e) To increase integration and reaching towards positive goals

In psychotherapy the relationship between the patient and the therapist is of utmost importance. The psychotherapist must have a good personality and excellent training. He must establish a good rapport with the patient. A good rapport enables a frank attitude on the part of the patient, which enables him to pour out his difficulties to the therapist. It implies a hope of being helped and an eagerness to co-operate for that end. In other words, therapy requires a good relationship between the patient and the therapist. The attitude of the therapist must be that of a person who listens to everything without criticising, condemning or censoring. Such an attitude assures the patient that he can say what he wishes. The patient thinks that the therapist is the only person to whom all secrets may be told. The patient also regards the therapist as stronger and superior in comparison. This way all the irrational attitudes, suspicions, hostilities and excessive demands which the patient has towards the world will unconsciously be focused upon the therapist.

Techniques of Psychotherapy

A variety of techniques have been developed in treating a patient psychologically. They are as follows:

Therapeutic Interviews

An interview is any type of prolonged contact between the therapist and the patient in which conversation plays a prominent role and which centres round the patient's problems. The set-up is such that it encourages the patient to unburden himself and talk about his complaints, and the stress and strain of his existence. Some patients do this almost spontaneously, whereas, others require a measure of guidance from the therapist. The aim of the therapist is to touch upon, sooner or later, on all significant aspects of the patient's life. He may guide the patient's conversation to further topics by repeating in the form of questions, something which the patient has already touched on or by raising new queries. In this procedure it is very important to observe the patient because he shows by facial expressions, changes in colour, and speech pauses or evasion, where the points of stress lie. Such signs guide the therapist in recognising what points should be taken up; if they become severe, what points should be left alone for the time being.

To know in what direction to guide or not to guide the conversation, the therapist must have a thorough knowledge of psychotherapy. It is obvious that in the interview the patient does most of the talking and that the interview is a diagnostic as well as a therapeutic procedure. The close inter-relation between diagnosis and therapy is a characteristic and unique aspect of psychotherapy.

Interviews of this type usually last about an hour and occur once or twice a week. If there is a great need for help, they may be given daily for a period of time. If they are effective in patients who do not require institutional treatment, beneficial results may be apparent after one interview. If improvement is not evident up to ten sessions, it is futile to continue. The total number of interviews needed depends upon the patient.

Why and how is the patient benefited by therapeutic interviews? The pertinent question has been raised by many psychologists. The answer lies in the fact that the patient talks to an individual whom he thinks strong and capable of giving help, who listens to everything and who encourages him to speak without condemning or punishing him, and this allays his fears and guilt and makes him feel more worthwhile and accepted. Together with this, there is an implicit development in spontaneity and frankness through the very fact of talking about forbidden and avoided subjects. He gradually feels that he has faced himself and his problems. The burst of emotions frequently occurring in interviews leads to release. The therapist is a trusted and sympathetic friend.

The interview therapy may be particularly effective in relieving the acute symptoms of any psychoneurotic disturbance of relatively recent origin. It can be very effective in patients who have mild disturbances of a psychotic type, but can still function in society. In addition to organic treatment, it can be of further benefit to patients with psychological disturbances complicating an organic ailment. If necessary, for organic diseases the therapist must advise physical examination and laboratory tests.

Psychoanalysis

The therapy of psychoanalysis was developed by Sigmund Freud. He developed this therapy in the course of his private practice as a physician over a period of years. The essential methods of this psychoanalysis therapy according to Coville are: (1) systematic utilisation of free association, (2) dream analysis, (3) the transference neurosis and (4) interpretation and re-education, with the goal of resolving the principal emotional problems of childhood. By these methods, the patient's repressed unconscious material is brought to the level of awareness, is explored and is interpreted in relation to his symptoms, his concept of self (ego) and his relationship with others.

Free Association. This follows the preliminary interview during which a case history is obtained and a working diagnosis is established. The patient is encouraged to relax by reclining on a couch, with the therapist in the background. He is then instructed to report to the therapist anything and everything that comes to his mind without censorship of any sort. In the early psychoanalytic sessions, the patient may experience great difficulty in achieving the free association—one or more sessions may pass in which he produces nothing which is suitable for the therapist's analysis and interpretation. As the therapeutic relation proceeds, however, the ability to associate freely is developed and this enables the patient to express ideas and feelings which have been repressed, some for a period of many years. The rapidity, with which this ability is related to the degree of resistance to therapy is displayed by the patient. Nor does free association always proceed evenly or in a chronological sequence; it may be interrupted by blocking, withholding of associations and purposive production of irrelevant and distracting material.

The associations, as ultimately produced by the patient and recorded by the analyst, gradually form a mosaic of ideas and feelings which, while they seem to be incoherent, illogical and faulty in time sequence, are nevertheless emotionally related. Equipped with his knowledge of the patient's life history and his observation of the patient throughout the therapeutic experience, the analyst recognises the dynamic meaning of these associations and from time to time guides the patient toward particularly meaningful areas of thought and feeling. The chief virtue of this method is its 'ventilating' effect, referred to as 'catharsis'.

Dream Analysis. Dream analysis is often a fruitful method of psychotherapy. Following the lead of Joseph Breuer (1842–1925), Freud perceived that in the dreams reported by his patients lay clues to significant unconscious material. The method has since persisted as a standard practice among psychoanalysts. During a therapeutic session, the analyst asks the patient to report his dreams. The difficulty of recalling the details of a dream is well known, but a patient who has been under analysis for some time and has gained the ability to free-associate readily, will also have developed a facility to recall the dreams. The content thus revealed by the patient, along with the substance of the underlying problems which the dream suggests, are then employed by the therapist as stimuli for further associations. Dream analysis may be conceived as a form of free association, but in the Freudian concept the dream is so highly organised a form of mental activity that it merits special listing.

According to Freud, dreams have both a manifest and a latent content. The dream images and their apparent meanings are the manifest content; the unconscious, conflictive material, for which the dream images are symbolic substitutes, is the latent content. Both levels have importance in the treatment process. The manifest content of dreams is often determined by immediate environmental circumstances and recent or remote life events. The symbols chosen to express the unconscious (latent) meaning of the dream may be universal or accidental. Universal symbols are those which have a generally accepted meaning for a given cultural group (such as phallic symbols); accidental symbols are those having a special meaning in terms of the life experiences of the individual relating the dream.

Two mental mechanisms characterise the manner in which a person works out a conflict or some other problem in his dream. Through condensation, a single composite image of the manifest content may stand for a number of ideas or feelings. In the mechanism of displacement, effect which is in reality associated with one respect of the dream is expressed in relationship to another aspect. These two mechanisms bring about a distortion of the dream content believed by Freud to be an unconscious device to disguise unacceptable thoughts and feelings and thus protect the ego against a sense of guilt.

The modes of dream interpretation and their application in psychotherapy differ among analytic therapists, depending on the school of analysis in which they are grounded, but the fundamentals are by and large the same.

Transference Neurosis: A transference neurosis exists when the patient transfers to the therapist the emotions which have been repressed since early childhood. In the treatment experience, such transferred emotions usually emerge as mild manifestations directed towards the analyst. As the therapeutic procedure continues, these emotions grow in intensity and duration. In the eyes of the patient, the therapist assumes the role of a stern parent (or other person who stood in this relation to the patient in childhood) This is an extremely valuable instrument for the therapist in his probing of the patient's subconscious because it encourages the patient to re-live the emotional experiences of his early years. Referred to as abreaction, the patient's response to this mechanism is the most critical phase of the psychoanalysis.

The transference neurosis may lead to attachment, to dependency on, and even love for the therapist (positive transference); or it may give rise to resentment, impatience and often violent antagonism toward the therapist (negative transference). The latter reaction brings about a severe, though usually temporary, disruption of the therapeutic process. The anxieties aroused by transference neurosis are among the unpleasant features of psychoanalytic therapy, and if they are not successfully resolved they may be harmful to the patient, in view of their 'out of the frying pan into the fire' effect. It should be noted that a counter transference from a therapist to patient may develop. To guard against this the therapist must in his own attitude remain as aloof as possible and must avoid being thrown into the morass of the patient's turmoil.

Interpretation: Interpretation is essential throughout the course of psychoanalysis; the therapist must be continually alert to opportunities to decipher and interpret the dynamic meaning of free associations, dreams and the behaviour of the patient. He pays particular attention to any feelings that are expressed by the patient and seeks to ferret out the relationship between these feelings and the nature of the material being discussed.

The interpretations offered by the analyst fall into two categories — those which call the patient's attention to the emotions he is expressing (the dynamic significance of which are then explained); and those which help the patient to recognise the defence he employs to keep threatening or unpleasant feelings repressed.

The analyst must have a keen sense of timing. He must be extremely careful to pick an opportune and appropriate time to share his interpretations, called the 'working through'. This constitutes an essential phase of psychoanalytic therapy. The unveiling of an interpretation at a point when the patient is unprepared to accept it and profit by it can be valueless or even dangerous.

Because interpretation is so critical a matter, the analyst must be completely aware of his own defence mechanism and drives; otherwise he will fall into the trap of interpreting the patient's dynamic feelings and thoughts in terms of his own life experience and underlying problems. This is one of the reasons why psychoanalysts are required to undergo a personal analysis.

Play Therapy

Play therapy is usually meant for children who find it difficult or impossible to speak out their conflicts. In play therapy, children are encouraged to engage in free play in which conflict can be more adequately expressed.

The essential methods of play therapy are offered by way of dolls, puppets, miniature household furniture, clay, sand, water, and other toys. Through the manipulation of these toys, the child reveals unconsciously his feelings of frustration and hostility.

The play with dolls is very helpful in understanding the dynamic relationships in the family as the child experiences them. Play therapy allows the child to express unconscious aggression. It also provides release of tension in the patients and is used in diagnosing the patient's trouble.

Group Therapy

Group therapy means psychotherapeutic procedure in which several individuals are simultaneously undergoing therapy. The size of the group may vary from 3 to 50. In practice, group therapy has as many variations as individual therapy. The earliest form of group therapy were largely didactic with the group leader lecturing, persuading and directing. With the new development in the field the group leader has come to serve the same function for the group as does the individual therapist for the patient. He encourages expression, examines motives, offers interpretation and gradually elicits participation of the individual member. According to Coville the essential features of group therapy are as follows:

1. The group is selectively screened to achieve some degree of homogeneity and congeniality. The factors considered are age range, gender distribution, diagnosis, general personality characteristics and prognosis. The controlling consideration and the weight given to any of these factors in selecting patients depends upon the therapist. Groups are usually small, the optimum number ranging from six to ten. Most groups meet once or twice a week for several months or longer.

2. Varying practices exist in the use of group therapy in relation to individual therapy. Thus, some therapists will select and prepare a patient for group therapy only after a course of individual therapy; others will maintain the patient in individual and group therapy concurrently; some will enter the patient directly into the group setting without individual therapy.

3. The therapist attempts to create a permissive atmosphere which encourages spontaneity of expression. In the beginning, patients relate their own symptoms and problems. Gradually, they embark upon discussions of significant emotional experiences in their outside life, and eventually, they evaluate and comment upon the experiences of their members.

4. In the group situation, conformation to a rigid pattern of participation is not required. Thus, patients can participate in their own manner, at their own pace and with varying degrees of resistance

The following example gives us an idea about group therapy. This example also shows that in small groups any personal problem, impulse, attitude, conflict, guilt, hostility or anxiety is discussed on the basis of personal experience.

1st Patient   :   As a little girl, I used to wet my bed. I used to hate to go to bed, fearing, may be, I would have an accident.

Therapist   :   Those were possible feelings.

1st Patient   :   What happens when even adults dream they are going to the lavatory and may wet the bed?

Therapist   :   That is miserable too.

2nd Patient :   My mother told me I was heartbroken in a year.

3rd Patient :   I remember when I was about 12 years old a girl friend pulled her pants down in the back of the garage and did her business. I thought it was awful.

4th Patient   :   When I was about ten, some of the boys would pull down their pants and the other boys would do acts with them. I think there is something in that that makes me shy with other men. I never connected it until this minute — a kind of fear of other men because of that.

At this point another patient volunteered:

I remember when I was a child, one day my dad came in and I wanted him to show me a picture. He showed me one of me sitting on the toilet and after that I never cared to have any one draw pictures any more.

Group therapy breaks down the patient's feelings of isolation and uniqueness of his illness. He comes to know that there are other individuals who also suffer from the same tension. This helps him in releasing the tension. Another advantage of group therapy is that it offers opportunities for social experience in which the patients may test their own growth in inter-social relations and the therapist may observe the patient's work.

Psychodrama

The technique of psychodrama was developed by J.L. Moreno. In psychodrama the patient is encouraged to act out before an audience. In psychodrama the patient is asked and instructed to act out an emotional constellation as if he were an actor on a stage. This therapy has also been used to prepare individuals for future situations. It has also been used in industry for training in handling inter-personal problems. The therapist acts as the director on the stage. He obtains information through an interview about the patient's symptoms and problems of life situations.

Insulin Shock Treatment

This is also known as insulin shock therapy. This was developed by M.J. Sakel. Insulin shock treatment is based upon the fact that when an individual is given a large dose of insulin, the amount of sugar in the bloodstream is rapidly diminished to a point where the patient goes into shock and becomes unconscious. As a result of this shock, the brain is deprived of sugar, its most important food, and the body is excessively stimulated to utilise all of its forces. When this occurs the normal pathways in the brain are somehow reinforced, and gradually the behaviour of a mentally sick individual subject to such treatment is restored to normal.

A patient with the type of illness known as manic–depressive psychosis—which is manifested by under-activity, loss of emotional control, swings of mood from extreme depression to extreme excitement—can often be speeded to recovery by the use of mental treatment. Involutional melancholia is another form of mental illness which is being treated successfully by the use of insulin. This mental illness occurs during the change of life period in both men and women and is characterised by depression of mood, severe anxiety and delusions that the body is being destroyed in strange and impossible ways.

Music Therapy

The use of music as a therapeutic measure in emotional and mental disorders began hundreds of years ago. The chief significance of music as a means of therapy lies in mechanism of the human brain and the way musical sounds reach and affect it. Music, according to Altshuler, is first perceived by the thalamus. The stimulation of thalamus automatically incites the cortex, which results in gaining the attention of the individual and this makes further therapy possible.

Humanistic Therapy

Humanistic therapy is a psychological perspective which rose to prominence in the mid-20th century in response to Sigmund Freud's psychoanalytic theory and B.F. Skinner's behaviourism. With its roots running from Socrates through the Renaissance, this approach emphasises and individual's inherent drive towards self-actualisation and creativity.

It typically holds that people are inherently good. It adopts a holistic approach to human existence and pays special attention to such phenomena as creativity, free will and human potential. It encourages viewing ourselves as a 'whole person' in the study of behaviour in other people. Humanistic psychology acknowledges spiritual aspiration as an integral part of the human psyche. It is linked to the emerging field of transpersonal psychology.

Humanistic psychology has sometimes been referred to as the 'third force' in psychology, distinct from the two more traditional approaches, which are psychoanalysis and behaviourism. In the context of post-industrial society, humanistic psychology has begun to be seen as more relevant than the earlier approaches. It is largely responsible for new approaches towards human capital, stressing creativity and human wholeness. Previously the connotations of 'creativity' were reserved for and primarily restricted to working artists. In the 1980s, with an increasing number of people working in the cognitive-cultural economy, creativity came to be seen as a useful commodity and competitive edge for international brands. This led to creativity training in-service trainings for employees, probably led by Ned Herrmann at G.E. in the late 1970s.

Humanistic psychology concepts were embraced in both theory and practice of education and social work, peaking in the 1970s–1980s, particularly in North America.

***

8

Personality and Sexual Deviations

Importance

Sex education is instruction on issues relating to human sexuality, including human sexual anatomy, sexual reproduction, sexual activity, reproductive health, emotional relations, reproductive rights and responsibilities, Sexual abstinence, and birth control. Common avenues for sex education are parents or caregivers, formal school programs, and public health campaigns.

Sex is a universally strong biological drive in the life of human beings. It plays an important role in preservation and building of human society. Since sex drive has powerful potentiality to influence human life it is important to harness this energy for the harmony and development of human personality. Much attention has been given to this drive by societies since the dawn of human civilisation. It has considerable influence on the human mind and sex needs, being more often frustrated than any of the other human needs, sex frustration is bound to affect development of human personality to a great extent

The importance of sex in the development of human personality has been emphasised by psychologists who profess psychoanalysis. They have tried to conceive a picture of the inner life of man in terms of sex energy which is a significant source of action of human beings. The dynamic interplay of inner life of a person, his behaviour, expressions and experiences are attributed to this source of energy. Maladjustment in life and psychopathology in human behaviour is attributed to unsatisfactory behaviour of sex life. Sex is supposed to provide certain influences that stress certain factors in human life. Normal and pathological behaviour is thus related to sex behaviour. Some have attributed marginal processes of powers to sex force.

Man's sexual activity in an urban society has been more and more reduced to certain vicissitudes. Attendant problem of learning how to be natural in this activity needs the help and organisation of sex education. Sex education should aim at developing proper attitudes and proper level of understanding on the sex activity among boys and girls in the juvenile age so that misconceptions and wrong notions may not mar the healthy understanding of sex as force in human life. Healthy and objective information on sex will not only help in ensuring better adjustments that are often marred by sexual frustration but will also help in securing satisfactory relationship among people when they get married. Experts have considerably emphasised the need for sex education among juveniles so that misinformation may not lead them to commit wrong actions which is likely to lead them to tragic goals of life. Therefore, we have to provide certain basic information on sex behaviour in human beings, the knowledge of which will enable boys and girls to understand the behaviour in proper scientific perspective.

Human sexuality has biological, physical, emotional and spiritual aspects. The biological aspect of sexuality refers to the reproductive mechanism as well as the basic biological drive, or, libido that exists in all species, which is strongly influenced by hormonal levels. The emotional or physical aspect of sexuality refers to the bond that arises between individuals, and is manifested physically or through emotions such as love, trust and caring. There is also a spiritual aspect of sexuality of an individual or as a connection with others. Experience has shown that adolescents are curious about aspects of their sexuality as well as the nature of sexuality in general, and that many will seek to experience their sexuality in some way.

Traditionally, adolescents in many cultures were not given any information on sexual matters, with discussion of these issues being considered taboo. Such instruction as was given was traditionally left to a child's parents, and often this was put off until just before a child's marriage. The progressive education movement of the late 19th century, however, led to the introduction of 'social hygiene' in North American school curricula and the advent of school-based sex education. Despite early inroads of school-based sex education, most of the information on sexual matters in the mid-20th century was obtained informally from friends and the media, and much of this information was deficient or doubtful value, especially during the period following puberty when curiosity of sexual matters was the most acute. This deficiency became increasingly evident by the increasing incidence of teenage pregnancies, especially in Western countries after the 1960s. As part of each country's efforts to reduce such pregnancies, programs of sex education were instituted, initially over strong opposition from parents and religious groups.

The outbreak of AIDS has given a new sense of urgency to sex education. In African countries, where AIDS is an epidemic (see HIV/AIDS in Africa), sex education is seen by most scientists as a vital public health strategy. Some international organisations such as Planned Parenthood consider that broad sex education programs have global benefits, such as controlling the risk of overpopulation and the advancement of women's rights (see also reproductive rights). The use of mass media campaigns, however, has sometimes resulted in high levels of 'awareness' coupled with essentially superficial knowledge of HIV transmission.

Physiology of Sex Behaviour

Sexual behaviour and its physiological aspects in human beings have been watched in past by observing the behaviour of animals. Sex behaviour in animals is simple to observe. It is not very much complicated by learning, experience, and ideas.

In the case of human beings, it can be modified a lot by experience, learning, etc. Sexual life is a psychological basis. It is demonstrated by the fact that sexual desires are felt to undergo waxes and wanes. There are life-cycles in both animals and human beings. Sexual desires are felt in human beings at the stage of puberty. The menstrual cycle in women is an 'oestrus' cycle. However, sexual desire in women is not completely controlled by the events of this cycle. In every normal individual, there is a single long period of mating activity, beginning with the maturation of the gonads at puberty. After puberty, the period of sexual activity is continued until it ends in the relatively sudden menopause of women or the rather gradual sexual senility of men.

Physiological events have been worked out in considerable detail during oestrus cycles. Under the influence of the follicle—stimulating hormone (FSH) of the anterior pituitary gland, the follicles of the ovaries begin to develop. As the immature follicle grows it secretes oestrogen, and this, in turn, helps the anterior pituitary body to reproduce a second hormone, the luteinising hormone (LH). The combined influence of FSH and LH helps the follicle develop and thus more oestrogen is secreted. Next, large amounts of oestrogen change the epithelium of the uterus and vagina and at the same time influences the pituitary gland to secrete more LH and less FSH. At this point in the cycle the follicle begins a new stage of development and under the influence of LH, becomes the corpus luteum. As the corpus luteum develops it continues to secrete oestrogen and in addition, elaborates a sew hormone, often called progesterone which causes more epithelial changes in the uterus until it is ready for the ovum to be implanted if fertilisation takes place. Progesterone also serves to stimulate production of the lactogenic hormone of the anterior pituitary, prolactin. Prolactin, finally, is important in the development of the mammary gland for milk production, should pregnancy occur.

Physiologically, oestrus or the phase of 'heat' are cyclic and in the case of animals they are seasonal. Birds mate in the spring; dogs in the spring and fall. In terms of bodily cycle, female mammals experience an oestrus cycle. During the major part of the cycle, the female is unreceptive to the male. The menstrual cycle in woman is an oestrus cycle. However, it is evident that existence or appearance of sexual desire in woman is not completely controlled by the events of this cycle. From various experiments carried out in human beings and animals on sex behaviour and sex needs are conditioned by presence in the blood of certain hormones. These hormones are secreted by internal endocrine glands. Regarding the role of the hormones in influencing sex behaviour, Boring states the following:

"There is strong evidence that mating in animals depends only secondarily on the perception of a mate. Being aware of the presence of a mate does not stimulate sexual desires unless the necessary hormones are present in the blood. Nor is any particular set of sensations requisite. Surely, sight and touch may act together, or one sense may act alone when the animal is deprived of others. In this respect, sexual desire is like thirst or hunger. Water is tantalising only when the animal or man is already thirsty, food only when he is already hungry. If he is thirsty or hungry and sees no food, then he gets restless, becomes more active than usual."

Sex desire and behaviour are determined by many factors in human beings. Reaction to sex behaviour tends to depend upon learning of responses. In this learning, emotions, thoughts, the sex behaviour in previous experiences and ideas considerably influence human beings. Boring reports further that 'habits' of thought and action are supposed in both men and women upon the activities of their hormones, that, having learned to want sexual relations, they continue to want them even when the power of procreation is missing. It states that sex behaviour can be modified through sex education. If education is rational, sex attitudes are developed on healthy lines, if they are distorted sex behaviour can lead to certain aberrations and abnormality. Accordingly, hormones alone do not influence sex behaviour. Habits, thoughts and action also determine the quality of sex behaviour in human beings.

Thus boys and girls can be trained in proper habits, thoughts and action. Physiology provides certain bases for sex behaviour. It is modified by experiences and learning available in the environment.

Psychological factors, besides physiological conditions, influence the activities of human beings including their sex behaviour. Not-withstanding the fact that in old age, when androgens diminish, many aged people are energetic and active. Their vigour and force in their behaviour can be attributed to healthy habits of activity, and to their strong motives and goals. Ideational habits sustain human beings when their bodily vigour has considerably diminished. Role of idealism and sentiments are always emphasised in society and in the growth of healthy personality of human beings.

Boring asserts that there "seems to be no question that androgens in a man increase his energy and efficiency, have thus an effect upon his usefulness and effectiveness in living." It would be wrong to emphasise, therefore, the basis of sex on physiological grounds alone. Habits and ambition also play some significant role. It cannot, however, be concluded that physiological bases of sex behaviour has to be minimised. It has been observed that castration vitally affects the body, impairs intellectual nerve and the power of creative thinking.

From the foregoing paragraphs, it is evident that physiology plays an important role in determining sex behaviour. But physiological basis do not exclusively condition sex behaviour. Many non-physiological aspects also affect sex activities in human beings. Learning, experiences, conditions in society and cultural norms considerably influence sex activities among human beings. Mating activities among human beings take place under sophisticated conditions and in certain parts of the world it has become highly organised and highly conditioned by time-old norms and cultural demands of society.

There are many wrong conceptions among boys and girls on physiological understanding of male and female reproductive systems. It would be highly appropriate to give accurate and correct information to them on the human reproductive systems.

Hormones and Sex Behaviour

Gonadal hormones have been produced by biochemists and injected into human systems. In castrated male guinea pigs, for example, sexual behaviour returns after treatment with testosterone. However, injection of hormones may not restore sexual potency in all castrated men. Castration sometimes may destroy sexual potency and sometimes not. It is apparent that psychological and other factors are important enough in men to obscure the effects of castration, and replacement therapy.

Oestrogen influences sex behaviour. In castrated female rats, the injection of oestrogen brings about oestrus and receptivity. There is definite relationship between the amount of hormone injected and the degree of sexual responsiveness induced. Many positive effects of hormone treatment are reported. There have been some failures also.

Use of gonadotropins or gonadal hormones to immature animals, both male and female, makes them sexually arrive at an early age. Pituitary extracts also provoke sex activity.

Regarding the relation between hormones and sex behaviour, Morgan reports the following findings:

1. In both male and female castrates, androgen brings out masculine sexual behaviour and oestrogen feminine behaviour;

2. Androgen can bring out feminine behaviour and oestrogen masculine behaviour in animals of both sexes; and

3. Male hormones given to males and female hormones given to females may inhibit the development of normal mating behaviour if they are administered in larger doses to animals castrated in early life.

Effect of pituitary gland on sex behaviour is also noticed. Removal of these glands lead to the genital glands showing a tendency to fatty denegation. Removal of the gland from female dogs during pregnancy causes abortion. Removal of glands also result in persistent sexual infantilism with failure of functional activity in sperm production in the testis.

Pineal gland also influences sex behaviour. The pineal is a small gland near the base of the brain. It is in contact with the roof of the third ventricle from which it develops embryologically. Tumorous growths on or near the pineal glands are associated in children, with the premature development of sex, precocious mentality, and an acceleration of growth of functions instead of at the normal time of puberty. Horrax reports the removal of the pineal gland furnishes some internal secretion which checks growth and especially checks sexual maturity. Extracts of the pineal body when injected into rats, developed evidence of precocity of sexual development.

Hormones are considered to be an organic component of relatively simple structure. Hormones produce profound physiological effects Hormones are sometimes considered to action a catalytic manner.

Hormonal regulation is an important faction in behaviour dynamics in human systems.

Nervous System in Sexual Behaviour

Considerable work has been done on the relationship between sex behaviour and nervous system. Morgan reports that findings on the relationship between natural and sex behaviour can be divided roughly into two parts:

(i) The sensory control and conditions of aroused sexual behaviour, and

(ii) The neuromuscular mechanisms for executing mating patterns.

It is felt that each one of the senses may contribute in one way or another to arousing sexual behaviour. Odours, sounds and visual cues all play their part in sex behaviour. Tactile and kinesthetic are also some part of that. When all findings are taken together, it becomes evident that it is the total amount of relevant sensory stimulation rather than any particular kind of stimulation that arouses sexual behaviour.

The spinal cord mediates certain elementary aspects of sexual behaviour.

Hypothalamus are known to be important in sexual behaviour. Sexual arousal is impossible in the absence of these centres. Gonadal hormones arouse activity in the hypothalamic centres.

Cortex is supposed to play its own role in sexual behaviour. It is also possible that different impulses arising from sensory stimulation may influence the excitability of the hypothalamus, either directly or through the cortex. In higher animals, in whose case they have a larger cortical contribution and have been made to learn to be aroused by a variety of responses many factors, in combination, play their role in sex behaviour. Thus, the hormonal sensory and cortical influences are additional.

Some studies have indicated that there are sex differences in maturational and personality traits. These differences may be aroused by differences in nervous system. While nervous system may influence sex behaviour, the presence of certain hormones in the blood may also arouse nervous system which, in turn, may precipitate sexual activity. Glands tend to activate nervous system in various ways. When secretion is added to blood system, it enthuses sex behaviour and this behaviour is supported by nervous activities.

Maladjustment in Sex Behaviour or Sexual Deviations

Lack of proper, objective and scientific education or sex may lead to many misconceptions on sex behaviour among boys and girls. Faulty education may lead to faulty habits and wrong attitudes may be fostered among boys and girls. It may lead to degeneracy. Violence and anti-social reaction may also follow faulty sex habits. Culture in a society has to be properly cultivated so that youngest generation develops healthy attitudes on sex. Since sex deviations are caused by wrong education or bad handling, majority of sex deviants are neither degenerate nor anti-social. It is, therefore, necessary that sex education at juvenile stage should be healthy and scientific and initiation into sex education should be considered as an anti-cultural act.

One of the obvious facts that is mostly responsible for sex deviation or maladjusted sex development is due to immaturity in person. The immaturity may be due to emotional reasons. Bad emotional states may hamper in the proper growth of sexual development in boys and girls. It may affect their life severely. Due to emotional reasons, sexual development may be arrested or distorted and emotional reasons operate more effectively when the child is young.

Psychoanalytical school of thought believe that early experiences during childhood days are instrumental in distorting the life vision and attitude of children. The school believes that often the child is exposed, when young, to conscious or unconscious seduction by an older child or an adult long before his own sexual development has reached a mature genital level. Such experiences of seduction may contribute to arrested or distorted developments. It may also lead to childhood fixation which may interfere with later maturational sequences and leaves the child to grow into an adult sex deviant.

During early adolescence, children with seductive experiences are prone to be reactive; their conflict may render them unable to display healthy sex adjustment. This may lead to various distorted sex behaviour and develop a fixed pattern of sex behaviour which may persist in their life. According to psychoanalytical school of thought, adult sex deviations are the result of experiences met during childhood days and therefore, like neurosis and psychosis, it may affect the adult personality to a great extent.

Psychologists believe that any form of sexual deviation or perversions is caused by faulty sex behaviour. This maladjustment may not lead to homosexual intercourse when this outcome is permissible and objectively possible. One of the forms of sexual maladjustment occurs when deviants prefer sex relations with persons of the same sex when there is an opportunity to get it gratified with the help of opposite sex who is easily available.

Those, whose sexual development is not normal, may find gratification of sex by indulging in activities like exhibiting sexual parts or looking at them. Some may get sexually excited by intimate things like shoes etc., other forms of sex deviations are displayed in behaviour like sadism or masochism suffering.

All civilisations have condemned sexual deviations as immoral and unnatural. Laws have been passed in various societies to make sexual deviation punishable by law. Attitudes of public have been constantly roused by societies to condemn sexual deviations.

Freud, the founder of psychoanalysis, has described sexual deviation or perversion as a behaviour in which a person acts out of conflicts and fantasies without suffering from anxiety. Psychosexual deviations are comparable to psychopathic desire loss.

Anxiety in a person towards sex life may lead to sex disorders. An arrested or distorted sexual pattern may result due to childhood anxiety which forces a child to select an abnormal object for sex love.

There are various types of sexual deviations which result from faulty concepts about sex from which the person may suffer. The common deviations are:

  (i)   Overt homosexuality
  (ii) Genital exhibitionism
  (iii) Sexual looking or voyeurism
  (iv) Fetishism

(v) Transvestism

(vi) Sadomasochism

Overt Homosexuality

Homosexuality is regarded as a commonly prevalent maladjustment. Technically, in overt homosexuality, the person prefers sex relations with his or her own sex in spite of the availability of potential partners of the opposite sex. In case of certain overt homosexual adults, they are normal males or females both having adequate genital development and as to secondary sex characteristics.

In early years, it was assumed that heredity was a decisive factor in homosexual behaviour. Freud attributed this deviation to archaic mechanisms. Sometimes, stress is placed upon pre-oedipal phases of development and upon oedipal conflicts.

Homosexuality may be also due to inborn constitutional factors and such individuals are rarely interested in members of the opposite sex. In some cases, homosexuality may be based on early childhood seduction by an adult homosexual or previous frustration in love relations with opposite sex.

Strong homosexual attitudes may get established in the nervous system in the process of maturing and this habit may become unalterable. Social pressures and will power may be too feeble to undo such strong habits and attitudes.

Genital Exhibitionism

Exhibition of genitals becomes one of the sources of sex gratification with some people. It is generally confined to men. It is usually a post-pubertal and post-marital phenomenon. The person, suffering from this maladjustment compulsorily shows his genital to young women or mature women in public places, streets, parks etc. It is said that he does this to stimulate women to do the same. There is some basic unconscious motivation behind this behaviour. People with such behaviour may be sexually inhibited and timid. From a psychoanalytical point of view, castration anxiety and narcissism are often quoted as factors responsible for this behaviour.

Voyeurism

Voyeurism is a sexual deviation in which a person tries to get sexual gratification through looking at the sexual organs, or naked body, or the sexual activities .of others. Male voyeurs are generally inhibited sexually. They are heterosexual as regards their object. Common behaviour patterns of voyeur are peeping at women who are undressed or undressing.

Psychodynamics behind voyeurism may be the same as those behind exhibitionism. The voyeur, like the exhibitionist, remains fixed at an infantile level.

Fetishism

In fetishism, a person tries sex satisfaction or gratification by fixation on an object. He selects an inanimate object as the source of love. The commonest fetish is a women's shoe. Fetishism may be predominantly asexual. Normal fetish behaviour seems to provide security to the person. There is a hypothesis that the fetish is a substitute for a sex partner, a substitute that makes no demand and is not itself dangerous. Hair fetishism is an interest in the hair of the Mons veneris, part of the external female genital, an interest in denying the absence of male genitalia in women.

Transvestism

It means literally cross-dressing. A person suffering from this deviation tries to obtain sex gratification with the opposite sex in a symbolised way by putting on the clothes of the opposite sex. This behaviour is largely confined to males. Women who dress like men are usually homosexually inclined. Stekel supports the view that transvestism is a homosexual behaviour. A minority of male transvestites are also fetishist who can achieve full potency only while they wear some item of women's clothing. Psychoanalytic thinking emphasises castration anxiety as responsible for this sex deviation.

Sadomasochism

By sadism is meant that the person tries to get sexual pleasure in inflicting pain, restriction or humiliation on others. By masochism is meant to get sexual pleasure by exposing oneself to suffering. It is generally considered that sadism is due to fixation in an infantile misinterpretation and distortion of the male role in sex intercourse which the adult as a child misinterprets as a brutal attack. Masochism is looked upon as fixation in an infantile misinterpretation of distortion of the female role. Both sadism and masochism are traditionally interpreted as defences against castration anxiety.

Masturbation as Sex Deviation

It is a form of sex behaviour in which most boys, when the sex tensions are strong, learn to relieve themselves by masturbation. Some men and women may continue this behaviour when sources of satisfaction are otherwise available. Continuance of this behaviour may give rise to psychological difficulties and may raise the problem of conscience. In some extreme situations when normal outlet for sex gratification is not available, small practice of masturbation in moderation, accompanied with day-dreaming, may form physically as a harmless mode of relief. But for most human beings, there are psychological difficulties inherent in this practice. It may arouse certain emotional feelings which may interfere with the efficient working. Masturbation is not rare. It is practiced by boys and girls, men and women at one stage of life or the other. Its practice does not lead to feeble mindedness or impotence as is generally believed. But, as a practice, it is bad and has to be guarded against as far as possible.

Impotence and Its Causes

Lack of getting erection in genital organ of male is called impotence. Mechanisms of erection are psychological in nature. There can be both psychological and physiological causes of impotence.

Physiologically, if erection centres in genital parts of the body are injured, they may ruin erection nerves and may lead to impotence. Erection centre can be injured by either destroying or damaging cells and nerves responsible for gaining erection or by blocking urine passage by urine or seminal discharge by sealing the mouth of penis through certain mechanical or manual means. By blocking the outlet, the pressure of water of seminal fluid inside genital organ will apply corresponding pressure on other sensitive duct and nerve passages which may then cause rupture in veins responsible for erection process. Leslie Brained Arey warns not to block the passage within the penis by applying force and its mouth as it would damage and rupture nerves inside genital system and may cause impotence. He has discussed the function of erection centres in genital organ in detail.

Impotence can be caused by psychological factors also. Some shock or traumatic experience may lead to psychic transformation, followed by impotence. Since impotence caused by psychological reasons is a vast subject to master, it is suggested to read a standard textbook on abnormal and clinical psychology on the subject.

Impotence, premature and retarded ejaculation are the commonest forms of sexual maladjustment in the male. Frigidity may be present in women. Anxiety, fear and guilt may interfere with masculine sex functions. Emotional ambivalence towards women or a feminine identification may lead to causes of impotence. There may be conscious as well as unconscious factors in producing guilt or anxiety. Sometimes, a strict super ego makes sexual activity seem sinful, dangerous, a id even unthinkable. There may be pathological guilt feeling about sex. Aggression aroused by anger sometimes leads to effective male malfunctioning. Unresolved oedipal fears of a father figure may sometimes result in an irrational inability to fulfil the male role adequately for adulthood.

Sexual malfunctioning in female may give her such problems like frigidity, menstrual difficulties, and pathological reactions to pregnancy. It may also lead to problems of breast feeding. Female psychosexual disorders have to be looked into properly for adequate treatment.

Sublimation of Sex Energy

Conversion of sex energy into constructive forms and socially approved ways is known as sublimation process. In sublimation, sexual desire is drained into the creative achievement or into wholesome direction. Any goal, pursued with enthusiasm has a sublimative effect upon sexual frustration. A person, sexually frustrated, may, throw himself into his work with full devotion and in this work he may seek emotional satisfaction of his needs. Sublimation may not provide a perfect adjustment as people may seem to lose themselves in the intense and emotional pursuit of other goals, accomplishing a reasonable, if imperfect, adjustment of their emotional lives.

Transfer or sublimation provides partially perfect substitute for the usual sexual life of a person, man or woman, during the normal productive period. In case of sexual frustration, the basic difficulty is to divert sex needs into constructive and socially approved channels. This can be done by sublimation which will consume the psychic energy and can be converted into constructive ways. This can be developed and fostered only at the juvenile stage. All these concepts it is presumed may be brought to the notice of juveniles and incorporated in regular class-room teaching. The advantages far outweigh the disadvantages.

Sex Adjustment

In our present society the child is likely to receive information from other children about his body structure and functions earlier than many parents suspect. It is, therefore, important that each child receive, before he is stimulated by misinformation, an understanding of the process of birth, of the parts and functions of his body, and of his maturing relations with their same and the opposite sex.

The establishment by the young infant of desirable health habits of elimination, cleanliness of body, and the prevention of body manipulation are forms of indirect sex education. Children are curious and tend to become unduly interested in matters which their elders appear to want to keep from them. Hence a young child should become accustomed to seeing, as a matter of course, the naked bodies of other children of both sexes. Structural differences between the male and the female should be observed by him and accepted so that later, curiosity concerning sex differences may be lessened.

He is entitled to know where babies come from and that sister is different from brother in some respects. He should be taught the correct names of body parts, such as navel, rectum, buttocks, anus, penis, testicles, and vagina. The child should know that a new baby is formed in its mother's body. He should know also the father's part in the creation of the new life. Information of this kind, however, should be given gradually, objectively and tactfully, and fitted to the child's maturing power to understand it and to appreciate its significance to himself and his own behaviour.

As the child nears puberty he needs to be prepared for the changes that will take place within him. New sex urges may cause him to want to experiment with his own body or with other boys' and girls'. The effect upon adolescents of the beginnings of adult sex life depends in great part upon the amount and kind of preparation that has been given them by their elders. To the erroneously informed or the non-informed young person, these changes may be accompanied by severe and often damaging shock. Although a boy usually does not experience the same emotional disturbance at the approach of puberty that may come to a girl who is unprepared for her first menstruation, he may develop feelings of anxiety as the result of the physiological changes of seminal emissions. Healthful, objective information concerning the probable appearance of these phenomena at puberty will do much to counteract the conflicts that may arise in the adolescent boy.

If he has received wise sex education in his pre-adolescent days, is given ample opportunity for association with members of the opposite sex, and is not exposed to distorted sex attitudes on the part of his elders, he will be able to make satisfactory adjustments to his developing sexual urges.

9

Personality Conflict and Mental Disorders

Adjustment

THE relationship which becomes established among the biological heritage or organism, the environment, and the personality is adjustment. The term adjustment refers to a harmonious relationship between the person and the environment. The degree of harmony depends upon two things: (i) certain potentialities within a person; and (ii) character of the environment. A person is said to be adjusted when he is so related to reasonably adequate environment that he is relatively happy, efficient and has a degree of social feeling. In simple words, adjustment is an all-inclusive term meaning relationship between an individual and his environment through which his needs are satisfied in accordance with social demands. The adjustment process is a universal sequence that can be identified in the behaviour of organism from the lowest species up to man. Boring says that if a paramecium (single celled animal) meets an obstruction while swimming, it will pack up, turn through a small angle and swim forward again.

If individual's experiences have so shaped his personality that he is well prepared to play the roles which are expected of the status assigned to him within a given environment, and if his basic needs are met by playing such roles, then we say that he is well adjusted. On the other hand, if experience has not prepared him to play the roles of his assigned status, or if the environment is such that he is denied the normal status for which his experience has prepared him, and his fundamental needs are not met, then we say he is maladjusted.

Needs and Goals in Adjustment

A need is a state of tension in the person which tends to direct his behaviour towards goals which will relieve the tension. A goal is an activity which satisfies the need. There are various needs, for example, (i) organic needs, i.e., food; (ii) personality needs, i.e., affection and belongingness; (iii) achievement; (iv) independence; and (v) social approval. Essential aspects of adjustment process are:

1. Existence of motive
2. Circumstances leading to thwarting
3. Varied response
4. Discovery of solution

As an example it may be said that an individual usually proceeds first in the direction of the goal; second, when he is blocked by an obstacle and makes varied response; thirdly, until he discovers some response and finally removes the obstacles and reaches the goal. It is a matter of common experience that adjustments are often complex and frustrating. When progress towards a goal is checked and there is unresolved tension, we have frustration. The consequences of frustration are many and varied. It may breed hostility and anger, destructive and aggressive impulses, delinquent and anti-social behaviour or it may lead to silence, restraint and withdrawal. Frustration breeds tense emotional states. Thwarting means non-fulfilment of aroused motive.

Frustration or thwarting may arise from various factors namely: (1) Physical factors in the environment; (2) social and societal factors; (3) economic factors; (4) personal defects; (5) incompatible goals; and (6) the person's normal standards.

Physical factors are obstacles from the environment which results in thwarting and frustration. In famine-infested areas people are compelled to go without food and their hunger needs are frustrated by the food. A prisoner in solitary confinement is frustrated as his need for company is not fulfilled. Frustrations from the social environment are strong and persistent. We all desire to be appreciated, loved and respected. If this desire for love and respect is not met, the result is frustration. Unemployment, lack of security in employment, inadequate wages and harsh treatment by employers and lack of opportunities cause widespread frustration. Poverty also causes frustration. Krech and Crutchfield stress the role of society and cultural moods as the causal factors of frustration. They point out that often "the very needs which a particular culture itself induces are thwarted by the structures and the institutions of that society." A person with bad features is not usually liked. This causes in him frustration. Incompatible goals which a person is not able to fulfil also cause frustration. The last factor is the person's normal standard. Sometimes the high moral standard of the family causes frustration.

Methods of Adjustment

There are two methods of adjustment: one is direct and the other is indirect. These methods are used in an attempt to restore harmony between the individual and his environment. When a person has been frustrated, deprived or humiliated, he is likely to reduce the tension of the need by taking certain kinds of actions. These methods are also known as methods of tension reduction. These methods are always pointed out towards the relief of a feeling of distress.

Direct Method

Direct methods are always conscious. They are also rational. The needs for which satisfaction is sought are also conscious. They are typically employed to solve a typical problem once and for all. The direct method includes the following:

Renewed Attempts to Reach the Goal: The behaviour of Demosthenes may be cited as an example of this. This example can be called the example of direct action against a barrier of personal deficiency. Demosthenes was a Greek statesman who was unable to make better speeches because of a weak voice and a minor speech defect. It is said that he practised speaking with pebbles in his mouth and tried to strengthen his voice by shouting against the sound of the breakers on the sea-shore. In time he became a great orator and a famous statesman. This was a conscious attempt to reach the original goal, i.e., to become a great orator.

Substitutions of other Goals

(A) If the attempt to reach the original goal fails, the person may consider a substitute goal. In many instances of vocational choice, one goal is consciously substituted for another. For example, a man who wants to become a physician or a surgeon, but is blocked by insufficient ability, may opt for the occupation of a laboratory technician as a substitute. Another example is that if married couples are unable to produce children, they resort to adoption.

(B) Substitution of partial goal: For example, a man who dreams of a palace, brings a few pieces of marble and keeps them in his house.

(C) Apparent Substitution: These are sometimes difficult to explain. The common example usually quoted is that of a wife who having unsatisfactory sexual relations with her husband indulges in candy (crystallised sugar). Another example is of a girl who purchases a new dress. She has failed in the examination, by purchasing a new dress she may reduce her tension.

Analysis and Decisions

When a person is confronted with two or more motives or goals, he has to renounce one goal for another or he has to make a compromise. In simple words he has to make a choice between one goal or another. An M.Ed. student who is in Government service may be confronted with two goals viz., whether to do M.Ed. or to resign from Government service. Apparently, he has to renounce either the M.Ed. degree or Government service. He has to make a choice. Thus this is a conscious method of adjustment. Gates has given an example from a story of Somerset Maugham. In Somerset Maugham's story the hero had to face two strong incompatible goals. The goals were marriage with a girl whom he loved and giving up service. He was an ambitious and rising young diplomat. He fell in love with a girl of questionable character and reputation. Hence, he had to either give up his sweetheart and continue his career or marry her and give up his career. He ultimately decided in favour of the career.

Indirect Methods

Indirect methods are also called mechanism. They are distinguished from direct methods because (i) they are typically unconscious; (ii) they do not solve the adjustment problem once and for all, but only for a particular period. Indirect methods include: (1) sublimation; (2) withdrawal (including regression and daydreaming); (3) identification; (4) becoming dependent; (5) rationalisation; (6) repression; and (7) projection etc.

1. Sublimation—Sublimation is a concept originated by Freud. Freud defined it as unconscious deflection of libido into other more socially acceptable channels. Libido means sexual instinct. "Heterosexual love can be conceived of as consisting of a fusion of the needs for sexual activity, belongingness, affection and desire for care and to the need to be cared for. But activities which compromise the fused needs unconsciously are nursing, child welfare, social work, teaching, religious activities, friendship with persons of both sexes and the care of pets. Sublimation releases the tension. In simple words, sublimation is the process by which unconscious and unacceptable desires are channelled into activity that have strong social approval.

The unacceptable desires are usually sexual in nature and their expression may be sublimated as creative efforts in music, art and literature.

2. Withdrawal—The primary object of withdrawal is to remove oneself from a distressing situation. The process may take many different forms and may vary in extent and in degree of performance. Examples are forest rangers whose is a solitary occupation.

3. Regression—Regression is the mechanism whereby the individual returns to an earlier and less matured level of adaptation. It is a reversion of progressive sequence of development and a return to primitive form of personality structure. This happens in schizophrenic patients who regress from the adult world to infancy and are unable to dress, wash and feed themselves. The other example is of a first born child in the family. The first child gets a lot of affection but when the second child arrives in the family he reverts to bed-wetting.

4. Day Dreaming—Day dreaming allows a person to achieve in infancy what he cannot achieve in reality. Day dreaming is always connected with specific frustrations. For example, a child, because of frustration by his parents, imagines that he is not their son or daughter but he is really the child of wealthy parents. Revelry is a reaction to boredom or monotony while day dreaming is likely to be connected with a specific frustration.

Forms of Partial Withdrawal

(a) Avoidance or Limitation of the Situation—Some individuals stay away from situations in which they have met defeats. A girl who has been humiliated at a dance party may avoid dancing altogether. (b) Restrain emotional environment—This is another type of partial withdrawal. One young man had fallen in love with a girl and this girl rejected him. Afterwards, he did not involve himself in any love situation, (c) Procrastination—Procrastination means avoiding a situation or postponing it. Procrastination is fairly common among those persons who hold that moral and religious perfection may be attained. Procrastination is routed in inferiority feeling. Some students have a strong tendency to avoid a test because they are hyper-sensitive to failure. Persons who are not sure of being selected in an interview send applications after the due date, (d) Plunging into a number of activities in order to become fully occupied with other needs. For example, women whose dearly loved husbands have died become occupied in a number of religious activities, (e) Becoming dreamy or sleepy—This we find usually among children, (f) Alcohol—Persons who are frustrated take to drinking or wine and whisky.

Identification

Identification may be defined as a process by which the individual allies himself emotionally or feels himself one with another person or group. Usually the boy identifies himself with his father and the girl with her mother. This is a sort of hero worship.

Rationalisation

Rationalisation is most commonly found after failure to achieve a goal. Through rationalisation an individual justifies his undesirable behaviour. For example, if a boy does not get any response from the girl whom he loves, he may say that she is of bad character or the boy who comes late to school thinks that the clock is slow.

Repression

Repression is especially operative during early childhood. Repression is that part of a conflict situation which is most unacceptable to the Ego and Super Ego and may be forced to the unconscious by the Ego. Repression is the process of complete exclusion from consciousness of impulses, experiences and feelings which are psychologically disturbing because they arouse a sense of guilt or anxiety. Repression always solves unconscious conflict. It must be distinguished from suppression. Suppression is the conscious control of undesirable impulses, feelings and experiences. Repression is also to be distinguished from inhibition. In inhibition the individual consciously and purposely refrains from any activity.

Projection

There is a tendency for all of us to seek our faults in others. This is projection. In projection the individual protects himself from awareness of his own desirable traits or feelings by attributing them to others. Projection is the inverse of introjection.

Introjection

Introjection is like identification except that in identification the individual wants to be like the object while in introjection he considers the individual a part of himself. In schizophrenic patients the individual believes that he has ability of others.

Reversal Formation

Reversal formation means conscious attitudes which are partially repressed. For example, a girl who is of bad character will say that she is being teased by boys or a bride will become angry with her husband when the child arrives in the family too early.

Aggression

Aggression is a method of reducing tension. It is not an inborn drive. It springs only from frustration. It may also arise from being humiliated. This is a recent theory. Previously it was considered to be an inborn tendency. For example, war could never be abolished because of the aggressive drive. It does not follow either the direct or indirect methods. Gates gives us the following examples of aggression.

He says that a child wants to go outdoors and play but is prevented from doing so by his mother. It responds by becoming angry and striking her. A precise analysis of this little episode reveals several features:

  (a) The child has an urge to go out to play. Play is its present goal
  (b) Mother frustrates it by preventing it from achieving its goal (to play outdoors). This has the effect of producing in the child an immediate impulse to aggression, in this instance an impulse to strike its mother.
  (c) Now the child has two tensions: that of the need to play outdoors and that of the need for aggression. The goal which would satisfy its first need has been blocked by its mother, but the second goal, that is, to express its aggression by striking its mother, is not blocked.
  (d) Consequently, the child responds by striking its mother, and thereby achieves the goal of its urge to aggression.

(e) Presumably this direct aggressive action satisfies the need for aggression and has the effect of discharging all tension connected with this secondary urge.

(f) The child, however, still has in full force its need (and the tension which accompanied it) to go out and play, which was originally thwarted by its mother. In short, striking its mother does not solve his original problem.

If aggression is turned inward it becomes dangerous.

The Dynamics of Psychological Adjustment of the Child

It is not our intention in this chapter to cite the many areas of psychological adjustment in which children may fail to meet the demands of our culture. Rather, we plan to describe some of the principles of psychological adjustment that may be applied to all areas of child life. These principles of adjustment are applicable to the molar, or goal-oriented, aspects of child behaviour. The dynamic features of psychological of the child are presented as follows:

1. We have a striving organism. The child's motivated to action by certain primary or secondary needs. These needs stimulate either covert or cover behaviour patterns which are selective on the basis of maturation (unlearned patterns) and or transfer from previous experience. (The manner in which these needs are met, or the manner in which striving behaviour declines without 'adequate' need-reduction defines the primary features of the adjustment process).

2. These behaviour patterns of the child become directed toward some goal which shows promise of satisfying his needs. The selection of appropriate goals is an extremely complex aspect of psychological adjustment, involving perceptual-growth-status, emotionalised attitudes, social values, level of aspiration, and numerous other variables. (The maladjusted child from a social-reference standpoint is often the child who selects socially verboten goals to satisfy his needs. From a personal point of view his immediate adjustment may be satisfactory; i.e., he is able to satisfy his current needs. However, the attainment of socially forbidden goals typically makes it difficult for him to satisfy other needs in the future.)

3. The child's efforts to reach this goal (which promises to satisfy his needs) are frustrated by a barrier of some kind. In a general sense, there is always a barrier between the child and the attainment of a goal, even if this barrier is nothing more than a minor expenditure of energy to raise his arm, blink his eye, or swallow food placed in his mouth. The barrier to a behaviour sequence is frustrating to the degree that it bars the child from direct and immediate access to the desired goal. The amount of frustration experienced by a child when confronted with a barrier is also a joint function of the intensity level of his needs and the desirability or adequacy of the chosen goal for satisfying his needs.

4. The resolution of this frustrating state of affairs defines the social and personal adequacy of the child's immediate psychological adjustment. If the child can attain the goal (or a personally acceptable substitute goal) and thereby satisfy his need, he has made a healthy personal adjustment. If this attained goal is also socially acceptable, he has made a personal-social adjustment. All other resolutions of the conflict situation are maladjustive in nature.

5. The behavioural consequences of an inadequate resolution of a conflict situation are 'typical of personal-social mal-adjustment. Although we must admit that a child is

making one kind of psychological adjustment to a conflict situation when he 'throws a temper tantrum,' his adjustment is likely to be inadequate from both a personal and a social point of view. His original needs which precipitated the conflict may be little altered by this form of behaviour. Further-more, as a consequence of this behaviour, his parents, teachers, and peers may place additional barriers between him and other goals that he will seek in the future. This latter is one of the most pernicious features of maladjustive behaviour. It frequently initiates, maintains, and augments a vicious circle of inadequate and inappropriate responses.

Symptoms of Chronic Maladjustment

The following kinds of behaviour may be symptomatic of major maladjustment:

1. Extreme restlessness, easily excited, destructive tendencies towards people and things, frequent emotional upsets, constant day-dreaming, feelings of 'differentness' extreme tenseness, feelings of inferiority, abnormal fears of many things, preference for playing alone, stubbornness, resentful of criticism, excessive sulking and pouting, feelings of inferiority, feelings of great importance, tendency to bully other children, constant need for attention; inability to work hard on anything, repeated truancy and inability to make decisions.

2. The physiological symptoms of chronic maladjustment may take the form of reversals or complications in toilet habits; the development of nocturnal enuresis, obstinate constipation diarrhoea, excessive urinary voiding, and so forth. Chronic maladjustment is also frequently reflected in feeding disturbances, obesity and anorexia.

3. Non-pathological withdrawal is characterised by the following kinds of behaviour: (1) the child prefers solitary activities at the expense of social interactions; likes to read, listen to music, go to the movies, collect things, and the like in the absence of other children and adults; (2) the child prefers to make his psychological adjustments on the reality level: likes to day-dream about a romantic and glorious future for himself, about being loved by his friends, about defeating his 'enemies' and about satisfying all of his psychological needs that are difficult to satisfy on the 'reality level. Most of these behaviour patterns are displayed at one time or another by all children.

4. The nervous habits in children living under conditions of extreme psychological stress usually appear as various combinations of the following kinds of behaviour: thumb sucking, finger-nail biting, nose picking, head scratching, head banging, face rubbing, nervous finger movements or hand wringing, restless pacing, frequent crying over minor circumstances, body rocking, lip biting, facial tics and/or grimaces, nervous singing or talking in the absence of others, frequent urination, and the like.

Conflict

Conflict has a broader significance especially in understanding maladjustment. Conflict has been defined, as a state of mind in which two or more incompatible behaviour trends are evoked that cannot be satisfied fully at the same time. In recent years psychologists have given much attention to the problem of conflict. Conflict is one of the types of thwarting. Frustration occurs in the individual as a result of the blocking of motives or by conflict. Conflict is usually a clash of motives. Conflict has been described in terms of interactions between the individual and his environment. This is the field of theory of behaviour, developed by Kurt Lewin. It emphasises the observation that behaviour does not depend upon the organism alone or on the environment alone, but what goes on between the two. Kurt Lewin says that tendencies behaviour may be represented by vectors which show the direction and strength of the individual's striving. Most impulses can be described as directed towards or away from an environmental event. This is stated in terms of valences of which positive (+) valences are tendencies to approach, and negative (–) are tendencies to withdraw and avoid. Valences and vectors are both field phenomenon and can be defined only in terms of both the character of the person and the environmental forces acting on him.

Types of Conflict

Field theory shows that there can be only three basic types of conflict: (1) approach-Approach conflict; (2) avoidance-avoidance conflict; and (3) approach-avoidance conflict.

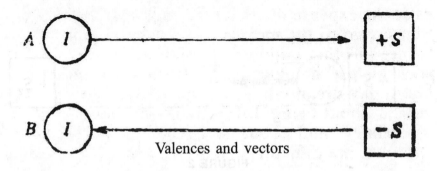

Valences and vectors

FIGURE 1

In A, the interaction of the individual (I) and the situation (S) may be described as a positive valence, in B as a negative valence. (After K, Lewin.)

Approach-Approach Conflict

The conflict is between two positive valences that are equal in strength. A child may have to choose between reading an interesting book and going out to play football. Approach-Approach conflict is a conflict between two equally attractive choices. The examples are: should I go to see a picture with a girl friend or play a tennis match with a prominent player of the college? This type of conflict may also be understood as double-approach-avoidance conflict. Girls in India have to face this type of conflict very often. Sumitra is a bright student in the college and is very keen to take a Ph.D. degree. It has always been her ambition to qualify for economic independence. But there is a prospect of marriage in a very respectable family and to a young man who seems to have everything a girl may aspire to in marriage, but who insists on immediate marriage. It appears that she has to choose one of the two attractive alternatives and is faced by approach-approach conflict. But each alternative is linked with a penalty. If she selects the goal of the Ph.D. degree and continues to study she has to forego a tempting offer of marriage which she may or may not get again, and if she chooses marriage she will never get the degree she has so ardently desired all her life. So the element of avoidance is there. (See Fig. 1).

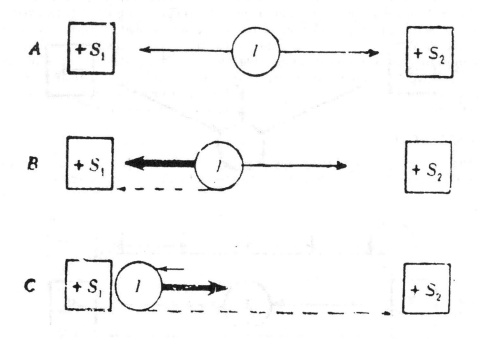

FIGURE 2

Approach-approach conflict

The approach-approach conflict, A, is solved easily. If some variation in behaviour brings the individual a little closer, physically or psychologically, to the attracting situation S_1 and away from the other attracting situation S_2 the vector for S_1 is increased in strength because of the decreased distance, and the conflict is resolved by the individual's going in that direction(B). In C, satiation of the S_1 motive may weaken its vector. The individual then vacillates to the S_2 choice. The dotted vectors indicate actual movements and the solid vectors motivational forces (After K. Lewin).

Avoidance-Avoidance Conflict

Conflicts of this type are evoked by two negative valences. Both tendencies are to retreat from or to avoid something. In simple words, the individual is caught between the devil and the deep sea. For example, a young boy may want to avoid doing an unpleasant task and also want to escape a threat of parental punishment, or a soldier in battle may have a conflict between his need to run away and save his skin and his need to avoid being dubbed as a coward.

The most usual solution of Avoidance-Avoidance conflict is the living field i.e., to take a third course of action. Most escape mechanisms are methods of leaving the field. The boy whose example has been given by us may develop a headache thereby avoiding both the task and parental displeasure or he may apparently work at the job but really be engaged in day-dreaming, which is a common way of escaping the unpleasant alternative. If this conflict is not solved it results in nervousness or anxiety and the like. (See Fig. 2)

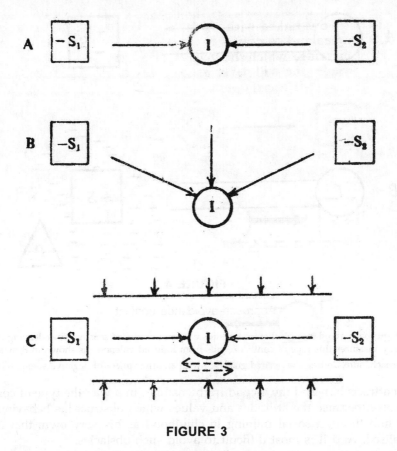

FIGURE 3

Avoidance-avoidance conflict

The usual response to this type of conflict in A is to leave the field, as shown by B. If material or psychological barriers prevent this, as in C, the individual shows vacillating behaviour (two dotted vectors at the choice point, and the unreduced tension (After K. Lewin)

Approach-Avoidance Conflict

In this type of conflict, approaching and avoiding tendencies are evoked simultaneously. For example, a child wants to play football but is afraid of being hurt or when it loves and fears his mother. Approach-avoidance conflict cannot be solved by leaving the field because the impulse for approach (positive valence) keeps the individual from retreating. An example may be that a young man from a very orthodox family is invited to a dinner at a modern hotel. He has been brought up in a family which looks down upon non-vegetarian food served in chinaware outside the kitchen. Nor has he ever eaten with shoes on with people of other castes and communities. He, therefore, looks upon such an invitation with anxiety, if not fear that he would lose his caste and incur the displeasure of his parents for indulging in a dinner which is considered impure and irreligious in his family. On the other hand, he does not wish to look old-fashioned and backward in the eyes of his friends. The attitudes and values of his parents have become his own and he is caught between the desire to be called modern and his orthodox attitudes and values.

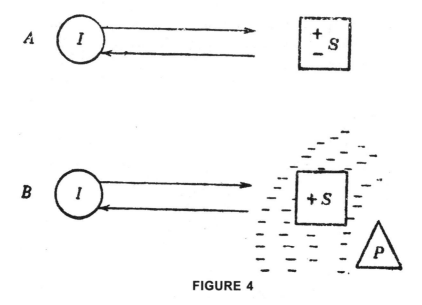

FIGURE 4

Approach-avoidance conflict

An unresolved approach-avoidance conflict in A results only in unreduced tension, since leaving the field is not a solution. In many instances this type of conflict results from induced valences, as shown in B, where a parent (P) forbids an approach, surrounding the desired goal (+S) with an atmosphere of negative valences (After K, Lewin)

The first attracts him and the second frightens him. In a way the type of conflict is most difficult to solve, because the attitudes and values which obstruct his behaviour have been adopted by him through social training in childhood as his very own; that is, they have been internalised. And it is most difficult to avoid such obstacles.

Approach-avoidance conflict often leads to inferior adjustment or unreduced anxiety.

Fact of Conflict

Life is a series of conflict situations on the basis of which the personality is formed. Some of the conflicts pointed out by Freud are those between pleasure seeking and reality, love and hate, passivity and activity. Growth towards maturity is dependent upon the individual's success in solving these conflicts. The cause of conflicts may arise from personal insufficiency such as inadequate intelligence, lack of physical strength, and disability and disease. But the fact cannot be avoided that conflict has some effect on the individual's ability to adjust. Mesearman has conducted experiments on cats. This is a valuable study and these experiments on conflict in cats have made valuable contributions to the understanding of human adjustment. Conflicts are not only the precipitating causes of adjustment difficulties, but also have a relationship and the ability to adjust when confronted by new problems. The experiments show that strong, unresolved early conflicts make enduring changes in personality and case studies of people confirm these findings. If a person persists over a period of years in making inferior excessively substitutive or non-adjustive responses, it is very probable that earlier disabling influences have reduced his general ability to adjust.

Common Sources of Conflict

In infancy and childhood, the family being the chief social background of the individual, it is the scene of most of these conflicts. Later on sex comes to determine many of the conflicts for the reason that the demands of our culture have not been well adjusted to the sexual needs of the individual. And there are many other ways in which cultural values can give rise to conflicts.

Family Conflicts

1. Interaction of personalities that take place within the family i.e., child's relations with members of the family.
2. Conflicts of insecurity. Insecurity is due to the conflicts of fear and dependency. If parents are cold and demanding the child feels rejection. This has a very bad effect on the child.
3. Parent's wrong handling.
4. Feelings of inferiority.
5. Conflicts also arise from sibling rivalry,
6. Over protection or parental submission.
7. Underprotection.
8. Bad personality results from constant financial strain.
9. Unattractive children.
10. Parents who have high moral standards.

Sex Conflicts

1. Gap between physical and social maturity. A person may want to marry earlier but parents may not agree.
2. Sexual needs and the sense of guilt.
3. Lack of manliness or unattractiveness.
4. Too strict early training.
5. Guilt of masturbation.
6. Difference between Indian culture and Western culture.
7. High personality or morality.

School Conflicts

1. Over-competition in school.
2. Over-restriction in the classroom.
3. Teacher's method of handling in the class.
4. Teacher's report of behaviour problems in the classroom.
5. Children with special problems of adjustment: the sickly child, the child with sensory defects, the intellectually gifted child, the dull child, the isolated child, the inferior child and the delinquent child.

Concept of Wholesome Personality

A wholesome person is a person who is physically strong and healthy, who is mentally alert, who is emotionally stable and whose home and school environment are well fitted to his needs and interests. Wholesome personality is one whose "concept of a self is realistic in that what he thinks of himself, agrees closely with what others think of him and with his achievements. He enjoys a kind of minor harmony when there is a degree of integration of his intellectual and emotional capacities. Children who are well-adjusted come from homes that are happy places, where discipline is used for more far-reaching purposes than merely deterring wrongdoing, where responsibility is a part of the routine of life, where the family enjoys recreations together, and where family relationships and attitudes towards children are wholesome. In such homes, children learn to take responsibilities on their own level, to be independent and take care of their own needs, to solve their own problems and to be well-adjusted, adults must know not only how to create a good environment for children, but once it is created, they must know how to maintain it. Thus, a person who does not suffer from anxiety and chronic discomforts, possesses normal personality.

In wholesome personality there may be two aspects, viz., functional and social. If the functions of an individual are well, he may be called well-adjusted because in functioning well there is a need of organised and whole personality. He thus acts with his whole mind and also wholeheartedly. This does not mean that juvenile delinquents, who may work with their whole minds, are also well-adjusted personalities. The reason is that they act against the society and are anti-social. So social factor also plays an important role in wholesome personality. A wholesome personality will never commit anti-social acts.

In conclusion, wholesome and well-adjusted personality is characterised by the harmony between the needs of individuals and demands of the environment.

Disorganised Personality and Mental Disorders

Disorganised personality means psychoneurosis. If the adjustment of the child is inadequate, he is maladjusted and inefficient; if he has chronic discomforts, then he may be called possessing a disorganised personality and is also known as a neurotic patient. The development of neurosis is due to the result of early patterns of personality adjustment in which inadequate balance exists between the drives of the individual, (the Id) and the counter drives, (Ego and Superego). Despite their differences some types of neurosis have much in common such as defences, repression, displacement, reaction formation, and rationalisation. There are, however, varying differences of opinion concerning the significance of these drives.

For example, Karen Homey suggests that in our culture the expression of hostility is of basic importance in personality integration, and that when it is inadequately expressed neurotic conflict results. Harry S. Sullivan emphasises the importance of the establishment of self-esteem if neurotic behaviour is to be avoided.

Recently W.V. Silverberg has stressed the importance of both inner and external sources in the development of self-esteem as well as the effective expression of hostile attitudes. When these are thwarted in their expression, neurotic behaviour results.

According to present knowledge, neurosis may be defined as follows:

1. A high degree of repetitiveness which is irrational in nature
2. Lack of true insight into the cause of the behaviour.
3. Conflicting drives which contribute to anxiety, self-disapproval and tension.

4. Impairment and reduced effectiveness in some physical functions.

Psychoneurosis is also characterised by anxiety, that anxiety which hampers social adjustment.

A distinction can be drawn between 'fear' and 'anxiety'

"Fear is a catastrophic response" that all persons make when faced with a highly motivated situation to which they can make no effective adjustment.

"Anxiety is distinguished from fear in that it is a response to an anticipated danger, or to a symbol of one, rather than to the threatening situation itself. Normal anxiety is present when the anticipated peril is imminent and probable. It is sometimes called situational anxiety, for it is relieved when the situation that aroused it is past. For a military aviator in wartime to suffer a severe emotional disturbance, when under enemy fire, is normal fear. For him to show signs of emotion as he contemplates the next combat mission is normal anxiety. But if in time of peace and in the safety of his own country, he trembles when an automobile backfires, or if he breaks into perspiration, when someone slaps him on the back, he is showing neurotic anxiety."

Types of Neuroses

Anxiety Neurosis:

This refers to the apprehension of danger by people e.g., a student near the examination hall begins to think that he might fail in the examination. Anxiety neurosis frequently results in various disagreeable and sometimes quite painful bodily sensations. The most common of these are:

1. Difficulty in breathing.
2. Pain in the region of the heart.
3. Palpitations.
4. Dizzy spells.
5. Increased perspiration.
6. Generalised weakness and exhaustion
7. Pains and cramps in the stomach.
8. Headaches.

What docs a person who is anxious complain of? The most common complaints are:

1. Fear of indescribable danger.
2. Fear of impending illness.
3. Irritability.
4. Insomnia.
5. Restlessness.
6. Loss of appetite.
7. Sluggish thinking.
8. Feeling of confusion.

What are the common signs observed in persons experiencing anxiety?

1. Cold, moist hands and feet.
2. Dry mouth and lips.

3. Variations of rate of the pulse.
4. Variations in blood pressure.
5. Tenseness.
6. The abdominal muscles are still and tense.
7. The reflexes are exaggerated.

If anxiety continues for any length of time it is likely to affect the various organs of the body—the heart, the stomach, the blood vessels, etc. At first these changes may be of a temporary nature, but if the anxiety persists, the organs may undergo structural changes. When anxiety is prolonged and abnormal it is indicative of emotional illness.

Neurasthenia or hypochondria:

It means when our bodily organs are upset, e.g., when the examination approaches fast, some of the students develop fever. This upsets their internal organs. According to Nice, neurasthenia is characterised by fatigue, dullness, depression and lack of interest, and may be found in the hypochondriac, and the hysteric, compulsive or anxiety state. There is a question as to whether it should be listed as a specific syndrome. There are, however, a large number of neurotic patients whose symptoms centre around complaints of fatigue. This fatigability also extends to the mental aspects of the individual's life. The fatigue of the neurasthenic differs in several ways from actual physical fatigue. First, neurasthenia is not due to actual physical exertion. Weeks of rest and idleness do not alleviate the symptoms.

Another characteristic of the disease is the presence of somatic symptoms. Binding sensations of the neck and shoulders are common complaints Lack of sleep and loss of appetite are also common features.

The question of aetiology is much involved. Heredity has long been considered as an important factor since mental disorders are found to be numerous in the ancestry of the neurasthenic patient. However, this can be taken with a grain of salt for we have no record of the prevalence of the disease in the ancestry of non-mental patients.

The nature of the continued emotional tension provides an adequate explanation for the symptomatology of the neurasthenic patient. Although the normal individual often exhibits the same symptoms the neurasthenic patient tends to retain the ills despite adequate sleep and rest. These symptoms may last for days or even weeks and in some severe chronic cases it is known that it lasted for years in the form of chronic psychological invalidism.

Nervousness

It is due to motor symptoms i.e., when hands tremble, fingers do not work etc.

Phobias

Phobias are real expressions of anxiety as compared with normal fears. When fear is attached to a specific type of situation, it is called phobia. "Mild phobias, which are very common, may be stimulated by almost every kind of situation imaginable. Among the more common phobias are fears of the dark, of small enclosed places, of heights, of animals, of crowds, of water and of thunderstorms. A person with a phobia admits that his fear is groundless but he is unable to control it. Although many normal people have minor phobias, the condition is regarded as psychoneurotic when it is severe and of long duration, and when it interferes with ordinary life activities to an appreciable degree." According to Nice, phobia is a fear of something which is not objectively a source of danger, but which the individual reacts to with real fear despite the fact that he realises this reaction is inappropriate. A phobia is an unrealistic and persistent fear, the origin of which has been for-gotten.

There are two theories regarding the origin of phobia: the conditioning theory and the dynamic interpretation theory. According to the conditioning theory in phobias, there is an emotional traumatic episode, feeling of guilt, repression from consciousness of the experience, and subsequent upsets whenever the individual is exposed again to the circumstances of the original emotional trauma.

In general, the dynamic theory holds that the phobia is a defence mechanism through which the individual gets rid of anxiety-arousing impulses. An unconscious impulse arouses an emotional state, this impulse is repressed, but the emotional state continues. The individual tries to explain his emotionally aroused visceral tensions, and their causes, and seizes upon some object, situation, or idea as the explanation. A real situation can be handled through avoidance, whereas the impulse, being unconscious, cannot be dealt with.

Thus the phobic individual purchases freedom from anxiety by avoiding certain objects or situations, if, as the conditioning theory maintains, phobias result from one or more fear-producing episodes, the individual should, by avoiding the fear producing object or situation, be free from anxiety and the whole problem would end there. It is here the conditioning theory fails as an explanation for phobic anxiety. It may be a progressive maladjustment which continues to operate and spread to other objects and situations. Anxiety attacks occur in many situations and each situation is seized upon as an explanation of the attack. Eventually, if the attacks continue, the patient becomes a 'phobic prisoner', finding no situation, even his own home, which does not provoke a fear response. A phobia is a psychological neurosis but as in neurosis the method of relief eventually becomes the disease itself.

In summary, a phobia is a morbid fear brought on by some experience in the past. It is a defensive mechanism against continual, severe anxiety.

Obsessions—When a compulsion occurs in connection with a phobia, its adjustive value is seen most clearly. To an individual who has a fear of being attacked in the night, tension is obviously reduced by examining all the bolts and locks repeatedly and by making several inspections of closets and under the beds. A compulsion is a routine that gives a sense of security. An obsession is a compulsive thought that keeps recurring, even when the person tries to banish it. The obsessive thought is annoying, sometimes because it is distressing in itself and sometimes because it seems foolish and irrational, e.g., washing hands again and again and still not being satisfied. There are a number of characteristics that denote obsessive compulsive neurosis. These are:

1. Compulsive rituals (e.g., hand-washing rituals).
2. Obsessive fear of dirt and germs (usually accompanied by cleansing and tidying rituals).
3. Obsessive fear that the patient may harm someone (usually accompanied by precautionary rituals).
4. Compulsive need to count, or repeat verbal formulae.
5. Obsessive rumination about trivial or irrelevant matters.

6. Compulsive drive to work, or to busy one's self in some activity.
7. Compulsive attendance to detail, often at the expense of the broader, more important aspects of the task.
8. Compulsive adherence to high standards of work, or morality or to regulations.
9. Pseudo at suicide.
10. Compulsive avoidance of feared situations (e.g., crowds) or obsessive fear of certain situations.
11. Compulsive habit of mannerism (e.g., tics).
12. Obsessive hypochondria.
13. Compulsive avoidance or obsessive fear of people.
14. Obsessive fears of being poisoned, swindled, attacked.
15. Obsessive doubts; vacillations and worrying.
16. Compulsive sexual behaviour (e.g., masturbation).
17. Compulsive aggressive or emotional outbursts (e.g., nagging or temper tantrums).

Compulsive behaviour is never modified by experience; it is repeated time and again for no logical reason. The individual cannot help behaving as he does. Some unconscious force or tension compels him to express his repressed needs or conflicts in distorted form. All neurotic behaviour, and much normal behaviour, is compulsive in this general sense.

Psychoses

"The most seriously non-adjustive conditions are the psychoses, popularly known as insanities or mental disorders . . . A psychoneurotic person is a discomfort to himself and may be a nuisance to others, but a person with a fully developed psychosis is dangerous to himself and to society. Psychoses are more common than is ordinarily realised."

Types of Psychoses

Organic Psychoses

These are the disorders "caused by identified organic conditions. They include brain injuries, syphilis of the nervous system, chronic addiction to alcohol and other drugs and brain deterioration associated with old age."

Functional Psychoses

It means lack of appreciation of reality. It is further classified into the following sub-divisions:

Schizophrenia or Dementia Praecox

"It has a seclusive personality with marked abnormality in the development of emotions and feelings. The patient manifests a gradual blunting of emotions and growing indifference towards persons and things. Situations that would arouse emotions of sorrow, anger, etc., leave him absolutely cold. If the news of his mother's death is conveyed to him he just mumbles "That's rather bad—isn't that so?" and again withdraws into his shell The patient does not appear to be in contact with reality and he is completely lost in his dream-like ideas . . . The most acceptable theory is that "Schizophrenia is the result of the failure of an individual to make an adequate adjustment to his environment." The patient may break out suddenly with emotional violence.

Manic-depressive Psychosis

"It consists either of over-activity and an elated feeling tone in the manic phase or of retardation and sadness in the depressed condition. Usually, a patient has an attack in one or the other of these forms, and then recovers. It has been suggested that manic- depressives are persons who have never learned how to compromise, who are either completely defeated by conflict or else deny it by an unreal elation."

Hallucination

It is when a person behaves in a silly or incoherent manner that he suffers from hallucination, e.g., a person who laughs or cries for nothing when there is no observable reason.

Delusions

"Delusions or false beliefs held without reference to reality occur frequently in schizophrenia. The most frequent delusion is persecution. The patient declares that he has been robbed, cheated or imprisoned by his family, or that people have conspired to cause him to lose his position. Delusions help to explain defeats and to build a sense of importance. They are tolerated by the patient because his distorted perception of reality prevents their critical appraisal."

Comparison of Seven Characteristics in Psychoneurotics and Psychotics

Characteristics	Psychoneurotics	Psychotics
Aetiology	Psychogenic factors are of primary importance; hereditary factors are undermined.	Constitutional and/or hereditary factors are critical in most cases; neurological and toxic factors are often determining agents: psychogenic factors are contributory.
General Behaviour	Speech and thought are logical and coherent; loss of contact with reality is limited; delusions and hallucinations are not observed.	Speech and thought processes are incoherent; behaviour is bizarre and irrational; delusions and hallucinations are common.
Social Adjustment	Behaviour is in general conformity with accepted standards of society.	Social habits are lost; behaviour is at odds with accepted standards of society.
Self-Management	Can manage self, although they are not always self-supporting; suicide is a possibility.	Institutionalisation is usually necessary to prevent harm to self or others.
Insight	Frequently is good.	Is practical at best, frequently totally lacking.
Treatment	Psychotherapy is the treatment of choice.	Emphasis is on controlling behaviour with chemical and physical agents prominent; when contact is established, psychotherapy should be used.
Prognosis	No deterioration: improvement can be expected.	Deterioration may be present in chronic cases; previous high incidence of life time hospitalisation is being lowered.

***

10

Balanced Personality

Importance and Types

MENTAL hygiene is concerned with realisation and maintenance of the mind's health and efficiency or in other words it deals with healthfulness of mind. Some psychologists have defined mental hygiene as 'Mental Health'. This does not mean that health of body be ignored. On the contrary, the physical basis of mental health is the fundamental concern of mental hygiene. In simple words, mental hygiene is concerned with the study of factors which go against mental health and efficiency. Mental hygiene is not exclusively a purely medical subject. It goes beyond the confines of hospital and invades the precincts of the home, the school, the factory and other institutions which influence human conduct. According to *Dictionary of Education,* mental hygiene means "establishment of environmental conditions, emotional attitudes and habits of thinking that will resist an onset of personality maladjustments. It is the study of principles and practices in the promotion of mental health and the prevention of mental disorders."

Mental hygiene means the balanced and integrated development of personality. "It is a science that deals with human welfare and pervades all fields of human relationships." The aim of mental hygiene is to "aid people to achieve more satisfying and more productive lives, through the preventive of anxieties and maladjustments." As a matter of fact, it is that growing body of knowledge and technique drawn from sciences of psychology, child study, sociology, psychiatry, medicine and biology, which has for its purpose, first, the understanding and evaluation of human personality, the promotion of mental health as an expression of optimal adjustment to one's self and the world resulting in the highest integration, and second, the personality maladjustments by suitable treatment. A mentally healthy person is one who has a wholesome and balanced personality free from schisms and inconsistencies, emotional and nervous tensions, discards and conflicts. Wallace Wallin has defined mental hygiene as "the application of a body of hygienic information and technique called from sciences of psychology, child study, education, sociology, psychiatry, medicine and biology for the purpose of observation and improvement of mental health of the individuals and of the community; (ii) for the prevention and care of minor and major mental diseases and defects and of mental, educational and social maladjustments." According to the dictionary, mental hygiene is the science or art of maintaining mental health and preventing the development of maladjustment and neurosis.

In the early 20th century there became apparent a commendable interest in the problems of mental health. This attitude encouraged the application of scientific knowledge to the therapeutic treatment of inmates of the hostels for the mentally ill. Prof W. Beers is called the father of the mental hygiene. Once, when he was suffering from some ailments, he realised that various ailments are caused due to failure of the individual to adjust himself with situations and requirements of environment. This maladjustment also leads to the development of various mental ailments. It is necessary to do away with them. With this aim in view an International Mental Health Society was established in 1908. The society believed in the slogan 'sound mind resides in sound body.'

Mental hygiene and education are not contradictory but are complementary. The common aim of mental hygiene and education is adjustment. It is a triumph of mental hygiene that education is coming to be looked upon more and more from the point of view of the development of the personality of the child. Few years ago it would have surprised people to know that a child had personality. Today guarding of this personality is the most precious right.

There are two spheres of mental hygiene: Prophylactic Hygiene and Meliorative Hygiene. Prophylactic side of hygiene is oriented towards the prevention of disease, breakdown, weakness, disaster and death. The meliorative side of hygiene is oriented towards the acquisition of better health, more energy and abundant life. It stresses the normal and the ideal as opposed to the abnormal and pathological. It is obvious, therefore, that mental hygiene is by no means restricted to the job of safeguarding people from actual mental disease. Its more positive task is that of the meliorative branch of the subject, i.e., to render to worried, serene—the efficiency and better health. It is interested in making the bad good and good better. Nothing is said about making the better the best. Just as a competent architect can suggest how a given house might be made better even though he is unable to describe the 'best house', so the meliorative hygiene may indicate how the given personality might be improved and yet find himself nonplussed if asked to specify the character of an absolutely ideal personality. The most important function of mental hygiene is to build up a 'moral'. Ultimately, the aim of mental hygiene is to promote 'moral'.

Place of Mental Hygiene in Educational Practices

Mental hygiene has an important part to play in educational practices. With the knowledge of mental hygiene school has a great opportunity to develop normal social attitudes, training social skills and better adjustment. During the period of childhood, prevention of mental ill health can be effected with the knowledge of mental hygiene. School work can become wholesome and pleasant. Whole personality of the child can be adjusted to better social environment. The detailed description of the place of mental hygiene in educational practices is given by Pintner and others as reported as follows:

The Meaning of Normal and Abnormal

(a) Normality is matter of degree—It is an error to suppose that a clear line can always be drawn between the normal and the abnormal. No universally satisfactory definition of 'normal' has yet been formulated. If we knew what 'normal' meant, we would, of course, know what 'abnormal' means. The words have been used in various ways.

(b) The normal at one's best—One view of 'normal' is what a given person may be at his best. According to this definition, when a person is below his best, he is abnormal. Such a view indicates that normality is a matter of degree. It does not show, however, what one's best really is.

(c) Statistical definition—A second view of the normal person is statistical. According to this view, the normal person is the average person.

The Opportunity of the School

The school has a golden opportunity to train pupils in good habits of living. The work of prevention is most productive during the period of childhood. Good attitudes, habits of taking proper care of the body, skilful development of efficient and economical work habits and the like may be taught in school. The school has a great opportunity to develop normal social attitudes, and training in social skills. The opportunities for preventive work in mental hygiene, under school conditions, are still largely unexplored, although many advances have been made within recent year

Conditions of Mental Health

The nature of mental health is not yet fully understood. Much is known about conditions of health. Some of the physical conditions of mental well-being are care of body, cleanliness, care of eyes and other sense organs, dental care, proper food, fresh air, adequate lighting, and types of activity, or exercise, suited to the nature and need of the individual. The conditions of mental health are not fully understood, but a large number of very simple and useful rules may help us in the task of maintaining poise, serenity and self-control.

The Hygiene of Instruction

The hygiene of instruction is an attempt to make school work wholesome and pleasant. This does not mean 'soft pedagogy.' It does not mean sentimentalism. It means that the new aim is to develop the whole personality to train the child to adjust himself to his social environment in a creative and cooperative way; and to discover and develop the child's superior abilities. Integration of personality by means of normal activities is the great aim.

Habit

Customary types of acting tend to persist. Thus, we come to speak of the 'force' of habit. The aim of hygiene is to put this force of habit to work in our best interests. The important thing is to form habits in the right sequence. Every step in the right direction makes the next step in the right direction easier. We retain our plasticity, our self-mastery and our freedom, if the force of right habits is on our side. If the habits are bad, the step in the right direction is much harder to take than if the habits previously learned had prepared us for it. We are likely to be sidetracked into a blind alley by habits of an undesirable kind. Good habits increase our freedom, skill and mastery. They help us achieve our best, namely, our normal performance.

Individual Differences

Standardisation has many good uses. To standardise often means to promote efficiency and economy. In the search for economy and efficiency in education care must be taken, however, to remember that people differ. The same methods cannot be used in the same way for everybody. To ignore the fact that people differ in ability, intelligence, early social training, physical ability, strength, as well as age and sex, would be a serious mistake. If training is to be suited to the nature and needs of the individual, care must be taken to keep the function of the school flexible and adaptable. We may learn from others, but standardisation should can copying others. The psychology of individual differences teachers us that we should be ourselves, and not copy others. The uniqueness of educational hygiene is to discover these differences among people and provide for them. Tests and other devices have been useful to help determine the kind and range of individual differences, so that educational, procedure could be planned and carried out in accordance with resultant implications.

Attitudes

This term has been defined as mental set or readiness to respond. By attitude we mean, broadly speaking, how one feels about things or people. Not only what we do, but also how we feel about what we do is important. The attitudes we form in connection with our habits, some writers have even gone to the length of suggestions that attitudes are primary in importance. Unless we have the right attitude towards what we are doing, our performance will probably not represent our best. It is apt to be a half hearted affair. We are likely not to put forth our best efforts. When we act wholeheartedly, not only the force of habit is 'pulling' us but our emotions also are pulling us along, if we can combine the force of strength in the struggle for superior adjustment and mastery. The task of educational hygiene is to develop the right attitudes of whole-hearted action.

Inhibition

Technically, inhibition refers to the complete or partial blocking of an activity or process. Inhibition may be more or less permanent. There are many types and conditions of inhibiting. Some are good, others are bad. Certain inhibitions are necessary. Self-control, for example, calls for the strength to say 'No' although there may be present a strong emotional pull in the direction of saying 'Yes'. We cannot do opposite things at the same time: we must say 'Yes' to one, 'No' to the other. Mental hygiene aims to develop our ability to discriminate as well as the strength that goes with self-control. The formation of normal habits of work involves the acquisition of normal inhibitions.

Fear

Fear is a common form of inhibition. To have fears is not always abnormal, but to be at the mercy of fear is dangerous. It is likely to paralyse our best efforts. Fear interferes with our work. Sometimes fear limits us even before we get startled. We do not try our best, because we are afraid of failure and perhaps ridicule. As a result, our superior abilities may never be discovered and developed. The task of educational hygiene is to teach us how to control our fears. Hygiene aims to prevent harmful fears from entering the child's life. The intelligent self-confidence that comes with success is an antidote to injurious fear. It teaches us to take a rational view of our limitations, and also where our greatest strength lies.

Discipline

Many people think of something disagreeable, when discipline is mentioned. Discipline is sometimes confused with stupid forms of punishment. Mental hygiene aims to develop self-control and self-discipline. Rational impulsion, not blind compulsion is the goal. The aim is to provide the student with worthwhile tasks which will discipline him. Discipline is necessary, if mastery of self is to be achieved. This idea is, of course, not new in education, but it has sometimes been obscured. Not 'soft pedagogy' but intelligent pedagogy is the aim. We learn to do difficult things, by doing them. Self-training, or discipline, does not mean self-indulgence. The methods of discipline are to be suited to the individual.

Motivation

Animal trainers often use fear as a method of motivation. What is psychologically possible is not always pedagogically and hygienically desirable. Because fear is a powerful means of control, people are sometimes tempted to use it without rhyme or reason. Not mere submissiveness, but creative and wholehearted cooperation, is encouraged by educational hygiene. The aim is to teach the child to motivate himself. This is done by providing interesting and absorbing tasks. Skill in getting and holding attention is important. Take care of attention, and interest takes care of itself. Skilful teachers have always appreciated the hygiene significance of this normal type of motivation. Here again individual differences must always be taken into account.

Training and Instruction

If instruction consists merely of giving out information, it is incomplete. Mere knowledge of mental health is not enough; good habits of mental health must be cultivated. Skill in action is essential as the understanding of the logic of action. The aim of hygiene is to combine training and instruction in the ways most useful for development of personality.

The Plateau

Progress in learning sometimes appears to come to a standstill long before we have reached the limits of what we can do. The standstill periods are called 'plateaus'. The task of hygiene is to find out what is blocking us, when we have reached a plateau. When we have discovered just what is wrong, we may set about to right it. Frequently, the trouble is fatigue. Wise alternation of work and rest periods, suited to the special needs of the individuals, is useful for avoiding plateaus. At times we become 'fed up', or bored. Our reason tells us that we ought to go on working; but we are blocked by our emotions. We go stale. The danger is that, when we are bored, our improvement may be arrested. Sometimes we make a rash decision and suspend effort altogether. When we are bored, we cannot give our best performance. Skilful change of activities, at the right time, is useful in avoiding the deadening effect of boredom. Complexity of the material is a third cause of the plateau. This factor probably does not mean that the material is too much for us: it is far more likely that we are not quite ready to deal with complex material successfully. The complexity of the material and the aim of mental hygiene is to promote the self-understanding we need in order to see clearly our problems. The aim is to develop normal habits of work. Plateaus in general may be due to faulty work habits. Here mental hygiene renders some of its most useful services in showing us how we may correct and constantly improve our methods of working and achieve greater mastery.

Recreation

One hundred years ago play was regarded by most people as a frivolous matter. Today our understanding of play has improved. With growth in understanding, our attitude toward play has changed. We have begun to find out a way "all work and no play makes Jack a dull boy." We have learned to appreciate the social significance of play. Cooperation, teamwork, and mutual understanding are important values to be derived from play. Play may also provide us with socially approved channels of energy discharge not provided by our work. Hobbies are useful. Artificial distinctions have sometimes been drawn between work and play. Work need not be disagreeable. Bad habits of work make work disagreeable. Mental hygiene attempts to develop wholesome attitudes by means of play. Play is more than a pedagogical device; it is nature's plan of growth and development. Children have the right to play and mental hygiene takes its cue from the way of nature

Fatigue

When we are fatigued, our performance suffers. Our spirits may be low. Mental hygiene aims to teach the individual how to conserve his energy and strength. To know when and how to rest is important. To rest before one is completely fatigued means quicker recovery. Mental hygiene tells us how to use our reserve strength wisely. Fatigue is largely controlled by controlling working conditions. Normal habits or rest and sleep are necessary. Sometimes people tire themselves out by worrying. To quarrel with oneself is another undesirable way of using one's energy. Mental hygiene attempts to help us build a pattern of living on the basis of intelligent insight into our own needs of mind and body.

Conservation of the Sensory Apparatus

Our senses keep us in touch with what is going on in the world about us. The senses of sight and hearing are especially important in normal education. The marvellous machinery we call the sensory apparatus is so efficient that we are likely to take it for granted. Only when the machine gets out of order that many of us appreciate its importance. The aim of hygiene is to teach us how to take care of our senses. Hygiene trains us to refrain from abusing our senses. Many people impair their efficiency and endanger their well-being by ignorant or careless abuse of the sensory apparatus. In the school, hygiene has rendered a useful service in conserving and training the senses. Eye and ear defects are discovered by hygiene and treated before they have threatened the health and happiness of the pupils. Defective eyesight and impaired hearing are often accompanied by undesirable mental attitudes. Frequently they are the roots of injurious inhibitions. Children with poor hearing are sometimes unfairly deprived of the opportunity to develop normal social attitudes: people mistakenly regard these children as stupid. Development may be arrested because a child cannot hear or see well. Conservation of the sensory apparatus means that children are to be taught to take wise care of their eyes and ears and other senses.

Teamwork and Group Adjustment

Groups can often do things better than individuals. The democratic idea is based on faith in wise group work. The leader today is he who integrates the superior abilities represented in the group. The rules and elements of superior teamwork can be taught in the school. The principle of integration may be applied to groups as well as to the individuals. Mental hygiene aims to develop the child by providing opportunity for normal group activity under school conditions. More and more this aim is appreciated as a major contribution on the part of hygiene.

Heredity

Since much remains to be learned about human heredity, extreme views are misleading. Some maintain that heredity is everything. "Blood will tell," is their theory. People who hold this view are likely to make the mistake of thinking that training is of negligible importance. They believe that 'genius will out'. Even a genius, however, needs training. We are born, not with skills, but with capacities. Skills imply training. At the other extreme are those who believe that anybody can be taught anything. These are likely to become the blind worshippers of method. The holders of this view are likely to ignore the individual difference among children. A third view of heredity and environment suggests that we learn all we can about the capacities of children and adapt the wisest courses we know in the work of developing these capacities. The important thing is to provide the child with suitable opportunities to grow and develop normally.

Sex Education

Sex education means more than mere instruction in matters concerning sex relations. It is an important part of training in the art of wholesome living. Much confusion exists at present in regard to the aims and methods of sex education. Mental hygiene has not yet solved the problem of sex education, but much useful work has already begun. Intelligent self-control, normal habits of work, skill in solving personal problems of mind and body, and so on, are included in sex education. The older methods sometimes made virtue odious. High personal standards of conduct may be taught in an intelligent and sympathetic way. Nowhere is the value of example more important than in sex education.

Seeking Worthwhile Goals

Unless our activity has a definite goal, we are likely to scatter our energies and waste our efforts in aimless wandering. A goal makes life a battle and a march. To have a goal is not enough: the goal must be such that it gives us a feeling that it is worth fighting for. Only when a goal is worthwhile, do we feel ready to make sacrifices. Only when we are convinced that the goal is good, can we muster our best energies in the work of achieving it. A worthwhile goal centres our attention. What we attend to determines largely what our behaviour is to be. When we are absorbed in a worthwhile task, we are too busy to worry or to be afraid. We are too preoccupied with the work in hand to quarrel with others. Our best powers are drawn into action. Mental hygiene has no rule of thumb for living, but it offers some broad working principles. It suggests to us the enormous importance of selecting worthwhile goals from the beginning. From these goals and purposes, we are to take our cues for action. In the beginning it is relatively easy to develop normal habits of attentive co-ordinated activity. The aim of educational hygiene is to suit the goal to the individual's stage of development and his peculiar needs. The ultimate goal may be obscure, but the immediate goals are clear, namely, the development of our superior abilities, individual and social.

The Concept of Balanced Personality

About balanced personality, Klein states:

"The key word balanced refers to an avoidance of extremes, to finding the happy medium. As applied to dress and personal appearance it calls for building up standards of 'good taste' allegiance to which will protect the individual from being catalogued either as an over-fastidious, perfumed fop or as an unkempt, slovenly hobo. Neither the fop nor the hobo represent a sartorial balance. As applied to learning the concept involves steering a middle course between crass, shocking, self-satisfied ignorance at one extreme and opinionated painfully detailed, complacent pedantry at the other. The pedant is unable to see the wood for the trees and the ignoramus sees neither the wood nor the trees—and both are unaware of this intellectual blindness. With respect to sex the concept implies adoption of an attitude of enlightened self-control that will enable its possessor to escape the difficulties of the over-inhibited, squeamish prude as well as the dangers of the over-indulgent, prurient libertine. Both the prude and the libertine symbolise divergently extreme failures to achieve a balanced sex life. The prude is so afraid of sex that ignorant fear prevents appreciation of its beauty, while the libertine is so engulfed by lust that the beauty of sex is never cultivated. The one has too many inhibitions and the other not enough; hence both are off balance. Similarly, in connection with monetary matters balance suggests avoidance of both the Scylla of stinginess and the Charybdis of extravagance; for the miser's potential spending impulses are crushed by powerful inhibitions, while the potential saving habits of the spendthrift are never born because he is unable to curb the impulse to spend.

"Almost every aspect of personality reveals such distortion by failure to achieve optimal balance between the extremes of overdevelopment on the one hand and underdevelopment on the other. The aspect of religion furnishes the extremes of the smug, uncritical, supercilious, pietistic bigot along with his antithetic scoffer. A glance at the aspect of patriotism reminds us that a personality can be so fervently and chauvinistically patriotic that his country appears to him to be the apotheosis of all national virtue or, contrariwise, a personality can be so hypercritical of his country that he magnifies its vices and is blind to its virtues. Neither the jingo nor the 'copperhead' is an ideal patriot. If we turn to the aspects of communicativeness, we find both garrulous and taciturn individuals. The former are such chatterboxes that they bore others by their ceaseless stream of talk, while the latter are so silent as to make ordinary conversation a laborious undertaking. Here, too, there is a golden chance mean between saying too much and saying too little, just as there is between talking too loud and not talking loud enough or too rapidly and not rapidly enough. In analogous fashion personalities can be too aggressive or to meek, too excitable or too phlegmatic, too serious or too flippant, too ambitious or too apathetic. Even in terms of the personality's evaluation of itself the need for balance can be detected. The conceited egotist exemplifies an exaggerated evaluation while the discouraged victim of acute feelings of inferiority exemplifies the other extreme. What we ordinarily call self-esteem refers to an optimal balance between these extremes."

The balanced personality is poised, because to be poised means to be balanced.

How Schools can Promote Mental Health?

The chief mental hygiene task of the schools is not so much to prevent actual mental breakdown as to reinforce and amplify the functions of the ideal home in building up wholesome and socially constructive attitudes. In other words, what we have called the programme of meliorative mental hygiene should be the schools' main concern with mental hygiene. This does not mean that an already crowded curriculum should be burdened with one more subject. We are not advocating the addition of a course in mental hygiene at either elementary or high school level. The scope of meliorative mental hygiene is such that it cannot very well be compressed within the confines of a series of lesson plans or formal school projects.

Mental hygiene is more like a philosophy of life than a fixed body of knowledge. A philosophy of life is not acquired by taking a course in philosophy. Nor is a philosophy of life ever finished. It is changed with and developed as new experiences makes for deepened insight and superficial values are discarded in favour of more profound values. Similarly, the mental hygiene perspective calls for adaptation all through the years as insight deepens and new problems loom up. But the basic setting for this perspective is rooted in the experiences of the developmental years in home and school. This setting is so pervasive that no array of pious mental hygiene maxims can furnish the child with the requisite knowledge. Schools can introduce fire drills and tooth brush drills and spelling drills, but not mental hygiene drills. Every class has mental hygiene implications. So does every good book, every friendship, every contest, every examination, every promotion, and every demotion.

The mental hygienist is more concerned about the attitudes built up in the child by school experiences—both curricular as well as extracurricular—than he is with formal academic success. Every teacher has a responsibility for shaping and influencing the child's attitudes. Wholesome personality development of every child should be the fundamental educational objective. In terms of such a mental hygiene ideal it is just as important to adjust the school to the child as it is to have the child adjusted to the school. Mastery of the curriculum should be regarded as a means for enhancing personality development rather than as an end in itself. Existing curricula should be evaluated on the basis of their efficacy in furthering this goal. It is particularly important to consider their range and flexibility; for an extremely rigid curriculum of narrow content cannot be adapted to the individual needs of individual students. Many of our so-called educational misfits are casualties of an unyielding curriculum. Very often it is the school rather than the child which is the misfit in question. Enlightened school officials have long been aware of this and have already made considerable progress in the difficult and expensive task of fitting the school to the vagaries of the individual child.

Even where lack of funds prevents an elaborate curricular change much can be done to promote child welfare as the mental hygienist views such welfare. The psychological atmosphere of the school can be made more like that of a congenial home atmosphere. The child ought to be made to feel safe and secure at home and at school. In a way the school is to be considered a projection and enlargement of the psychological values of the well-administered family. It is the child's training ground for communal living. To achieve the utmost from his activities on this training ground he must be given a sense of belonging to the school community. He must be made to feel a part of it just as he is made to feel his identification with the family group.

***

Bibliography

Abeles, M., Prut, Y., Bergman, H., & Vaadia, E. (1994). Synchronisation in neuronal transmission and its importance for information processing. *Progress in Brain Research*, 102, 395-404.

Adler, A., *Understanding Human Nature*, New York: Greenburg Publishing, Inc., 1927.

— — —, *The Education of Children*, London: Allen and Unwin.

Ainsworth, Stanley, *Speech Correction Methods*, New York: Prentice-Hall, Inc., 1948.

Anastasi, Anne, *Differential Psychology* (3rd Ed.), New York, The Macmillan Company, 1958.

— — —, *Psychological Testing* (2nd Ed.), New York: The Macmillan Company, 1961.

Anderson, B. (1994). Speed of neuron conduction is not the basis of the IQ-RT correlation: Results from a simple model. *Intelligence*, 19, 317-323.

Anderson, B., & Donaldson, S. (1995). The backpropagation algorithm: Implications for the biological bases of individual differences in intelligence. *Intelligence*, 21,327-345.

Anderson, B., & Rutledge, V. (1996). Age and hemisphere effects on dendritic structure. *Brain*, 119, 1983-1990.

Anderson, Richard C., "Educational Psychology", *Annual Review of Psychology*, 18, 129-64, 1967.

Atkinson, John W., *Motive in Fantasy, Action and Society*, Princeton N.J., D. Van Nostrand Co., Inc., 1958.

Bansal, V.P., *Text Book of Educational Psychology*, Allahabad: India Press, 1958.

Bartlett, F., *Thinking: An Experimental and Social Study*, London: Allen and Unwin, 1958.

Bauham, K.M., "Senescence and Emotions: A Genetic Theory", *J. Genet, Psychol.*, 78, 175-183, 1951.

Beale, R., & Jackson, T. (1991), *Neural computing: An introduction*, Bristol, England: Adam Hilger.

Bear, M. F., Connors, B.W., & Paradiso, M.A. (1996). *Neuroscience: Exploring the brain*, Baltimore: Williams & Wikins.

Benjamin, Zoe, *Emotional Problems of Childhood*, London: University of London Press Ltd.

Berlyne, D., "Recent Development in Piaget's Work," *Crit. J. Educ.*, 26, 1-12, 1957.

Bernstein, J. (1973). *Einstein*. Glasglow: Wm Collins. Blinkov, S.M., & Glezer, I. I. (1968). *The human brain in figures and tables: A quantitative handbook*, New York: Plenum.

Bhatia, B.D., *Behaviour Problems in Children at Home and School*, Delhi: D.E.S., C.I.E.

Bhatia, H R., *Elements of Social Psychology*, Bombay: Manaktala.

Bhatnagar R.P., *Educational Psychology*, Gorakhpur: Vishva Widhya Prakashan.

Bhattacharya, P.N., *A Text Book of Psychology*, 1964.

Blair, G.M., *The Psychological Interpretation of Teaching Educational dministration and Supervision*, 33, 321-338, 1947.

Book, William F., *The Psychology of Skill*, University of Montana Publications in Psychology, No. 53.

Borg, Walter R., *Education Research: An Introduction*, New York: David Mckay Co. Inc., 1963.

Boring, *Foundations of Psychology*, New York: John Wiley & Sons, Inc., 1948.

Bose, G., "Delinquency in India" In Eissler, K.R., (Ed), *Searchlight on Delinquency*, New York: International University Press, Inc., 1949.

Bossard, J.H.S. and E.S., Boll, *Child Development*, 1957.

Bouchard, T. J., Jr. (1997). I.Q. similarity in twins reared apart: Findings and responses to critics. In R.J. Sternberg & E.L. Grigorenko (Eds.), *Intelligence, heredity, and environment* (pp. 126-160), Cambridge, England: Cambridge University Press.

Brand, C. (1996). "g," genes and pedagogy: a reply to seven (lamentable) chapters. In D. K. Detterman (Ed.), *Current topics in human intelligence: Volume 5* (pp. 113-120), Norwood, NJ: Ablex.

Bridges, Katherine, M.B., *Social and Emotional Development of Pre-School Child*, London: Kegan Paul, 1931.

Brit, J. Educ. Psychol. 25, 158-177, 1956.

Brody, N. (1992). *Intelligence* (2nd ed.), San Diego, CA: Academic Press.

Brown, M. C., Hopkins, W. G., & Keynes, R. J. (1991). *Essentials of neural development*, Cambridge, England: N. M. Weinberger, & G. Lynch (Eds.), *Brain and memory: Modulation and mediation of neuroplasticity* (pp. 239-249), New York: Oxford University Press.

Bruner, Jerome S., Jacqueline J. Ooodnow and George A. Austin, *A Study of Thinking*, New York: John Wiley & Sons, Inc., 1956.

Burks, B., *Foster-Family Resemblances in Intelligence*, Chap. 15 in Child Behaviour and Development, Ed., Darker, R. Kounion, J. and Wright, H., New York: McGraw-Hill, 1943.

Burt, C., "The Differentiations of Intellectual Ability," *Brit. J. Educ. Psychol.*, 24, 76-901954. *The Evidence for the Concept of Intelligence*.

Burt, S.C., *The Backward Child*, London: University of London Press Ltd., p. 133, 1951.

– – –, *The Young Delinquent*, New York: Appleton, 1925.

Caroll, J.B. (1993). *Human cognitive abilities: A survey of factor-analytic studies.* Cambridge, England: CAmbridge University Press.

Carroll, J. B., Kohlberg, L., & De Vries, R. (1984). Psychometric and Piagetian intelligences: Toward resolution of controversy. *Intelligences, 8,* 67-91.

Cattell, R. B. (1987). *Intelligence: Its structure, growth and action.* Amsterdam: North Holland.

Cattell, R.B., *Personality,* McGraw-Hill. 1951.

Caudill, M., & Butler, C. (1990). *Naturally intelligent systems.* Cambridge, MA: MIT Press.

Changeux, J. P. (1985). *Neuronal man: The biology of mind.* New York: Oxford University Press.

Churchland, P.S., & Sejnowski, T.J. (1992). *The computational brain.* Cambridge, MA: MIT Press.

Comb. A., and Snygg, D., *Individual Behaviour,* Rev. Ed., New York: Harper and Row Publishers, Inc., 1959.

Coville, W.J. et al., *Abnormal Psychology,* New York: Barnes and Noble, Inc., p. 237.

Cronbach, Lee J., *Essentials of Psychological Testing* (2nd Ed.), New York: Harper & Row, Publishers, 1960.

– – –, *Educational Psychology* (2nd Ed.) New York: Harcourt Brace & World, Inc., 1963.

Crutcher, K.A. (1986). Anatomical correlates of neuronal plasticity. In J.L. Martinez, Jr., & R.P. Kesner (Eds.), *Learning and memory: A biological view* (pp. 83-123). Orlando, FL: Academic Press.

Davis, R.A., "Applicability of Applications of Psychology with Particular reference to Classroom Learning;" *Journal of Educational Research,* 37. 19-30, 1943.

Dayhoff, J.E. (1990). *Neural network architectures: An introduction.* New York: Van Nostrand Reinhold.

Deary, I.J., Egan, V., Gibson, G.J., Austin, E.J., Brand, C.R., & Kellaghan, T. (1996). Intelligence and the differentiation hypothesis. *Intelligence, 23,* 105-132.

Dececco, J.P., "The Psychology of Learning and Instruction". *Educ. Psychology,* Prentice-Hall of India Pvt. Ltd., 1970.

Detterman, D. K., & Daniel, M. H. (1989). Correlations of mental tests with each other and with cognitive variables are highest for low I.Q. groups. *Intelligence. 13,* 349-359.

Detterman, D.K. (1991). Reply to Deary and Pagliari: Is *g* intelligence or stupidity? *Intelligence, 15,* 251-255.

Detterman, D.K. (1993). The case for the prosecution: Transfer as an epiphenomenon. In D. K. Detterman & R. J. Sternberg (Eds.), *Current topics in human intelligence: Volume 4* (pp. 85-115). Norwood, NJ: Ablex.

Diamond, M. C. (1991). Environmental influences on the young brain. In UNDERSTANDING THE GENERAL FACTOR OF INTELLIGENCE 129 K. R. Gibson & A. C. Petersen (Eds.), *Brain maturation and cognitive development* (pp. 107-124). New York: Aldine de Gruyter.

Diamond, M. C., Scheibel, A.B., Murphy, G. M., Jr., & Harvey, T. (1985). On the brain of a scientist: Albert Einstein. *Experimental Neurology, 88,* 198-204.

Dinkmeyer, C. Don, *Child Development, The Emerging Self,* Prentice-Hall Psychology Series, 1967, p. 252.

Dodwell, P.C., *Children's Understanding of Number and Related Concepts.*

Dollard, J., and Miller, N.E., *Personality and Psychology: An Analysis in Terms of Learning, Thinking and Culture,* New York, McGraw-Hill, 1950.

Dossay, M.L., *Advanced Educational Psychology, Oriential Jullunder, Education of the Backward Child,* National Council of Educational Research and Training, 1964, p. 4.

Dutt, N.K., *Psychological Foundations of Education,* Doaba House, Delhi, 1974.

Ellis, Henry, *The Transfer of Learning,* New York: The Macmillan Company, 1965.

Ellis, R., & Humphreys, G. W. (1999). *Connectionist psychology: A test with readings.* Hove, East Sussex: Psychology Press.

Elman, J. L., Bates, E.A. Johnson, M. H., Karmiloff-Smith, A., Parisi, D., & Plunkett, K. (1996). *Rethinking innateness: A connectionist perspective on development.* Cambridge, MA: MIT Press.

Encyclopaedia of Educational Research, New York: The Macmillan Company, 1952.

Epstein, H.T. (1979). Correlated brain and intelligence development in humans. In M.E. Hahn, C. Jensen, & B.C. Dudek (Eds.). *Development and evolution of brain size: Behavioural implications* (pp. 111-131). New York: Academic Press.

Everitt, V., 'Good Habits and Well-being of School Children", *Elementary Sch.,* 52, 344-50.

Eysenck, H. J. (1994). A biological theory of intelligence. In D. K. Detterman (Ed.), *Current topics in human intelligence: Volume 4* (pp. 117-149). Norwood, NJ: Ablex.

Flavell, J. H. (1963). *The developmental psychology of Jean Piaget.* Princeton, NJ: VAn Nostrand.

Flavell, John H., *The Developmental Psychology of Jean Piaget.* Princeton, N.J.: D. Van Nostrand Co. Inc., 1963.

Fleigher, Louis A,, and Bish, Charles, E., "Summary of Research on the Academically Talented Student", *Review of Educational Research,* 29 December, 1958, p. 409.

Flynn, J.R. (1996). What enviornmental factors affect intelligence: The relevance of I.Q. gains over time. In D. K. Detterman (Ed.), *Current topics in huamn intelligence: Volume 5.* (pp. 17-29). Norwood, NJ: Ablex.

Fodor, J.A. (1983). *The modularity of mind.* Cambridge, MA: MIT Press.

Fodor, J.A., & Pylyshyn, Z.W. (1988). Connectionism and cognitive architecture: A critical analysis. *Cognition, 28,* 3-71.

Frank, L.K., and others, *Personality Development in Adolescent Girls,* Manager, Soc. Res: Child Develop 16m No. 53, 1-316, 1951.

Fredenburg F.A., *The Psychology of Personality and Adjustment,* California: Cummings Publishing Co.

French, J. W., Ekstrom, R. B., & Price, L. A. (1963). *Manual for Kit of reference tests for cognitive factors.* Princeton, NJ: Educational Testing Service.

Freud, S., *An Outline of Psycho-analysis,* New York: W.W. Norton and Co. Inc., 1949.

Gabriel John, *Children Growing Up,* University of London Press, 1969, pp. 10.

Gallagher, J.J., *The Child in the Elementary School,* Washington: American Education Research Association, National Education, 1949.

Gardner, H. (1983). *Frames of mind.* New York: Basic Books.

Garrett, Henry, E., *Statistics in Psychology and Education,* New York: David MaKay Co., Inc., 1958.

Gates, *et al,, Educational Psychology,* New York: The Macmillan Company.

Gessel, A. and Shirley, *Child Development,* New York: Harper, 1949.

Gessel, A.F.L. Iig, and L.B., Ames: *The Years from Ten to Sixteen,* New York: Harper and Row, 1958.

Getzels, W.J., *Creativity and Intelligence,* London: B. John Wiley and Sons, Inc., 1962 p. 8.

Glees, P. (1988). *The human brain.* Cambridge, England: Cambridge University Press.

Gold, M., "Suicide and Socialisation of Aggression," *Amer J. Social,* 33,651-661, 1958.

Grimshaw, G. M., Adelstein, A., Bryden, M. P., & MacKinnon, G.E. (1998). First-language acquisition in adolescence: Evidence for a critical period for verbal langage development. *Brain and Language, 63,* 237-255.

Gustafsson, J. E. (1999). Measuring and understanding G: Experimental and correlational approaches. In P. L. Ackerman, P. C. Kyllonen, & R. D. Roberts (Eds.), *Learning and individual differences: Process, trait, and content determinants* (pp. 275-289). Washington, DE: American Psychological Association.

Haier, R.J. (1993). Cerebral glucose metabolism and intelligence. In P.A. Vernon (Ed.), *Biological approaches to the study of human intelligence* (pp. 317-373). Norwood, NJ: Ablex.

Haikarwal, B.S., *Economic and Social Aspects of Crime in India,* London: George'Allen & Unwin, 1934.

Hathaway, W., and Lowenfeld, B., *Teaching the Visually Handicapped in Education of Exceptional Children, Forty-ninth Year Book,* Part II, 135.

Havighurst Quoted in Henry, N.B. (Ed.), *Education for the Gifted,* Fifty-seventh Yearbook of National Society for the Study of Education. Part II, Chicago: University of Chicago Press, 1958, p. 19.

Havighurst, Robert, J., and Hilda Taba, *Adolescent Character and Personality,* New York: John Wiley & Sons, Inc , 1949.

Hebb, D. O. (1949). *The organisation of behavior: A neuropsychological theory.* New York: Wiley.

Hebb, D.O., *The Organisation of Behaviour: A Neurological Theory,* New York: John Wiley & Sons, 1949.

Hemphill, J.K., *The Leader and His Group Leadership,* Penguin Books, 1969.

Herrnstein, R.J., & Murray, C. (1994). *The bell curve: Intelligence and class structure in American life.* New York: Free Press.

Hollingworth, *Gifted Children, Their Nature and Nurture,* New York, Macmillan.

Horn, J. (1998). A basis for research on age differences in cognitive capabilities. In J.J. McArdle & R. W. Woodcock (Eds.), *Human cognitive abilities in theory and practive.* Chicago: Riverside.

Horn, J., & Noll, J. (1994). A system for understanding cognitive capabilities: A theory and the evidence on which it is based. In D. K. Detterman (Ed.), *Current topics in huamn intelligence: Volume 4* (pp. 151-202). Norwood, NJ: Ablex.

Humphreys, L. G., & Parsons, C.K. (1979). Piagetian tasks measure intelligence and intelligence tests assess cognitive development: A reanalysis. *Intelligence, 3,* 369-382.

Hunt, E. (1997). Nature vs nurture: The feeling of *vuja de.* In R. J. Sternberg & E. L. Grigorenko (Eds.), *Intelligence heredity, and environment* (pp. 531-551). Cambridge, England: Cambridge University Press.

Hunt, Earl B., *Concept Learning: An Information Processing Problem,* New York: John Wiley & Sons, Inc., 1962.

Hunt, J., *Intelligence and Experience,* Ronald Press, New York: 1961.

Hurlock, E.D., *Child Development,* New York, McGraw-Hill Book Company, Inc., p. 106.

Huttenlocher, P. R. (1990). Morphometric study of human cerebral cortex development. *Neuropsychologia, 28,* 517-527.

Huttenlocher, P. R. (1991). Dendritic and synaptic pathology in mental retardation. *Pediatric Neurology, 7,* 79-85.

Huttenlocher, P. R., & Dabholkar, A. S. (1997). Regional differences in synaptogenesis in human cerebral cortex. *Journal of Comparative Neurology, 387,* 167-178.

Inhelder, B., & Piaget, J. (1985). *The growth of logical thinking from childhood to adolescence.* New York: Basic Books.

Jack, L.M., *An Experimental Study of Adolescent Behaviour,* Child Welfare, 1952.

Jacobs, B., Schall, M., & Scheibel, A. B. (1993). A quantitative dendritic analysis of Wernicke's area in humans: II. Gender, hemispheric and environmental factors. *Journal of Comparative Neurology, 327*, 97-111.

Jalota, S., *Educational Psychology*, Banares, 1951.

Jenkins, J.J., *Studies in Individual Differences*, New York: Appleton, Century-Croft* 1961.

Jensen, A. R. (1980). *Bias in mental testing.* New York: Free Press.

Jensen, A. R. (1981). *Straight talk about mental tests.* London: Methuen.

Jensen, A. R., & Johnson, F. W. (1994). Race and sex differences in head size and I.Q. *Intelligence, 18*, 309-333.

Jensen, A.R. (1998). *The g factor.* Westport, CT: Praeger.

Jersild, A.T., *Emotional Development, Child Psychology*, 4th edition, London: Staples Press, Ltd.

Jersild, A.T., *In Search of Self*, New York: Teacher College Columbia University, 1952.

John Gabriel, *Children Growing Up*, London: University Press, 1969 p. 138.

Johnson, J. S., & Newport, E.L. (19890. Critical period effects in second language learning: The influence of maturational state on the acquisition of English as a second language. *Cognitive Psychology, 21*, 60-99.

Johnson, *Speech Problems of Children*, Prepared by the American Speech and Hearing Association for the National Society of Crippled Children and Adults, New York.

Judd, J. S. (1990). *Neural network design and the complexity of learning.* Cambridge, MA: MIT Press.

Kandel, E.R., Schwartz, J. H., & Jessel, T.M. (Eds.). (1991). *Principles of neural science* (3rd ed.). London: Prentice Hall.

Kasabov, N.K. (1996). *Fundations of neural networks, fuzzy systems, and knowledge engineering.* Cambridge, MA: MIT Press.

Katz, Barney and Lehner, George F.J., *Mental Hygiene in Modern Living*, New York: The Ronald Press Co.

Katz, L. C., & Shatz, C. J. (1996). Synaptic activity and the construction of cortical circuits. *Science, 274*, 1133-1138.

Kaufman, A. S. (1990). *Assessing adolescent adult intelligence.* Boston: Allyn and Bacon.

Kennedy, Lou and Carr Anna: *The Rehabilitation of Speech*, New York: Harper & Bros, 1947 (revised).

Killackey, H. P. (1995). Evolution of the human brain: A neuronantomical perspective. In M. S. Gazzaniga (Ed.), *The cognitive neurosciences* (pp. 1243-1253). Cambridge, MA: Press.

King, W.H., "The Development of Scientific Concepts in Children," *Brit. J. Educ. Psychol.* 1961, 2, 1-10.

Kirk, Samuel, A., *Educating Exceptional Children*, New Delhi: Oxford and IBH Publishing Company.

Klein, D.B., *Mental Hygiene*, Henry Holt, 1966.

Kohler, W.H., *Gestalt Psychology*, 2nd edition, Liverright, 1947.

Kolb, B., & Whishaw, I. Q. (1998). Brain plasticity and behaviour *Annual Review of Psychology, 49*, 43-64.

Konner, M. (1991). Universals of behavioral development in relation to brain myelination. In K. R. Gibson & A. C. Petersen (Eds.), *Brain maturation and cognitive development* (pp. 181-223). New York: Aldine de Gruyter.

Kostovic, I. (1990). Structural and histochemical reorganisation of the human prefrontal cortex during perinatal and postnatal life. *Progress in Brain Research, 85*, 223-240.

Krech, D. and Crutchfield, R., *The Structure and Function of Social Groups*, London: McGraw-Hill Book Company, 1948.

– – – "Group Morale and Leadership" in *Theory and Problems of Social Psychology*.

Kritzer, M. F., & Goldman-Rakic, P.S. (1995). Intrinsic circuit organisation of the major layers and sublayers of the dorsolateral prefrontal cortex in the rhesus monkey. *Journal of Comparative Neurology, 359*, 131-143.

Kumria, R.R., *The Indian Child in Home and School*, Jalandhar: University Publishers.

Kundu, C.L., *Personality Development. A Critique of Indian Studies*, Kurukshetra: Vishal Publications, 1976.

Kuppuswami, B., *Educational Psychology*, Delhi: Sterling, 1974.

Kurt Lewin, *A Dynamic Theory of Personality*, New York: McGraw-Hill Book Company, Inc.

Kyllonen, P. C., & Christal, R. E. (1990). Reasoning ability is (little more than) working-memory capacity? *Intelligence, 14*, 389-433.

Lenneberg, E. (1967). *Biological foundations of language.* New York: Wiley.

Lester, Grow D., & Alice Grow, *Educational Psychology*, American Book Company, pp. 566-69.

Levine, D. S. (1991). *Introduction to neural and cognitive modeling.* Hillsdale, NJ: Erlbaum.

Li, S. C., & Lindenberger, U. (1999). Cross-level unification: A computational exploration of the link between deterioration of neurotransmitter systems and dedifferentiation of cognitive abilities in old age. In L. G. Nilsson & H. Markowitsch (Eds.), *Cognitive neuroscience of memory* (pp. 104-146). Toronto: Hogrefe & Huber.

Linton, R., *Cultural Background of Personality*, New York: Appleton Century Co. Inc., 1945.

Loehlin, J. C., Horn, J.M., & Willerman, L. (1997). Heredity, environment, and I.Q. in the Texas adoption project. In R. J. Sternberg & E. L. Grigorenko (Eds.), *Intelligence, heredity, and environment* (pp. 105-125). Cambridge, England: Cambridge University Press.

Lovell, K., *The Growth of Basic Mathematical and Scientific Concepts in Children*, London: University of London Press, 1961.

Lynn, R., & Gault, A. (1986). The relation of musical ability to general intelligence and the major primaries. *Research in Education*, 36, 59-64.

Mackintosh, N. J. (1986). The biology of intelligence? *British Journal of Psychology*, 77, 1-18.

Mackintosh, N. J. (1998). *I.Q. and human intelligence*. Oxford, England: Oxford University Press.

Marchman, V. (1993). Constraints of plasticity in a connectionist model of the English past tense, *Journal of Cognitive Neuroscience*, 5, 215-234.

Maslow, A., *Motivation and Personality*, New York: Harper and Row Publishers, Inc., 1954.

Mathur, .S.S., *Educational Psychology*, Agra: Vinod Pustakmandir.

McClelland, David D. (Ed.): *Studies in Motivation*, New York: Appleton-Century Crofts, 1955.

McClelland, David D., John Atkinson, W. Russell Clark, A., and Edgar Lowell, L., *The Achievement Motive*, New York: Appleton- Century Crofts, 1953.

– – –, *The Achieving Society*, Princeton, N.J.: D. Van Nost-rand Co., Inc., 1961.

– – –, "Toward a Theory of Motive Acquisition," *American Psychologist*, 20, 321-33, 1965.

McClelland, J. L., & Jenkins, E. (1991). Nature, nurture, and conncetions: Implications of connectionist models for cognitive development. In K. VanLehn (Ed.), *Architectures for intelligence: The twenty-second Carnegie Mellon symposium on cognition* (pp. 41-73). Hillsdale, NJ: Erlbaum.

McClelland, J.L., & Rumelhart, D. E. (Eds.). (1986). *Parallel distributed processing: Explorations in the microstructure of cognition. Vol. 2: Psychological and biological models*. Cambridge, MA: MIT Press.

McDonald, Frederick J., *Educational Psychology* (2nd Ed.), Belmont Calif.: Wadsworth Publishing Co., Inc., 1965.

McDougall, W., *Social Psychology*, Methuen, 28th Edition, 1946.

McGoech, John A., *The Psychology of Human Learning*, New York: David McKay Co., Inc.,1942.

McLeod, P., Plunkett, K., & Rolls, E. T. (1998). *Introduction to connectionist modelling of cognitive process*. Oxford, England: Oxford University Press.

Mednick and Mednick (Ed.): *Research in Personality*, Holt Rinehart and Winston, Inc., 1963.

MeGoeth, J.A., *The Psychology of Human Learning*, Longmans, 1942.

Merrill, M.A., *Problems of Child Delinquency*, New York: Houghton-Milton and Co., 1947.

Miller, C., *Psychoanalysis and Its Derivatives*, Home University Library.

Miller, E. M. (1994). Intelligence and brain myelination: A hypothesis. *Personality and Individual Differences*, 17, 803-832.

Mitchell, D. E. (1980). The influence of early visual experience on visual perception. In C.S. Harris (Ed.), *Visual coding and adaptability* (pp. 1-50). Hillsdale, NJ: Erlbaum.

Morgan, B., & Gibson, K. R. (1991). Nutritional and environmental interactions in brain development. In K. R. Gibson & A. C. Petersen (Eds.), *Brain maturation and cognitive development* (pp. 91-106). New York: Aldine de Gruyter.

Mountcastle, V. B. (1998). *Perceptual neuroscience: The cerebral cortex*. Cambridge, MA: Harvard University Press.

Moustakas, C.E., *Psychotherapy with Children*, New York: Harper and Bros., 1959.

Mrzljak, L., Uylings, H. B. M., Van Eden, C.G., & Judas, M. (1990). Neuronal development in human prefrontal cortex in prenatal and postnatal stages. *Progress in Brain Research*, 85, 185-222.

Murray, H.A., *et al.*, *Explorations in Personality*, 1939, p. 74-75.

Neisser, U., Boodoo, G., Bouchard, T. J., Jr., Boykin, A. W., Brody, N., Ceci, S.J., Halpern, D. F., Loehlin, J. C., Perloff, R., Sternberg, R. J., & Urbina, S. (1996). Intelligence: Knowns and unknows. *American Psychologist*, 51, 77-101.

Nelson, C.A. (1999). Neural plasticity and human development. *Current Directions in Psychological Science*, 8, 42-45.

Nelson, M. M., & Illingworth, W. T. (1991). *A practical guide to neural nets*.Reading, MA: Addison-Wesley.

Nettelbeck, T. (1987). Inspection time and intelligence. In P. A. Vernon (Ed.), *Speed of information-Processing and intelligence* (pp. 295-346). Norwood, NJ: Ablex.

Nettelbeck, T. (1999). Savant syndrome—Rhyme without reason. IN M. Anderson (Ed.), *The development of intelligence* (pp. 247-273). East Sussex, England: Psychology Press.

Neville, H. J. (1991). Neurobiology of cognitive and language processing: Effects of early experience. In K. R. Gibson & A. C. Petersen (Eds.), *Brain maturation and cognitive development* (pp. 355-380). New York: Aldine de Gruyter.

Nice, R.W., *A Handbook of Abnormal Psychology*, Vision Press Ltd., 1959.

Noll, Victor H., *Introduction to Educational Measurement* (2nd Ed.,) Boston: Houghton Mifflin Company, 1965.

O' Reilly, R. C., & Munakata, Y. (2000). *Computational explorations in cognitive neuroscience: Understanding the mind by simulating the brain*. Cambridge, MA: Bradfor.

Palmer, C.E., "The Development of Normal Children," *Jr. of Speech Disorders*, Vol. V, pp. 185-191.

Pasricha-Prem, *Educational Psychology*, New Delhi: Sterling Publishers, 1963.

Piaget, J. (1952). *The origins of intelligence in children*. New York: International Universities Press.

Piaget, Jean, *The Moral Judgement of the Child*, London: Routledge & Kegan Paul Ltd., 1932.

– – –, *The Origins of Intelligence in Children*, New York: International Universities Press, Inc., 1932.

Pinker, S. (1994). *The language instinct*. New York: William Morrow.

Pinker, S., & Prince, A. (1988). ON language and connectionism: Analysis of a parallel distributed processing model of language acquisition. *Cognition, 28,* 73-193.

Plomin, R., & Petrill, S. A. (1997). Genetics and intelligence: What's new? *Intelligence, 24,* 53-77.

Poliakov, G. I. (1959). Progressive neuron differentiation of the human cerebral cortex in ontogenesis. In S. A. Sarkisov & S. N. Preobrazenskaya (Eds.), *Development of the central nervous system* (pp. 11-26). Moscow: Medgiz.

Rakic, P. (1995), Corticogenesis in human and nonhuman primates. In M.S. Gazzaniga (Ed.), *The cognitive neurosciences* (pp. 127-145). Cambridge, MA: MIT Press.

Ribble, M.A., *The Rights of Infants*, New York: Columbia Univ. Press, 1943.

Riessman Frank, *The Culturally Deprived Child*, New York: Harper & Row Publishers, Inc., 1962.

Rosenzweig, M. R. (1979). Responsiveness of brain size to individual experience: Behavioral and evolutionary implication. In M. E. Hahn, C. Jensen, & B. C. Dudek (Eds.), *Development and evolution of brain size: Behavioral implications* (pp. 263-294). New York: Academic Press.

Rumelhart, D. E., & McClelland, J. L. (Eds.). (1986). *Parallel distributed processing: Explorations in the microstructure of cognition. Volume 1: Foundantions.* Cambridge, MA: MIT Press.

Ryle, G., "Freedom, Language and Reality", *Proceedings Soc.*, 1951, Supp. Vol. 25.

Sandstrom, C.I., *The Psychology of Childhood and Adolescence*, London: Methuen and Co. Ltd, 1966, pp. 149.

Schade, J. P., & Van Groenigen, W.B. (1961). Structural organisation of the human cerebral cortex. *Acta Anatomica,* 47, 74-111.

Schonell, F., *Backwardness in the Basic Subjects*, Edinburgh: Oliver and Boyd, 1948.

Sejnowski, T. J., & Rosenberg, C.R. (1986). NET talk: A parallel network that learns to read aloud. In J. A. Anderson & E. Rosenfeld, *Neurocomputing: Foundations of research* (pp. 663-672). Cambridge, MA: MIT Press.

Shaffer, L.F., and Shoben, E.J., *The Psychology of Adjustment*, 2nd Edition, Boston, Houghton Mifflin, 1956.

Shanker, Uday, *Exceptional Children*, New Delhi: Sterling Publishers (P) Ltd., 1976.

– – –,*A Study of Child Delinquency*, Studies in Education and Psychology,' Publication No 5, 1955, C.I.E. Delhi, pp. 3-4.

Siegler, R. S. (1976). Three aspects of cognitive development. *Cognitive Psychology,* 8, 481-520.

Siegler, R. S. (1981). Developmental sequences within and between concepts. *Monographs of the Society for Research in Child Development,* 46, (2, Serial No. 189).

Simonton, D. K. (1999). Talent and its development: An emergenic and epigenetic model. *Psychological Review,* 106, 435-457.

Sirevaag, A. M., & Greenough, W.T. (1987). Differential rearing effects on rat visual cortex synapses: III. Neuronal and glial nuclei, boutons, dendrites, and capillaries. *Brain Research,* 424, 320-332.

Sohafer, H.R., and Emerson, P., *The Development of Social Attachment in Infancy*, Monograph of the Society for Research in Child Development, 1964, 29, No. 3 (Serial No. 94).

Sontag, L.W., Baker, C.T., and Nelson, V.L., *Mental Growth and Personality Development*, Society for Research in Child Development Monograph, 1958, 23, No. 2.

Spearman, C. (1904). General intelligence, objectively determined and measured. *American Journal of Psychology,* 15, 201-293.

Spearman, C. (1927). *The abilities of man: Their nature and measurement.* New York: Macmillan.

Spearman, C., *The Abilities of Man*, London: Macmillan, 1927.

Stagdill, R.M., "Personal Factors Associated with Leadership: A Survey of the Literature," *Jr of Psychology*, Vol. 25, 1948.

– – –, "Leadership, Membership, Organisation" in *Leadership*, edited by G.A. Gibb, Penguin Books.

Stankov, L., & Roberts, R. D. (1997). Mental speed is not the "basic" process of intelligence. *Personality and Individuall Differences,* 22, 69-84.

Stankov, L., Boyle, G. J., & Cattell, R.B. (1995). Models and paradigms in personality and intelligence research. In D. H. Saklofske & M. Zeidner (Eds.), *International handbook of personality and intelligence* (pp. 15-43). New York: Plenum.

Stein, D. G., Brailowsky, S., & Will, B. (1995). *Brain repaid.* New York: Oxford University Press.

Sternberg, R. J. (1985). *Beyond I.Q.: A triarchic theory intelligence.* New York: Cambridge University Press.

Sternberg, R. J., & Detterman, D. K. (Eds.). (1986). *What is intelligence? Contemporary viewpoints on its nature and definition.* Norwood, NJ: Ablex.

Sternberg, R.J., & Kaufman, J. C. (1998). Human abilities. *Annual Review of Psychology,* 49, 479-502.

Symonds, P.M., *The Psychology of Parent-child Relationships*, Appleton-Century Co., 1966.

– – –, *The Dynamics of Human Adjustment*, 1946, New York: Appleton Century Crofts, Inc.

Szentagothai, J. (1978). The neuron network of the cerebral cortex: A functional interpretation. *Proceedings of the Royal Society of London, B,* 201, 219-248.

Taanenbaum R., and *et al,, Leadership and Organisation,* A Frame of Reference, p. 23, London: McGraw-Hill Book Co., 1961.

Taneja, V.B , *Educational Psychology and Statistics,* Chandigarh: M.C. Publication, 1975.

Tead, O., *The Arts of Leadership-. Whai is Leadership?* London: McGraw-Hill Book Company, Inc.

— — —, *The Art of Leadership: How to Train Leaders?* London: McGraw-Hill Book Company, Inc., 1935.

Terman, L.M., and Oden, M.H., *The Gifted Child Grows Up,* Stanford University Press, 1947.

Terman, L.M., *Genetic Studies of Genius,* Stanford: Stanford University Press, Vol. I. 1925.

Terman, Lewis, M. and Maud A,, Merrill, *Measuring Intelligence,* Boston: Houghton Mifflin Company, 1937.

Thompson, *Child Psychology,* New York: H.M. Company, 1952, p. 22.

— — —, *The Psychology of Thinking,* Pelican, 1959.

Thompson, R. F. (1985). *The brain: An introduction to neuroscience.* New York: W. H. Freeman.

Thorndike, E.L., *Foundations of Learning,* Columbia University Press.

— — —, *Selected Writings from a Connectionist's Psychology,* Appleton-Century Crofts, 1949.

— — —, *Animal Intelligence,* New York: The Macmillan Company, 1911.

— — —, *The Psychology of Learning,* New York: Teachers College Press, Columbia University. 1973.

Thorndike, Edward, L., and Irving Lorge: *Teachers World Book of 30,000 Words,* New York: Teachers College Press, Columbia University, 1944.

Thorndike, Robert, L., and Elizabeth Hagen, *Measurement and Evaluation in Psychology and Education,* Nrew York: John Wiley & Sons, Inc., 1961.

Thorndike, Robert, L., *The Measurement of Creativity,* Teachers College Record, 64, 422-24, 1963.

Thurstone, L.L., "Primary Mental Abilities" in *Psychometric Monograph,* No. 1, Chicago: University of Chicago Press, 196.

— — — "Factorial Studies of Intelligence" in *Psychometric Monograph,* No. 2, Chicago: University of Chicago Press, 1941.

— — — *Multiple Factor Analysis,* Chicago: University of Chicago Press, 1947.

Torrance, E., Paul, *Creative Thinking Throush the Language Arts.* Educational Leadership, 18, 13-18, 1960.

— — — "Priming Creative Thinking in the Primary Grades" *Elementary School Journal,* 42, 34-41, 1961.

— — —, *Guiding Creative Talent,* Englewood Cliffs N.T. Prentice-Hall, Inc., 1962.

— — — *Creativity: What Research Says to the Teacher:* Washington, D.C.: Department of Classroom Teachers and American Educational Research Association, National Educational Association, 1963 (a).

— — —, *Education and the Creative Potential,* Minneapolis: University of Minnesota Press, 1963 (b).

— — —, *Gifted Children and the Classroom,* New York: The Macmillan Company, 1963.

— — —, *Torrance Tests of Creative Thinking, Norms Technical Manual,* Princeton, N.J.: Personnel Press, 1966.

Torrance, Paul, E., and Harmon, J.A., "Effects of Memory Evaluative, and Creative Reading Sets on Test Performance," *Journal of Educational Psychology,* 52, 207-14, 1967.

Toyama, K., Komatsu, Y., & Tanifuji, M. (1995). In vitro studies of visual cortical plasticity. In J.L. McGaugh, N. M. Weinberger, & G. Lynch (Eds.), *Brain and memory: Modulation and mediation of neuroplasticity* (pp. 222-238). New York: Oxford University Press.

Tutoo, D.N., A *Text Book of* Education, Srinagar: Ali Mohamad and Sons, 1965.

Valentine, G.W., *The Psychology of Early Childhood,* Cleveland Sherwood Press, 1942.

Vernon, P. A. (1992). Intelligence, reaction times, and peripheral nerve conduction velocity. *Intelligence,* 16 273-288.

Vernon, P.E., *The Structure of Human Ability,* London: Methuen, 1927.

Vinacke, W.E., *The Psychology of Thinking,* New York: McGraw-Hill, 1952.

Wallance Wallin, A *Text Book of Mental Hygiene,* Hountrias.

Waltz, D., & Feldman, J. A. 9Eds.). (1988). *Connectionist models and their implications: Readings from cognitive science.* Norwood, NJ: Ablex.

Wastson, Robert, I., *Psychology of the Child,* New York: John Wiley and Sons, Inc.

Whitehouse Conference on Child Health and Protection.

Wickett, J.C., Vernon, P. A., & Lee, D.H. (1994). *In vivo* brain size, head perimeter, and intelligence in a sample of healthy adult females. *Personality and Individual Differences,* 16, 831-838.

Wiesel, T. N., & Hubel, D. H. (1963). Single-cell responses in striate cortex of kittens deprived of vision in one eye. *Journal of Neurophysiology,* 26, 1003-1017.

Willerman, L., Schultz, R., Rutledge, J. N., & Bigler, E. D. (1991). *In vivo* brain size and intelligence, *Intelligence,* 15, 223-228.

Williams, R. W., & Herrup, K. (1988). The control of neuron number. *Annual Review of Neuroscience,* 11, 423-453.

Woodworth, *Psychology* (13th Edition).

Woodworth, R.S., *Contemporary School of Psychology.*

Young, K., *Personality and Problems af Adjustment,* London: Rout- ledge and Kegan Paul, 1947.

INDEX

• • •